BMW Art Guide by Independent Collectors.

The global guide to private yet publicly accessible collections of contemporary art.

Revised edition with 49 additional collections

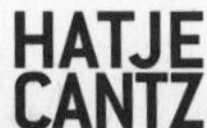

"Why had no one done this before?"

A collector's comment on the idea for this book

A little over a year ago we launched the first *BMW Art Guide by Independent Collectors*, the first global guide to private yet publicly accessible collections of contemporary art. But what might "publicly" mean in this context? That edition highlighted over 170 collections open to the public, but also collections whose owners agreed to open their private homes, by appointment, to readers of this guide—an absolute novelty in the world of international art. This unprecedented openness was generated because the *BMW Art Guide by Independent Collectors* is not a guide for tourists, but rather a guide for art lovers, culled from careful research, with discretion, and attention to detail. That we were urged to so quickly to produce a second, revised edition evidences the enormously positive response to the first. Whoever held the book in their hands confirmed the incredible work our team had achieved. Research for this new edition has yielded 49 new collections, among them very private places you simply won't find in any other travel or art guidebook. The result is a volume containing 217 magical places completely dedicated to art. Above all, we wish once again to thank the collectors for the immense trust they have placed in us, in our guide, and in the visitors to their collections. Access to these stunning places is a privilege, and one we aim never to take for granted.

Dr. Steven Althaus
Senior Vice President
Brand Management BMW,
Marketing Services BMW Group

Jana Hyner
Director,
Independent Collectors

We should also mention that the *BMW Art Guide by Independent Collectors'* blog is now online, featuring background information on collections, posts about collecting, and current news. For more information, please visit www.bmw-art-guide.com.

Contents

Argentina
Buenos Aires … 009–013
Salta … 014

Australia
Hobart … 015
Melbourne … 016
Sydney … 016

Austria
Gars am Kamp … 017
Klosterneuburg … 018
Lebring … 018
Neuhaus … 019
Vienna … 019

Bangladesh
Dhaka … 020

Belgium
Brussels … 021–023
Deurle … 024
Kemzeke … 025
Ostend … 025

Brazil
Brumadinho … 026
Rio de Janeiro … 027
São Paulo … 027

Canada
Toronto … 028
Vancouver … 029

China
Beijing … 030
Shanghai … 033

Denmark
Copenhagen … 034

Finland
Helsinki … 035
Tampere … 036

France
Alex … 037
Avignon … 038
Flassans sur Issole … 038
Marines … 039
Paris … 039–040
Saint-Paul-de-Vence … 043
Senlis … 043

Germany
Aschaffenburg … 044
Augsburg … 045
Baden-Baden … 045
Bedburg-Hau … 046
Berlin … 046–057
Bremen … 058
Donaueschingen … 058–059
Dörentrup … 059
Duisburg … 060
Düsseldorf … 061–062
Eberdingen-Nussdorf … 062
Freiburg … 063
Hamburg … 064
Hünfeld … 067
Künzelsau-Gaisbach … 067
Leinfelden-Echterdingen … 068
Leipzig … 069
Munich … 069–071
Neu-Ulm/Burlafingen … 071
Neumünster … 072
Neuss … 073
Reutlingen … 074–075
Riegel am Kaiserstuhl … 075
Sindelfingen … 076
Soest … 076
St. Georgen … 077
Traunreut … 078
Ulm … 078–079
Waldenbuch … 079

Great Britain
Edinburgh … 080
London … 083–084
Wolverhampton … 084

Greece
Athens 085–090
Paiania 090

Hungary
Veszprém 091

Iceland
Hafnarfjordur 092

Independent Collectors 093

India
Gurgaon 094
New Delhi 095

Indonesia
Jakarta 096
Magelang 097

Israel
Tel Aviv 098

Italy
Alzano Lombardo 101
Briosco 102
Busca 102
Camogli 103
Catania 104
Città della Pieve 104
Florence 105
Forlì 105
Gaiole in Chianti 106
Lucca 106
Malo 107
Milan 107–108
Naples 108
Reggio Emilia 111
Rome 111–112
Santomato di Pistoia 113
Turin 114–115
Varese 115
Venice 116
Verzegnis 116

Japan
Ichikawa 119
Kagawa 120
Tokyo 120

Luxembourg
Luxembourg City 121

Mexico
Ecatepec 122

Netherlands
Heerlen 125
Rotterdam 126
The Hague/Scheveningen 127
Venlo 128
Voorschoten 128
Wassenaar 129
Wijlre 129

New Zealand
North Auckland Peninsula 130

Norway
Henningsvær 131
Høvikodden 132
Oslo 132

Poland
Poznań 135
Warsaw 136

Portugal
Cascais 137
Lisbon 138

Puerto Rico
San Juan 141

Qatar
Doha 142

Russia
Moscow 143–145
St. Petersburg 145

Singapore
Singapore 146

South Africa
Klapmuts 147
Stellenbosch 148

Spain
Barcelona 151–152
Cáceres 153
Huesca 154
Madrid 154
Pontevedra 155
Valencia 155

Sweden
Knislinge 156

Switzerland
Appenzell 157
Langenbruck 158
Lucerne 159
Rapperswil 159
Riehen 160
Schaffhausen 161
Zuoz 161

Turkey
Istanbul 162–165

Ukraine
Kiev 166

United Arab Emirates
Dubai 167–169
Sharjah 169

United States of America
Cleveland 170
Dallas 171–172
Denver 172
Fort Lauderdale 173
Geyserville 174
Greenwich 174
Houston 175
Long Island City 175
Los Angeles 176
Miami 176–181
Napa 181–182
New York 182–185
Oaks 185
Reading 186
San Antonio 186
Santa Monica 187
Seattle 187
West Palm Beach 188

The Authors 191
Index 192–200

A

B

C

D

E

F

G

H

I

J

K

L

M

N

O

P

Q

R

S

T

U

V

W

X

Y

Z

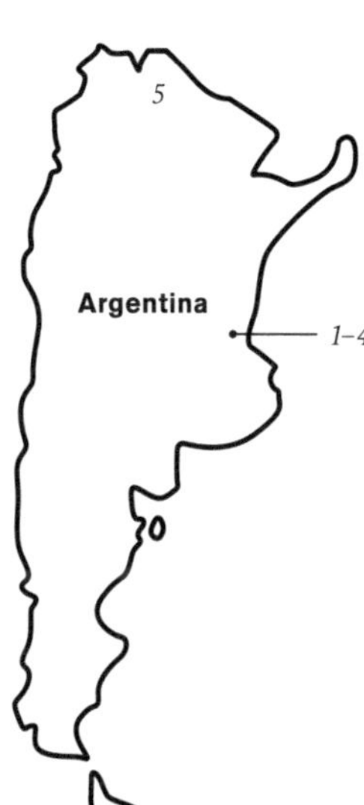

1   Colección de Arte
      Amalia Lacroze de Fortabat

*Argentina's richest woman presents six decades
of art-treasure collecting*

Collector:
Amalia Lacroze de Fortabat

Address:
Olga Cossettini 141
Puerto Madero Este
C1107CCC Buenos Aires
Argentina
Tel +54 11 43106600
info@coleccionfortabat.org.ar
www.coleccionfortabat.org.ar

Opening Hours:
Tues–Sun: 12–9pm

The Colección de Arte Amalia Lacroze de Fortabat lies in
the middle of Porto Madero, the newly trendy quarter
of the Argentine capital. Until the end of the 1990s, this
neighborhood was still a no-go area of rundown houses
ringing the harbor. It's been heavily restored and added
to over the past few years by world-class architects like Sir
Norman Foster, Philippe Starck, and Santiago Calatrava.
The architect of the Colección Fortabat, which opened in
fall 2008, is the Uruguay-born New Yorker Rafael Viñoly.
He built a modern, light-filled house for the art collection
of Argentina's richest woman: 1 000 works ranging from
Pieter Brueghel to Andy Warhol, who made a portrait of
her in 1980. The socially critical artist Antonio Berni has
a gallery all to himself.

A   *2*   Fundación Federico Jorge Klemm

*The idiosyncratic collection of an artistic multi-talent
with opulent leanings*

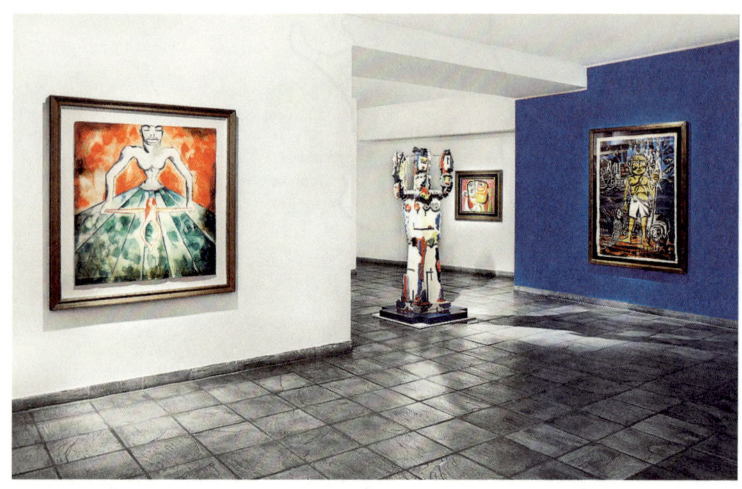

Opera singer, organizer of happenings and performances, painter, photographer, author of television series about artists from Rembrandt to Jean-Michel Basquiat, gallerist, collector, and patron. Frederico Jorge Klemm (1942–2002), a flashy Argentine with German-Czech roots, was all of these things—at night. During the day, he lorded over a chemical company founded by his father. The part-time eccentric with platinum blonde hair was a wild mixture of Gianni Versace, Andy Warhol, and Liberace. His art collection reflects his unconventional style: blasphemous works of photography by Andres Serrano meet knick-knack sculptures by Jeff Koons and naked men by Robert Mapplethorpe. Additionally: Argentine artists emerging onto the international scene, like Guillermo Kuitca or Nicola Costantino. In 1995 Klemm started a foundation dedicated to supporting, above all, young Argentine art.

Collector:
Federico Jorge Klemm

Address:
Marcelo T. de Alvear 626
C1058AAH Buenos Aires
Argentina
Tel +54 11 43123334
admin@fundacionfjklemm.org
www.fundacionfjklemm.org

Opening Hours:
Mon–Fri: 11am–8pm

There is no shortage of museums, galleries, and other art venues in
Buenos Aires, the bustling metropolis on the Río de la
Plata. Too bad, then, that they are spread across so many different
quarters, with melodious names like Recoleta, Retiro, Palermo, and
Belgrano. Carefully planning your art sojourn, therefore, is crucial. The
comparatively cheap black-and-yellow taxis and their friendly drivers
will do the rest. Aside from the private museums presented in this
guide, one should definitely visit the Museo Nacional de Bellas Artes,
with its extensive collections of European and Argentine art from the
Middle Ages to the twentieth century.
International art discourse continues at the private Fundacíon Proa, in
the colorful harbor district of La Boca. Whether Rosemarie Trockel,
Louise Bourgeois, or the Argentine rising star Leandro Erlich—all have
had a big show in this gleaming white building. Even the bookstore is
worth a visit. You can also find a fine selection of Argentine and
international art books and magazines in the well-stocked Librería
Purr, on the grand boulevard Avenida Santa Fe. The galleries Ruth
Benzacar and Jorge Mara-La Ruche, both regular exhibitors at Art
Basel Miami Beach, offer Argentine avant-garde at the highest level.
Each year in late May, right in Argentina's autumn, the art fair Arteba,
which specializes in Latin American art, attracts up to 120 000 visitors.
Friends of photography will find fine works at the photography fair
Buenos Aires Foto, at the end of October.
This fair is organized by the team behind the website Arte Online,
which also organizes gallery nights on the first Thursday of each
month. There are also off-spaces, but here they have a rather nomadic
character or are open for one show only. It's best to pay attention to
local flyers to discover what's going on.

Nicole Büsing & Heiko Klaas

More Information: www.bmw-art-guide.com

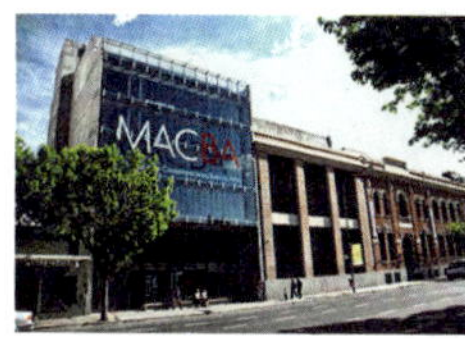

Collector:
Aldo Rubino

Address:
Avenida San Juan 328
C1147AAO Buenos Aires
Argentina
info@macba.com.ar
www.macba.com.ar

Please check the website
for most current information
on opening hours.

3   MACBA—Museum Art Center Buenos Aires   A

A focus on international Geometric Art at a brand new art center

MAMBA, MALBA, MACBA. Anyone flaneuring through Buenos Aires on a museum tour could get them mixed up. While the first two have been around for a long time, the MACBA arrived on the scene in 2012. The Museum Art Center Buenos Aires was founded by native Aldo Rubino, who now lives in Miami and is a frequent guest on the collectors' panel at Art Basel Miami Beach. Rubino's private collection concentrates on geometric abstraction: Op Art, Hard Edge, and Neo-Geo, from Manuel Álvarez Bravo and Victor Vasarely, all the way to the American Sarah Morris. Special exhibitions feature all varieties of current art. Shows take place in the 2 400-square-meter translucent building brought to life by local architect duo Vila/Sebastián. The location is great: the MACBA, which sits adjacent to the MAMBA, is in the lively flea-market quarter of San Telmo.

Collector:
Eduardo F. Costantini

Address:
Avenida Figueroa Alcorta 3415
C1425CLA Buenos Aires
Argentina
Tel +54 11 48086500
info@malba.org.ar
www.malba.org.ar

Opening Hours:
Wed: 12–9pm
Thurs–Mon: 12–8pm

4   MALBA—Fundación Costantini (Museo de Arte Latinoamericano de Buenos Aires)

A grandiose view of a century of Latin American art

Unaware "gringos" come across places in South America that they couldn't have imagined in their wildest dreams. The Museo de Arte Latinoamericano de Buenos Aires (MALBA) is one such place. The museum of art features work from the Caribbean to Tierra del Fuego and is located in the posh district of Palermo Chico. It looks like an outpost of New York's Museum of Modern Art. Here, too, people know how to erect elegant structures; here modernism is self-consciously defined—naturally, from a Latin-American perspective. Nearly 300 key works from businessman Eduardo F. Costantini's collection are on permanent display: politically charged Conceptual Art by Léon Ferrari; the Chilean surrealist Roberto Matta is also well represented, as is the Brazilian Lygia Clark, whose fragile metal objects have leapt to premium prices internationally.

A

5   Museo James Turrell—
The Hess Art Collection, Colomé
*Turrell's largest Skyspace and additional light rooms
in breathtaking surroundings*

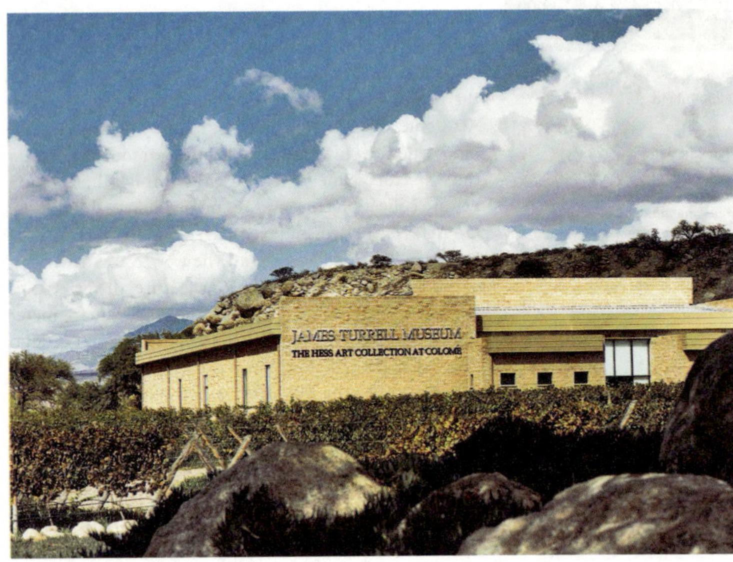

Far away from all the art metropolises, in a majestic location underneath the bright blue sky of the Argentine Andes, lies the world's first James Turrell Museum, opened in 2009. Here the light-and-land artist from Arizona completed the biggest *Skyspace* at his collector and friend Donald M. Hess's vineyard, Colomé: 2 300 meters up a mountainside sits a Turrell observatory with an open roof, joined by an orchestration of subtle light. Eight more light rooms, works acquired by Hess over the past forty years, are grouped around the spectacular centerpiece. Here you experience pure meditative inwardness. The Museo James Turrell, which Hess maintains along with his collections in South Africa and North America, is a truly magical space in a fascinating location.

Collector:
Donald M. Hess

Address:
Ruta Provincial 53
km 20 Molinos 4419
Salta
Argentina
Tel +54 3868 494200
reservas@bodegacolome.com
www.bodegacolome.com

Opening Hours:
Tues–Sun: 2–6pm
Reservations encouraged.

Additional exhibition locations:
Klapmuts, South Africa, p. 147
Napa, United States of America,
p. 181

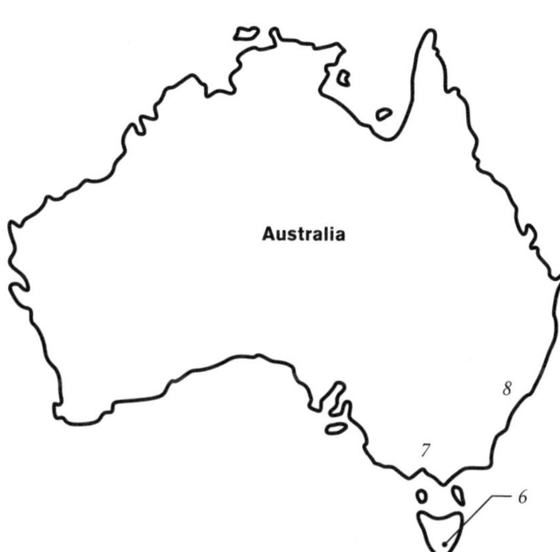

6   Museum of Old and New Art (MONA)
*A collection that puts personal predilection
over speculative intention*

Collector:
David Walsh

Address:
655 Main Road
Berriedale TAS 7011
Hobart
Australia
Tel +61 3 62779900
info@mona.net.au
www.mona.net.au

Opening Hours:
October–April
Wed–Mon: 10am–6pm

Small gestures are not his thing: Australian millionaire David Walsh owns one of the largest museums in the southern hemisphere. This building without daylight is burrowed deep into the Tasmanian bedrock. Aside from contemporary art, the museum also houses Egyptian mummies and Greek coins. Walsh, who made his fortune developing complex winning-systems for gambling, combines antique treasures with Australian contemporary art, as well as works by internationally renowned artists like Jannis Kounellis, Hans Bellmer, Anselm Kiefer, the Viennese group Gelitin, or Wim Devoye's excrement machine, *Cloaca*. Walsh prefers works that confront viewers immediately with subjects like sex and death. Walsh conceives his Museum of Old and New Art (MONA), opened in 2011, as a kind of secular temple in which one is snapped back into humanity's existential conditions.

A

7 Lyon Housemuseum

*The private house as museum: living with art
and showing it to strangers*

If you want to visit Corbett and Yueji Lyon, you first have to
make an appointment. For good reason: the architect built
a house for his family which also functions as a museum.
In the cavernous rooms that remind one of galleries, the
artworks are arranged biannually anew. Lyon draws upon
a long tradition, such as Peggy Guggenheim's Venetian
house where she showed her private collection. The Australian pair has specialized in the artists of their own country,
collecting paintings from the likes of Tim Maguire, sculptures by Peter Hennessey, or large C-print photographs
by Anne Zahalka. Two decades ago the Lyons decided to
collect the work of a new generation, such as that by Peter
Atkins and Patricia Piccinini, both who have since become
established internationally.

Collectors:
Corbett & Yueji Lyon

Address:
219 Cotham Road
Kew VIC 3101
Melbourne
Australia
Tel +61 3 98172300
museum@lyonhousemuseum.com.au
www.lyonhousemuseum.com.au

By appointment only. To arrange
an appointment, send an e-mail,
or call on Mondays or Tuesdays
between 9:30–11:30am.

8 White Rabbit—Contemporary Chinese Art Collection

*One of the largest collections of Chinese art
since the beginning of the millennium*

Judith and Kerr Neilson have chosen to limit themselves:
they only collect Chinese art, and of that, art only created
after the year 2000. When Judith Neilson travelled to Beijing in 2001 she realized that her understanding of Chinese
art was based on an outdated cliché. When she returned,
she restructured their existing collection and, together
with her husband, she bought an old factory in Sydney's
industrial district. There she began to systematically acquire contemporary work by artists like Ai Weiwei, Huang
Zhen, Qi Zhilong, or Huang Yan. Each artist's age did not
matter; it was rather "creativity and quality" Neilson
was after. Instead of buying at art auctions, the couple buys
directly in China from gallerists and artists' studios. Their
collection, which held just a handful of Chinese works in
2000, now counts as one of the most important and focused
in the world.

Collectors:
Judith & Kerr Neilson

Address:
30 Balfour Street
Chippendale NSW 2008
Sydney
Australia
Tel +61 2 83992867
info@whiterabbitcollection.org
www.whiterabbitcollection.org

Opening Hours:
Thurs–Sun: 10am–6pm

— **A**

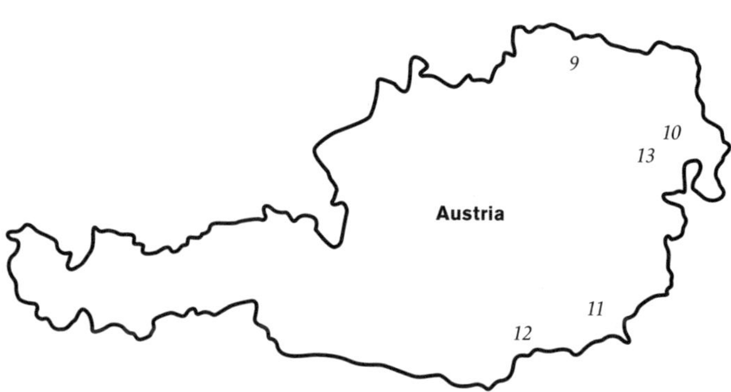

9   Kunstraum Buchberg
*Permanent contemporary installations
and projects in the park*

Collectors:
Gertraud & Dieter Bogner

Address:
Buchberg am Kamp 1
3571 Gars am Kamp
Austria
Tel +43 1 5128577
office@bogner-cc.at
www.bogner-cc.at/projekte/
kunstraum

By appointment only.

Gertraud and Dieter Bogner are museum experts. The couple runs an international agency for museum planning in Vienna. Some of their prestige projects of the last years include the New Museum in New York City and the new Folkwang Museum, in Essen. Of course, if you have such a background, you also want to surround yourself with art projects privately. The Bogners do this—but far away from Vienna, in their twelfth-century castle, Buchberg, located in lower Austria, where since 1979 they have invited artists to modify its rooms. Thus far there have been eighteen permanent room-alterations: color interventions, wall works, and sculptures. And in the green environs surrounding the castle, stars like Dan Graham or Heimo Zobernig have executed distinctive works relating to the architecture.

A

10 Essl Museum—Kunst der Gegenwart
Museum-level international art since 1945

The entrance into the world of contemporary art could not have been more perfect: the collector couple Essl met by chance in New York City at the end of the 1950s. Agnes Essl worked at the renowned Zabriskie Gallery, and Karlheinz Essl, who would later establish a chain of building-supply stores, was there to study the phenomenon of supermarkets. Museum visits and encounters with artists and gallerists were the basis of their enthusiasm for art. With over 7 000 works, this private collection is one of the biggest in Austria. Since 1999 it has been hosted at the Essl Museum in Klosterneuburg, near Vienna. "We assume the freedom to collect what excites us, without a claim to completeness." Eight to ten exhibits a year feature works by artists as diverse as Jonathan Meese, Tobias Rehberger, or Valie Export.

Collectors:
Agnes & Karlheinz Essl

Address:
An der Donau-Au 1
3400 Klosterneuburg
Austria
Tel +43 2243 37050150
info@essl.museum
www.sammlung-essl.at

Opening Hours:
Tues: 10am–6pm
Wed: 10am–9pm
Thurs–Sun: 10am–6pm

11 Schlosspark Eybesfeld
Carefully executed art projects in a palace garden setting

A palace, a garden, and an enthusiastic couple. Christine and Bertrand Conrad-Eybesfeld do not buy their art off the rack. It originates on site, sometimes in a few weeks, sometimes over a period of years. The owners of a culture-management agency do not consider themselves collectors or patrons, but rather artists' partners for these outdoor projects. Indeed, the couple has enough space: the castle is located in the sparsely populated state of Styria, in southeastern Austria. It all started with the artist Heimo Zobernig, who in 1989 made his mark on the castle's former tennis court with a fifteen-centimeter-thick concrete plate. Sol LeWitt executed a large-scale work shortly before his death, in 2007. For the Conrad-Eybesfelds, at least as important as the end result is getting people involved in the whole process, including the local community.

Collectors:
Christine & Bertrand
Conrad-Eybesfeld

Address:
Jöss 1
8403 Lebring
Austria
Tel +43 3182 240812
Tel +43 3182 240818
cce@eybesfeld.at
bce@eybesfeld.at
www.eybesfeld.at

By appointment only.

12   Museum Liaunig   **A**
*Austrian art after 1950 and prominent works
by international artists*

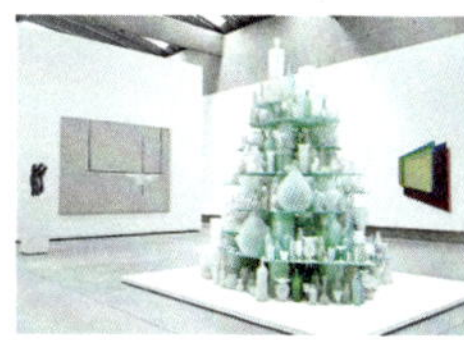

Collector:
Herbert W. Liaunig

Address:
Neuhaus 41
9155 Neuhaus
Austria
Tel +43 4356 21115
office@museumliaunig.at
www.museumliaunig.at

Opening Hours:
Wed–Sun: 10am–6pm

Only guided tours by appointment
(10am, 12pm, 2pm, 4pm).

With its slim, slightly rounded form, the Museum Liaunig resembles a gigantic USB-stick plugged into green hills. Outside the metropolises, in a quiet corner of Austria, the Carinthian businessman Herbert W. Liaunig opened this radically modern looking museum in the summer of 2008. The 160-meter-long, 30-meter-wide building was master-minded by the Viennese architectural firm Querkraft. Liaunig collected "what resulted from personal encounters and predilections." The roughly 3 000 works include key pieces of Austrian postwar art by figures like Arnulf Rainer or Maria Lassnig, but also undiscovered or over-looked work, as well as young positions. Since the museum was founded, Liaunig has collected with more focus and closed some previous gaps, such as his acquisition of some Viennese Actionists. His goal is to bring Austrian art since 1950 alive for the visitor.

13   Thyssen-Bornemisza Art Contemporary—
Atelier Augarten (T-B A21)
*Worldwide support of art projects, local cooperation
with Vienna's Belvedere*

Collector:
Francesca von Habsburg

Address:
Scherzergasse 1A
1020 Vienna
Austria
Tel +43 1 51398560
exhibitions@tba21.org
www.tba21.org

Opening hours vary depending on
exhibition. Please check the website for most current information.

For seven years, Thyssen-Bornemisza Art Contemporary operated out of a historic apartment in the heart of Vienna. Since the summer of 2012, the private foundation has been located in the Atelier Augarten, working in conjunction with the state-run museum Belvedere. Three exclusive projects take place in the new rooms each year, projects that often blossom at the interstice between exhibition and performance. But that's not all they do: here, at the nerve center of a worldwide foundation, the mission is to work closely with international artists, from Vienna to Reykjavik to New Delhi. Chairwoman Francesca von Habsburg, daughter of the super-collector Baron Hans Heinrich Thyssen-Bornemisza, grew up with art. And now the former "it girl" of London society has become one of the most experiment-friendly patrons of contemporary art since the foundation opened, in 2002.

B

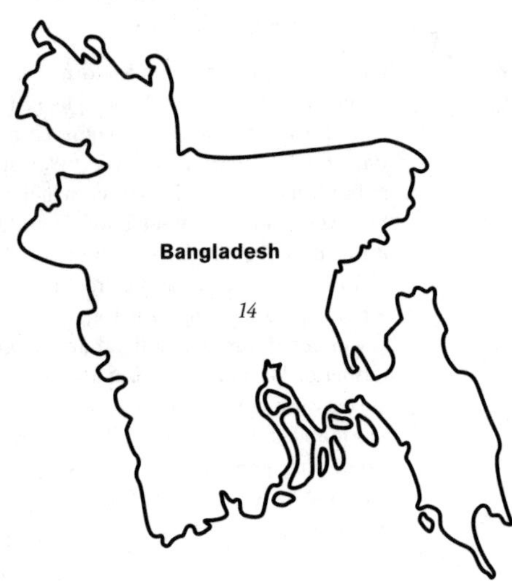

14   Samdani Art Foundation
A discovery of modern and contemporary art
from Bangladesh

Globalization has put previously ignored countries on the art map—Bangladesh, for example. Bangladeshi industrialist Rajeeb Samdani and his wife, Nadia, are well aware of this, so their aim is to acquaint an international audience with art from their country. In April 2011 they opened a foundation to promote local art via exhibitions, film screenings, and events like the Dhaka Art Summit. Their collection, spread over three floors of their private home, includes local artists such as Tayeba Begum Lipi, Mahbubur Rahman, and Naeem Mohaiemen, alongside international artists such as Rashid Rana, Jitish Kallat, or Tracey Emin. Samdani, who is also a member of the South Asian Acquisitions Committee of the London Tate, has an additional project: a sprawling sculpture park in the country's northeast.

Collectors:
Nadia & Rajeeb Samdani

Address:
Level 5, Suite 501 & 502
Shanta Western Tower
186 Gulshan – Tejgaon Link Road
Tejgaon I/A, Dhaka-1208
Bangladesh
Tel +8802 8878784-7
info@samdani.com.bd
www.samdani.com.bd

Opening Hours:
Mon–Thurs: 3–7pm
Sat–Sun: 3–7pm

B

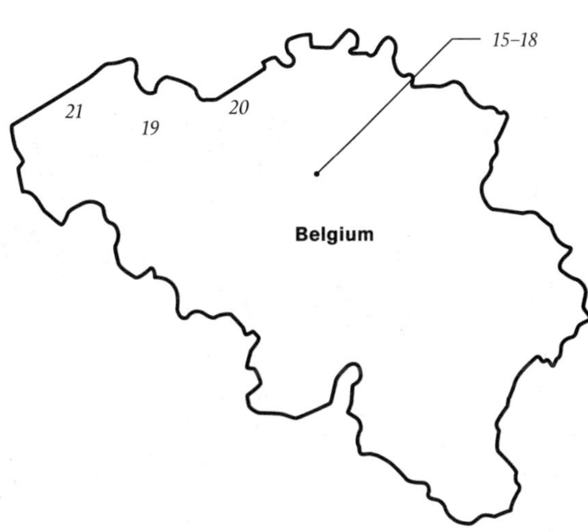

15   Frédéric de Goldschmidt Collection
*Reduced aesthetics and humble materials in three
locations in the center of Brussels*

Collector:
Frédéric de Goldschmidt

Address:
Brussels, Belgium
frederic@frederic.net

Visitation permitted only
occasionally. Please inquire
by e-mail.

He had purchased art before, but only since 2009 has
Frenchman Frédéric de Goldschmidt considered himself a collector. That's when he first acquired works that
blew the dimensions of his loft apartment, located in a
seventeenth-century building in central Brussels. Today
he owns two additional showrooms: one of 70 square meters and the other 160. The conceptual core of his collection is the group Zero and their associates, with works by
Günther Uecker, Heinz Mack, or Piero Manzoni. In the
meantime, de Goldschmidt, who works as a film producer,
has begun collecting mostly younger artists, such as the
Berliner Stef Heidhues or Joel Andrianomearisoa, from
Madagascar. The collection's common thread is a reduced
aesthetic and great sensitivity to rather humble materials.
De Goldschmidt rearranges his collection each year in
time for Art Brussels.

16   Maison Particulière
*Exhibitions in a private home curated by collectors,
artists, and men of letters*

B

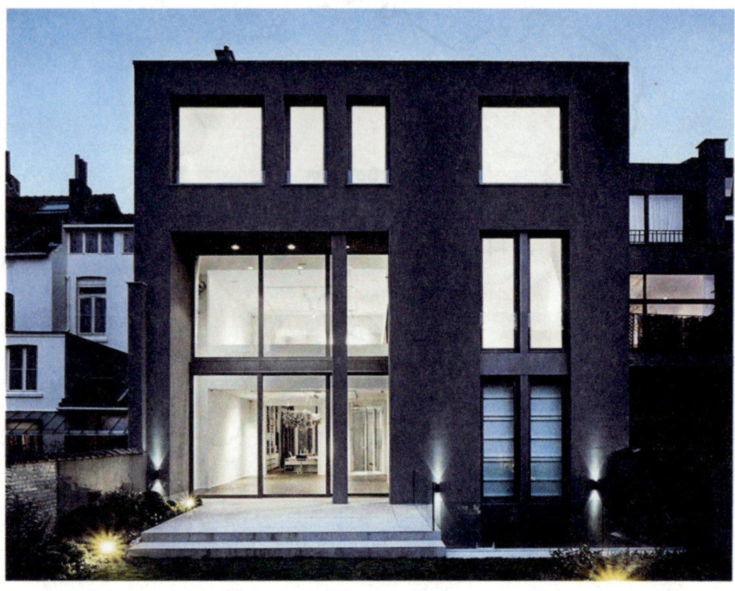

It would be hard to be more innovative. The Brussels-based
French couple Amaury and Myriam de Solages assigns
a thrice-yearly team of four collectors and one artist to
curate an exhibition based on a predetermined theme. A
sixth person, an *Homme des Lettres*, chooses related texts.
The location is as unique as the idea: an uninhabited aristocratic domicile in the lively district of Châtelain. Three
storeys, dark hardwood floors, high ceilings, lots of light,
and chock-full of premium furniture by Ludwig Mies van
der Rohe, Arne Jacobsen, and young designers. The whole
project has been applaudingly received in Brussels: since its
opening, in April 2011, the Maison Particulière has become
an absolute hotspot of the city. Works as varied as those by
Cindy Sherman, Kiki Smith, and Hans Bellmer can be seen
alongside young Belgian artists, African sculptures, and
porcelain objects. Eclecticism with style.

Collectors:
Amaury & Myriam de Solages

Address:
Rue du Châtelain 49
1050 Brussels
Belgium
Tel +32 2 6498178
info@maisonparticuliere.be
www.maisonparticuliere.be

Opening Hours:
Tues–Sun: 11am–6pm
Thurs: 11am–7:30pm

B

17 Charles Riva Collection
*Charming presentation of contemporary art
in a private Brussels mansion*

Collector:
Charles Riva

Address:
Rue de la Concorde 21
1050 Brussels
Belgium
Tel +32 2 5030498
info@charlesrivacollection.com
www.charlesrivacollection.com

Opening Hours:
Thurs–Sat: 1–6pm

The Frenchman Charles Riva is co-owner of galleries in Brussels, Paris, and London. He sees his Charles Riva Collection, in Brussels, as a nonprofit space. Here he lives with his collection in a centrally located luxurious nineteenth-century townhouse. In the spring of 2009 Riva began to organize twice-yearly or quarterly exhibitions generated from within the collection, including of Leipzig painter and printmaker Christoph Ruckhäberle, as well as of Californian performance artist and pop-culture antagonist Paul McCarthy, or of the fictional New York artist Reena Spaulings, whose true identity remains a riddle. To go to galleries is a serious thing, Riva says, kind of like going to church. Whoever visits his collection should experience the novel ways in which art unfolds when viewed in private rooms.

18 Vanhaerents Art Collection
*Art and film since the 1970s: Warhol, Naumann,
and the consequences*

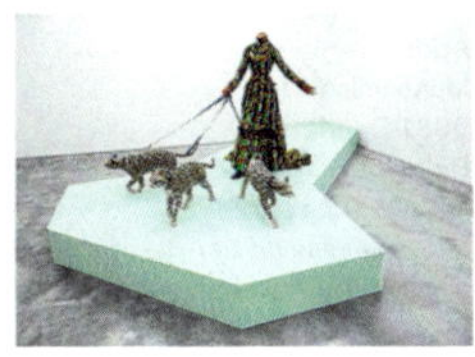

Collector:
Walter Vanhaerents

Address:
Rue Anneessens 29
1000 Brussels
Belgium
Tel +32 2 5115077
www.vanhaerentsartcollection.com

Online registration required.
Group tours every Saturday at
11am, 2pm, and 4pm; individual visits every first Saturday of
the month from 2–5pm.

Walter Vanhaerents's family has been in the construction business for eighty years; naturally he went into the business, too. But as a young man he had studied film. He was so impressed with Andy Warhol's five-hour-long *Sleep* that he wanted to see other works by the Pop icon. No surprise, then, that Warhol, along with Bruce Naumann, is one of the anchors of the Vanhaerents Art Collection. How did younger artists react to the impulses unleashed by these giants? They were further investigated by Cindy Sherman, Matthew Barney, and Ugo Rondinone, all up to the provocative neo Pop-Art businessman Takashi Murakami. The collection is housed in a charmingly remodeled 1926 industrial building on the outskirts of the hip fashion and gallery district Dansaert. Starting in 2007 new exhibitions have been shown biannually on three floors.

19 Museum Dhondt-Dhaenens

In the middle of Flanders, international art stars shown in quick succession

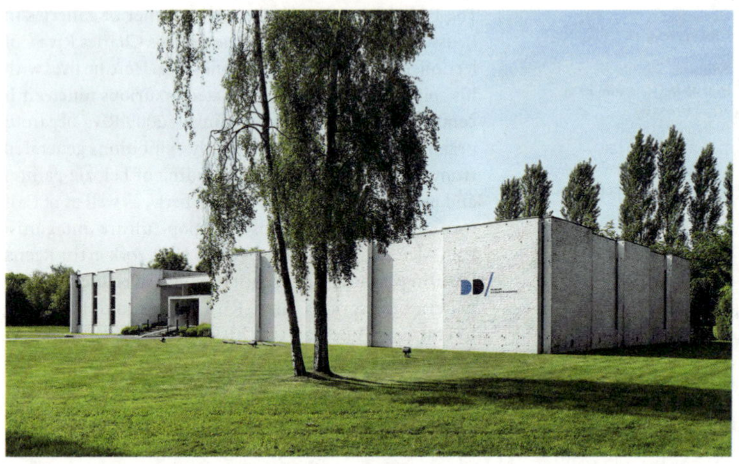

The Flanders industrialist couple Jules and Irma Dhondt-Dhaenens began collecting art in the 1920s. Belgium was just as divided then as it is today, which is why the couple focused almost exclusively on Flemish artists from 1880 to 1950, including James Ensor and Frits Van den Berghe. Toward the end of their lives, the collector couple decided to have a museum built to house their collection. Not in Brussels or Ghent, but in the countryside at Deurle, a beautifully located village on the river Leie and close to the artist colony Sint-Martens-Latem. The bright white, flat-roofed modernistic structure was opened in 1968. Today the museum continues to sharpen its contemporary profile with around eight annual exhibitions devoted to such international artists as Thomas Hirschhorn, Wade Guyton, and Monika Sosnowska.

Collectors:
Jules & Irma Dhondt-Dhaenens

Address:
Museumlaan 14
9831 Deurle
Belgium
Tel +32 9 2825123
info@museumdd.be
www.museumdd.be

Opening Hours:
Tues–Sun: 10am–5pm

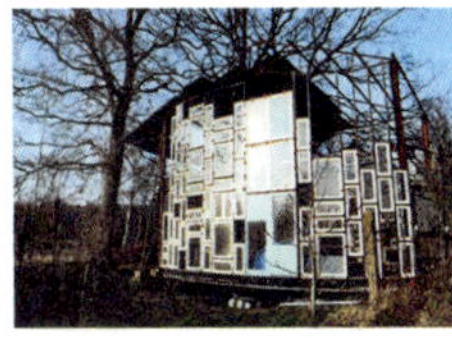

Collectors:
Geert & Carla Verbeke-Lens

Address:
Westakker
9190 Kemzeke, Stekene
Belgium
Tel +32 3 7892207
info@verbekefoundation.com
www.verbekefoundation.com

Opening Hours:
Thurs–Sun: 11am–6pm

20   Verbeke Foundation
An impressive terrain for hiking and discovering unorthodox art

B

Dynamic, not static. This is the motto of the Belgian collector pair Geert and Carla Verbeke-Lens. "Our exhibition space does not aim to be an oasis. Our presentation is unfinished, in motion, unpolished, contradictory, untidy, complex, inharmonious, living, and unmonumental," says Geert Verbeke. The former logistics businessman opened a twelve-hectare art park in 2007 on his company's property. Storage buildings and greenhouses offer 20 000 square meters of covered space for two enormous special exhibitions per year. The Verbekes started with collages and assemblages, but now they prefer "Bio-Art"—art that includes living animals, plants, and even scents. Visitors unable to see the whole display in a single day can even spend a night in a truly new environment: Joep van Lieshout's eccentric polyester sculpture *CasAnus*, a gigantic reconstruction of a human rectum.

Collector:
Mark Vanmoerkerke

Address:
Oud Vliegveld 10
8400 Ostend
Belgium
Tel +32 473 997745
info@artcollection.be
www.artcollection.be

E-mail appointment only.

21   Collection Vanmoerkerke
Highlights of European and American Post-Conceptual art

He is a manic collector, admits businessman Mark Vanmoerkerke from the seaside resort town of Ostende, in Belgium. He has managed to group together over 1 000 works in just fifteen years, mainly European and American Post-Conceptual art. What is that? Works by artists like Francis Alÿs, Sophie Calle, or Andreas Slominski, all of which contain degrees of humor and irony. Following the carte blanche principle, every six months an established curator is allowed to come up with a new way to present the collection. Vanmoerkerke refrains from interfering. Moreover, the acting curator decides which curator will be next—a surprise not just for the collector, but also for visitors. The cult curator Jan Hoet was one of the first figures allowed to mix it up in the former airplane hangar that houses the collection.

B

22 Inhotim—Instituto de Arte Contemporânea & Jardim Botânico

The harmony of art and nature at one of the world's most sensual locations

Admittedly, it's hard to get here. All the same, it's worth it. Inhotim completely redefines the production, exhibition, and experience of major outdoor-art projects. The collector, commodities magnate and philanthropist Bernardo Paz, invites well-known artists to his 600-hectare tropical expanse to unleash their most extravagant ideas. His team, led by a German, Jochen Volz, supports artists however it can. Cildo Meireles, Matthew Barney, Olafur Eliasson, Yayoi Kusama, and Chris Burden have all left their traces. Getting to Doug Aitken's *Sonic Pavilion*, which funnels the sounds of inner earth to the surface, or Hélio Oiticica's color-orgy *Magic Square #5*, both take a while to get to. Best is to take one of the many golf carts available, but if you decide to walk, there are plenty of benches along the way to let your dreams fly.

Collector:
Bernardo Paz

Address:
Rua B 20
Brumadinho, MG
35460-000
Brazil
Tel +55 31 32270001
info@inhotim.org.br
www.inhotim.org.br

Opening Hours:
Tues–Fri: 9:30am–4:30pm
Sat–Sun: 9:30am–5:30pm

23   Casa Daros—
Daros Latinamerica Collection

B

*Contemporary art from Latin America at
Sugarloaf Mountain*

Collector:
Ruth Schmidheiny

Address:
Rua General Severiano 159
Botafogo, Rio de Janeiro RJ
22290 040
Brazil
Tel +55 21 2275-0246
rio@casadaros.net
www.casadaros.net

Opening Hours:
Wed–Sat: 12–8pm
Sundays and holidays: 12–6pm

In March 2013, the Casa Daros opened at the Botafogo district in Rio de Janeiro. It shows Latin American art on 12 000 square meters in a converted neoclassical orphanage from the nineteenth century. With 1 200 works by 120 artists, the Daros Latinamerica Collection is the largest collection of contemporary Latin American art held by European collectors. It was founded in 2000 by the Zurich business couple Ruth and Stephan Schmidheiny. Since 2003, Ruth Schmidheiny has run the collection without her husband, supported by the South America expert Hans-Michael Herzog as artistic director and curator. The Casa Daros is an open place with education programs, artist talks, and discussions. Two annual exhibitions with art from across Latin America enrich the artistic offerings of the Copacabana.

24   Coleção Particular

*One of the few private collections open
to the public in Brazil*

Collector:
Oswaldo Corrêa da Costa

Address:
Rua Artur de Azevedo 51
Pinheiros, São Paulo, SP
05404-010
Brazil
Tel +55 11 23659575
www.colecaoparticular.com

Online registration required.

In Brazil, people don't really like to show off their possessions; it might arouse envy. This is why most of the private collections in São Paulo are hidden behind thick walls and hedges. Surveillance cameras and private security companies keep uninvited guests at a distance. But Oswaldo Corrêa da Costa is making an exception. In early 2010 he opened his Coleção Particular in a modern building made of exposed concrete in the middle of the upscale nightlife neighborhood of Pinheiros. The collector comes from a family of diplomats and has long resided abroad. After returning to São Paulo he was able to reunite the 500 works of his collection that had been separated in various depots. Now Brazilian Conceptual Art figures such as Valeska Soares or Cildo Meireles meet international positions like Sherrie Levine and Thomas Demand—an enviable combination.

C

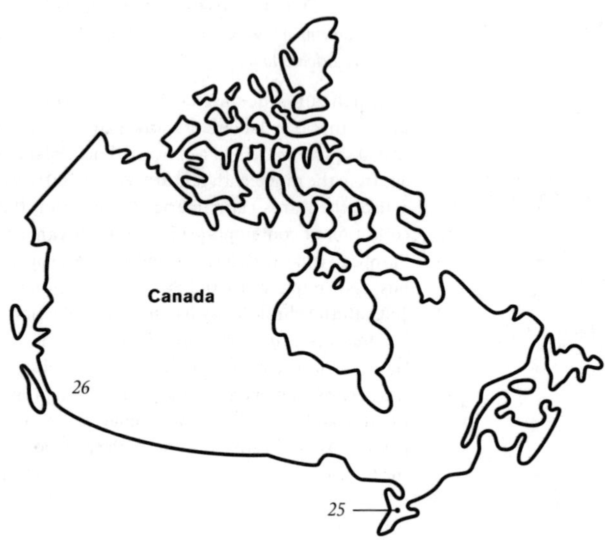

25 Scrap Metal Gallery
*Art focused on the relationship between word
and image in an industrial hall*

The name of the collection is doubly misleading: investor Joe Shlesinger and his wife, Samara Walbohm, did not, in 2011, open a "gallery" for their collection, but rather a private showroom, where they put on three to four exhibitions a year. Secondly, while much is presented here, none of it is "scrap metal," as the space's name advertises with a wink. The focus is rather on Canadian and international artists whose work is similarly humorous, subtle, and ambiguous. This includes art by the collective General Idea, Bill Viola, Jeff Wall, or other global players. The names Dave Dyment, Micah Lexier, or Laurel Woodcock, however, are not so well known. Their works all interrogate the complex relationship of language, text, and image.

Collectors:
Samara Walbohm &
Joe Shlesinger

Address:
11 Dublin Street
Unit E, M6H 1J4 Toronto
Canada
Tel +1 416 5882442
info@scrapmetalgallery.com
www.scrapmetalgallery.com

Opening Hours:
Fri–Sat: 12–5pm

26   Rennie Collection at Wing Sang
*Continuity since 1972: from trailblazing giants
to new talents*

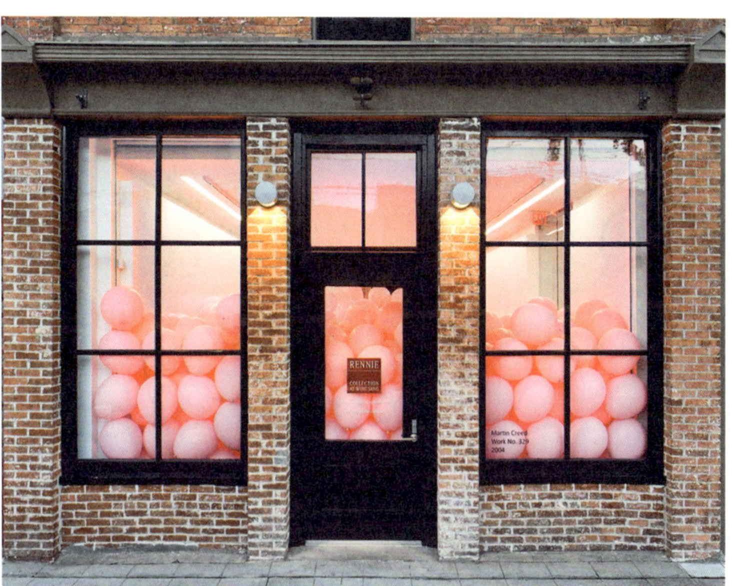

Collector:
Bob Rennie

Address:
51 East Pender Street
Vancouver BC V6A 1S9
Canada
www.renniecollection.org

Only guided tours with prior
online registration.

A guided tour through Chinatown's Wing Sang Building, whose renovation was commissioned by collector Bob Rennie, takes exactly fifty minutes—not nearly enough time if you know that the real-estate developer owns one of the largest collections in Canada. But Rennie made his money by deciding fast and keeping a quick pace. In a rush, and after you first register, you pass by works by John Baldessari, Mike Kelley, Louise Lawler, Rodney Graham, or by the Belgian artist David Claerbout, who ironically extends seconds-long film sequences from Hollywood classics to last an entire day. Rennie has been collecting since 1972 and owns many works later considered trailblazing. He now spends his time catching up with contemporary art by purchasing work by figures such as the Turner-prize-winning talents Martin Creed and Simon Starling.

C

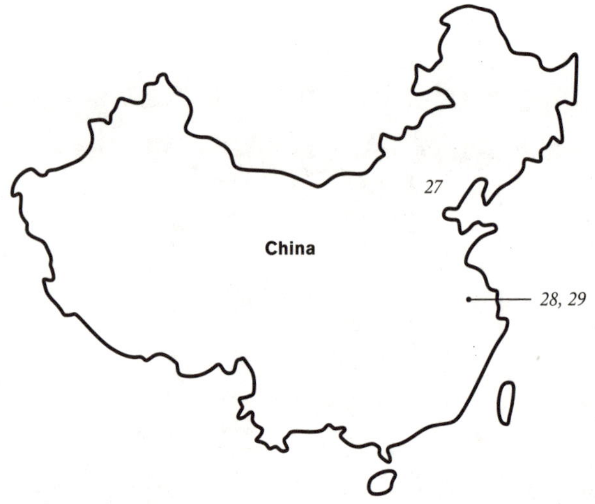

27   Domus Collection

*A global collection as an entry-point into a discussion
of international art*

The core of Richard Chang's collection is Asian art, even if
his Domus Collection, founded in 2008, contains roughly
800 works by international contemporary artists from the
1990s to the present. Among these representative works—
mostly painting and sculpture—are big names like Zhang
Xiaogang, Yang Shaobin, Tatsuo Miyajima, Anish Kapoor,
Olafur Eliasson, or Damien Hirst. A younger generation
is also represented, like the 1974-born American Matthew
Day Jackson. Parts of the collection are shown in regular
intervals and in new constellations in a peppering of museums across Asia, the United States, and Europe. By appointment, art lovers can take a tour of the Domus Collection
in its impressive 700-square-meter space, in Chang's Beijing
office building.

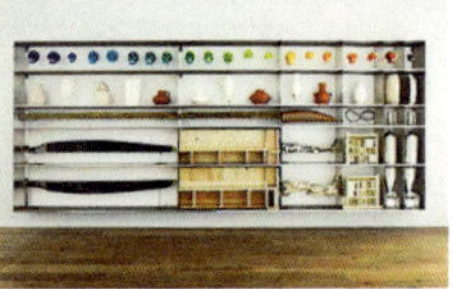

Collector:
Richard Chang

Address:
Airport Service Road 255
Caochangdi
Beijing 100015
China
info@domuscollection.com.cn
www.domuscollection.com.cn

E-mail appointment only.

Since the opening of the Chinese economy in the 1980s, the Chinese art market has been rapidly expanding, later experiencing a boom and eventually making headlines around the world. Works by Chinese artists command record prices, and the local **Beijing** scene has grown like wildfire. But asking where the "hot spot" of Chinese contemporary art is yields no reliable answer; it's seemingly everywhere. Coinciding with attention paid to Chinese artists is the exploding price of Chinese real estate, which often forces artists to move elsewhere. New artist neighborhoods and complexes are constantly emerging, and the art scene develops as quickly as the Chinese economy itself.

The most well known art address is 798 Art Zone, also called Dashanzi Art District, in the northeast part of the city. The former factory site has evolved in recent years as a magnet for galleries and creative people. Not far away are other artist quarters, like the Jiuchang Art Complex, the Caochangdi district, or the artist colony Songzhuang Art Community.

Among the important galleries in Beijing are the Aye Gallery, the Long March Space, White Space Beijing, and, of course, the international galleries that have opened branches here, including Pace of New York, the Italian Galleria Continua, or the Swiss galleries Boers-Li Gallery and Galerie Urs Meile.

If you're looking to learn more about Chinese art history, visit the National Art Museum of China (NAMOC), which features Chinese art from antiquity to today. More contemporary is the program of the Ullens Center for Contemporary Art (UCCA), which was founded by the Belgian collectors Guy and Myriam Ullens. New art can also be discovered in exhibitions at the CAFA Art Museum of the Beijing Art Academy, or during the Art Beijing art fair, in April, and during the Beijing Biennale, in October.

Silvia Anna Barrilà

More Information: www.bmw-art-guide.com

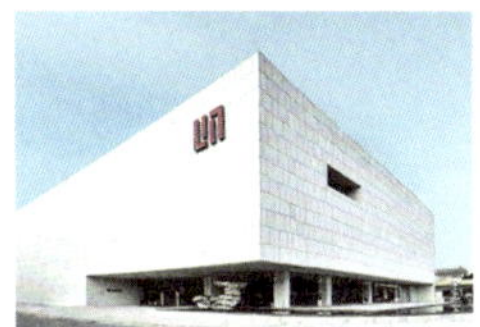

Collectors:
Liu Yiqian & Wang Wei

Address:
No. 210, Lane 2255
Luoshan Road
Shanghai
China
Tel +86 21 68778787
info@thelongmuseum.org
www.thelongmuseum.org

Opening Hours:
Mon–Sun 9:30am–5pm

28   Long Museum
An overview of Chinese art history and contemporary art

The first collectors from Mainland China to make it onto the 2012 *Artnews* list of the 200 top collectors were the investor Liu Yiqian and his wife, Wang Wei. In December of that same year the billionaires made their collection of Chinese art public, in the Long Museum, in Shanghai. Liu Yiqian's story began in the late 1980s, with the opening of the Chinese market. First he turned his mother's small shop into a thriving business. Then a friend familiarized him with the newly created financial sector, where he augmented his fortune. For the last twenty years the couple has bought art from China, mainly at auctions. According to the BBC, their collection is now worth more than one billion dollars. It ranges from traditional art to Revolution-era works to contemporary pieces by artists such as Zhou Chunya, Wang Guangyi, Zhang Xiaogang, and Yue Minjun.

Collector:
Qiao Zhibing

Address:
Shanghai Night
Caobao Road 400
Xuhui District
Shanghai
China
qiaozhibing@gmail.com

E-mail appointment only.

29   Qiao Zhibing Collection
An idiosyncratic presentation of new Chinese artists amid Shanghai's nightlife

In a nightclub called Shanghai Night, in the southwestern part of the city, lives a modest but uniquely displayed collection of Chinese and international art. The roughly thirty works, in a variety of categories, spread over four floors and 10 000 square meters, are supplied courtesy of Qiao Zhibing, who's been collecting since 2006. The glaring ambiance agrees with the artwork—and offers a particularly interesting ocular experience. The collection's central concern is new Chinese art—artists born in the 1970s and '80s—including Qiu Xiaofei, Li Hui, Xu Zhen, or Gao Lei. An additional focus is on Shanghai, with painters like Ding Yi and Zhang Enli. Among the internationally known figures are light artist Tatsuo Miyajima and Adel Abdessemed.

D

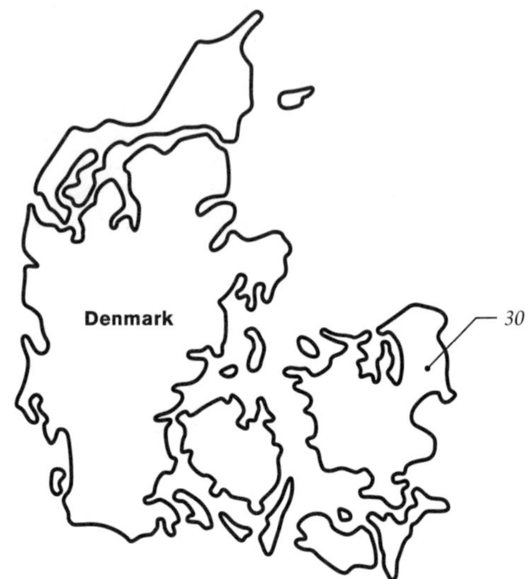

30 Djurhuus Collection
*International contemporary art tending toward irony
and the grotesque*

If you have reservations, don't do it! This is the maxim of
the Copenhagen lawyer and art collector Leif Djurhuus,
who has been devoid of doubt roughly 2 000 times, the
number of works in his collection. He does not own a
private museum; they are stored in a warehouse. A selection of 200 works was exhibited from August 2011 to Janu-
ary 2012 at the ARoS Aarhus Art Museum: works by the
1960s Danish avant-garde, such as Poul Gernes or Sven
Dalsgaard. There are also international sky-rocketers like
Robert Kusmirowski or Kendell Geers, along with plenty
of young artists from all over the world. What interests
Djurhuus is "cutting edge," border-crossing, provocative young art. If you make an appointment with him,
Leif Djurhuus will show you his collection wherever it is
being exhibited.

Collector:
Leif Djurhuus

Address:
Copenhagen, Denmark
sf@djurhuuscollection.com
www.djurhuuscollection.com

Visitation permitted only
occasionally. Please inquire
by e-mail.

F

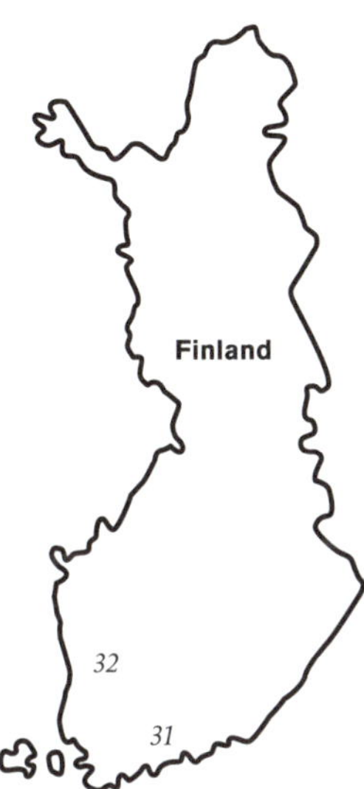

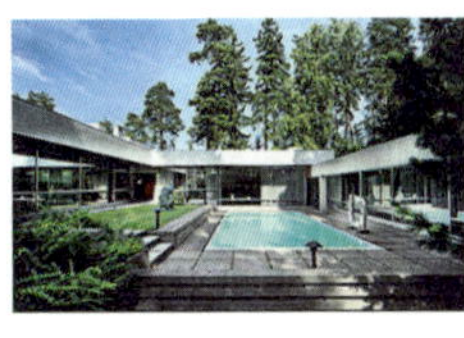

Collector:
Gunnar & Marie-Louise Didrichsen

Address:
Kuusilahdenkuja 1
00340 Helsinki
Finland
Tel +358 9 4778330
office@didrichsenmuseum.fi
www.didrichsenmuseum.fi

Opening Hours:
Tues–Sun: 11am–6pm

Due to renovation, the collection
will be closed until May 2014.

31   Didrichsen Art Museum
*International and Finnish art in a once very
modern Finnish home*

A house in the elegant International Style, flooded with
light, overlooking the ocean and a garden dotted with sculptures by Henry Moore. This dreamy house is not located in
the Pacific Palisades, California, but rather on a bay near
Helsinki. The modernist villa, built in 1958, belonged to
the collector pair Gunnar and Marie-Louise Didrichsen. Its
architect, Viljo Revell, once an assistant to Alvar Aalto, later
added a structure that in 1965 was opened as the Didrichsen
Art Museum. Gunnar Didrichsen, a Dane who moved to
Finland in 1928 and started a lucrative business, began collecting with his wife, Marie-Louise, and he loved progress
as much as he liked art. The comprehensive collection includes classical modernist works alongside pre-Columbian
art and Chinese antiquities.

32   Sara Hildén Art Museum
*One of the most important Finnish art hubs,
located on a beautiful lake*

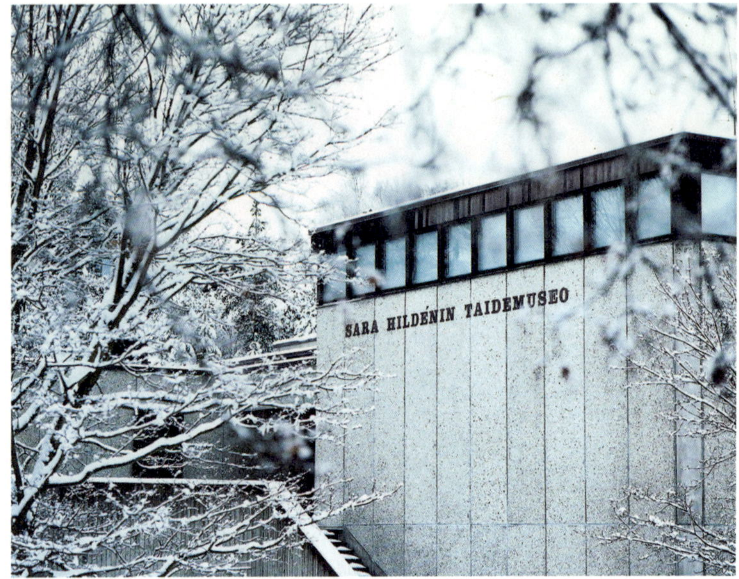

Typical Finland: the Sara Hildén Art Museum, in Tampere, is nestled harmoniously in an expansive sculpture park backed up to a lakeshore. Sara Hildén (1905–1993) was a successful entrepreneur in the fashion industry who collected Finnish and international artists of her time. In 1962 she established a foundation. The museum was commissioned by the city of Tampere in 1979, and was designed by the local architect Pekka Ilveskoski as a two-storey, low-rise building with large windows. Over 1 500 square meters serve to showcase the collection's works, some 4 500 objects. The focus remains on Finnish art: from the "Finnish Frida Kahlo," Helene Schjerfbeck (1862–1946), to very young artists. Wide-ranging special exhibitions show internationally known artists like Alex Katz, Subodh Gupta, or Wilhelm Sasnal.

Collector:
Sara Hildén

Address:
Laiturikatu 13, Särkänniemi
33230 Tampere
Finland
Tel +358 3 56543500
sara.hilden@tampere.fi
www.tampere.fi/english/sarahilden

Opening Hours:
Tues–Sun: 11am–6pm

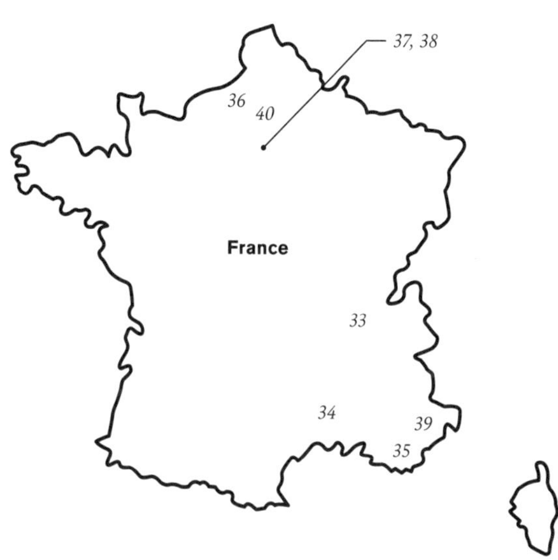

F

33 Fondation pour l'art contemporain—Claudine & Jean-Marc Salomon

Contemporary art in a castle, and sculpture in the garden amidst the Savoyard Alps

Collectors:
Claudine & Jean-Marc Salomon

Address:
191 Route du Château
74290 Alex
France
Tel +33 4 50028752
www.fondation-salomon.com

Opening Hours:
Thurs–Sun: 2–7pm

Claudine and Jean-Marc Salomon chose a beautiful, secluded location for the presentation of their contemporary art collection: encircled by small streams and earthy ponds, the Château d'Arenthon looks out onto the 900-soul village Alex in the Savoyard Alps. Winter-sports fans are familiar with the name Salomon, the company that invented the modern ski-binding. The company was sold to Adidas in 1997, and Jean-Marc Salomon is the grandson of the company's founder. The Fondation Salomon opened with a drum roll in 2001: forty works by the eccentric artist duo Gilbert & George caused quite a stir in the tranquil mountain valleys—and bestowed the collection with the added attention from which it profits today. The two annual exhibitions feature either a single artist or a part of the collection. The sculpture park with works by Jan Fabre and Antony Gormley is also worth seeing.

34   Collection Lambert

*Museum-quality international contemporary art
since 1960*

The inventory list of the Collection Lambert reads like
the Who's Who of recent art history: from Francis Alÿs
to Lawrence Weiner, and a slew of top names in between
that would make any museum director jealous: Louise
Bourgeois, Anselm Kiefer, and Jenny Holzer, just to name
a few. Yvon Lambert is one of the most trendsetting gallerists in all of France. His gallery, founded in 1966, remains
one of the hot spots of the Parisian art scene. With the
Collection Lambert, in Avignon, he has fulfilled the dream
of bringing his collection to his hometown in southern
France. It opened in 2000, when Avignon had been designated a "European Capital of Culture" for the year. Here
350 works from Lambert's 1 200 are housed in the Hôtel de
Caumont, an eighteenth-century palace, where two exhibitions are presented each year.

Collector:
Yvon Lambert

Address:
5 Rue Violette
84000 Avignon
France
administration@collectionlambert.com
www.collectionlambert.com

Opening Hours:
Tues–Sun: 11am–6pm

35   Peyrassol—Parc de Sculptures

A sculpture park on a centuries-old vineyard in Provence

Located on the historic vineyard estate Peyrassol, northwest of Saint-Tropez, in the Var Département of the Provence region, is one of France's youngest private sculpture
parks. In 2001 the Brussels entrepreneur Philippe Austruy
and his wife, gallery owner Valérie Bach, acquired the
vineyard, which dates back to the year 1256. For the Franco-
Belgian couple, wine, food, and hospitality are equally as
important as contemporary art. Nestled on the wooded
grounds are over twenty sculptures by Jean Dubuffet, Cesar,
Jean Tinguely, and Jaume Plensa, among others—and the
collection is being constantly expanded. In recent years,
works by French artists like Jeanne Susplugas or Fabrice
Langlade have been added. The perfect blend of art, Pro-
vencal flavors, and warm Mediterranean sun comprise the
charm of this special place.

Collectors:
Valérie Bach & Philippe Austruy

Address:
Commanderie de Peyrassol
RN 7
83340 Flassans sur Issole
France
Tel +33 4 94697102
contact@peyrassol.com
www.peyrassol.com

Opening Hours:
Early May–mid-September:
Mon–Fri: 9am–7pm
Sat–Sun: 10am–7pm
Mid-September–end of April:
Mon–Sat: 10am–6pm

36 Le Silo

*Minimal and Conceptual Art arranged perfectly
in a former grain silo*

Collectors:
Jean-Philippe & Françoise Billarant

Address:
Route de Bréançon
95640 Marines
France
lesilo@billarant.com

By appointment only.

They don't consider themselves pure collectors; they're more artists' companions and contemporaries. For over thirty years the Parisian business couple Jean-Philippe and Françoise Billarant have been intensely engaged with Minimal and Conceptual Art. Their friendships with artists have played a central role: Carl Andre, Robert Barry, François Morellet, and Michel Verjux are all pals. In Marines, a small city northwest of Paris, the couple had a 1948 grain silo transformed into exhibition spaces by the young architect Xavier Prédine-Hug, a former employee of Philippe Starck, who remodeled the simple structure into a reductive cathedral. And the artists? They thanked the collectors for their decades-long loyalty with perfect site-specific installations.

F

37 La Maison Rouge

*Attractive guest collections in Paris
and exciting artist projects*

Collector:
Antoine de Galbert

Address:
10 Boulevard de la Bastille
75012 Paris
France
Tel +33 1 40010881
info@lamaisonrouge.org
www.lamaisonrouge.org

Opening Hours:
Wed: 11am–7pm
Thurs: 11am–9pm
Fri–Sun: 11am–7pm

If you stroll along Boulevard de la Bastille, you will not come upon this "red house," as the name implies. The only thing red is a neon sign designating the private museum, which was opened in 2004 by the political scientist and supermarket-dynasty heir Antoine de Galbert. Once inside the 2 000-square-meter complex, however, you will find that red house, after all: in the covered courtyard stands a bright red structure—housing the café. De Galbert enjoys enigmatic staging. He also plays this kind of hide-and-seek game with his collection, which is not on permanent display, but rather rotates with those of his friends. Numerous top collections, like those of Thomas Olbricht or Harald Falckenberg, have made appearances at La Maison Rouge. Thematic and monographic exhibitions also take place here, as well as projects with artists ranging from Arnulf Rainer to Gregor Schneider.

38 Rosenblum Collection
Emerging artists alongside established names

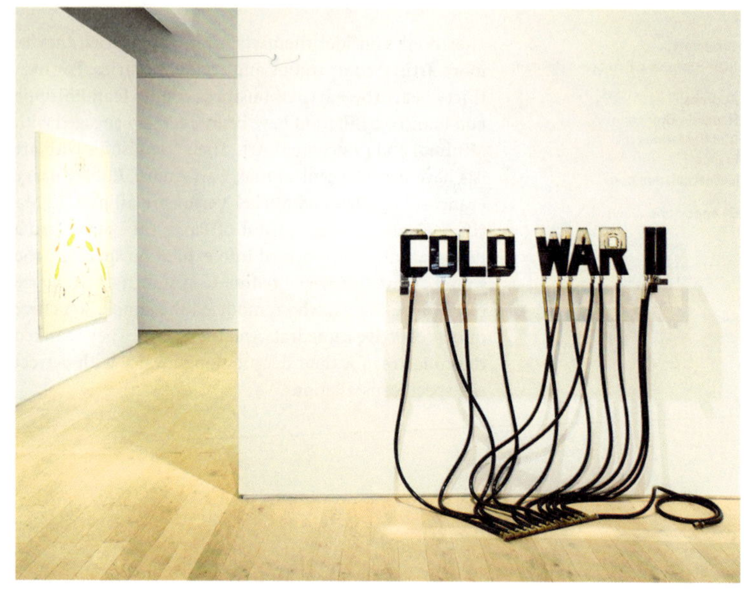

Art in a bunker. Not above ground, like the one Christian Boros has in Berlin, but rather discretely hidden underground, in Paris. Steve Rosenblum, the founder of an Internet start-up, and his wife, Chiara, commissioned award-winning architect Joseph Dirand to convert the sprawling rooms of a 1950s fallout shelter into a museum and private home. After traversing forty meters through a dark tunnel, one arrives at the empire of the young collector couple, who favor art of their own generation: Christoph Büchel, Gregor Hildebrand, or Aleksandra Mir are hip. At the Rosenblum collection, they meet established art by Duane Hanson or Christian Boltanski. Another great idea: friends of the couple are asked to add to the collection. Not least, an accessible audio-video archive library is equipped with the featured artists' favorite books, CDs, and DVDs.

Collectors:
Steve & Chiara Rosenblum

Address:
183 Rue du Chevaleret
75013 Paris
France
Tel +33 1 44245417
info@rosenblumcollection.fr
www.rosenblumcollection.fr

Only guided tours with prior online registration, every Saturday 11am and 3pm. Individual group tours by e-mail appointment.

"Paris is simply fantastic," says the young Parisian artist Jeanne Susplugas. "You fall in love again and again with this city. The cultural scene is extraordinarily rich. From the museums to the opera, from the galleries and art centers to private art initiatives, like the Maison Rouge." In 2012, the Palais de Tokyo was reopened after an expansion: an 8 000-square-meter laboratory for new international contemporary art—perfect for night owls, as it's open until midnight. There you'll also find one of the most popular art bookstores in the city, with a huge selection of art catalogs, magazines, and editions. Major exhibitions of modern and contemporary art are on show at the Centre Pompidou, the Jeu de Paume, and the Musée d'Art Moderne de la Ville de Paris, all in the city center, as well as the Fondation Cartier, which lies a bit further south, in the 14th Arrondissement. In addition, every summer the extensive monographic exhibition Monumenta, at the Grand Palais, which has included stars like Daniel Buren and Anish Kapoor, attracts throngs of visitors. The Grand Palais is also the venue of two high-profile autumn fairs: the FIAC art fair and Paris Photo. The biannual Mois de la Photo (Month of Photography) draws

photo enthusiasts from all over the world to **Paris** with dozens of photo exhibitions in museums and galleries. Since 2006, the Paris Triennial for contemporary art has breathed new life into the city. If you want to visit commercial galleries, head to the Marais district. Here you'll find the established gallery Yvon Lambert with a nice bookstore containing rare catalogs and editions. In recent years, a hip new gallery district has also popped up in the dynamic neighborhood of Belleville. And uncompromisingly contemporary galleries like Bugada & Cargnel or Balice Hertling are always worth a visit.

Nicole Büsing & Heiko Klaas

More Information: www.bmw-art-guide.com

39 Fondation Maeght
*Key figures of the twentieth-century avant-garde
and a grandiose sculpture park*

Collectors:
Aimé & Marguerite Maeght

Address:
623 Chemin des Gardettes
06570 Saint-Paul-de-Vence
France
Tel +33 4 93324596
contact@fondation-maeght.com
www.fondation-maeght.com

Opening Hours:
April–June
Mon–Sun: 10am–6pm
July–September
Mon–Sun: 10am–7pm
October–March
Mon–Sun: 10am–1pm,
2–6pm

It all started in the 1920s. Aimé Maeght, a lithographer, moved from the outskirts of Lille to Cannes and opened a small printing company with his wife, Marguerite, where they also sold radios and furniture. The then-unknown painter Pierre Bonnard asked them to take a few of his paintings on commission. They sold out in an instant, leading to one of the biggest success stories of twentieth-century art dealing. In 1946 the couple opened their legendary gallery in Paris and organized shows with Henri Matisse, Marc Chagall, and Wassily Kandinsky, and with Americans like Alexander Calder. The Fondation Maeght, founded in 1964, centers on works by all these artists and acts as a gift to posterity. With aesthetic assistance from the likes of Marc Chagall, Joan Miró, and Georges Braque, Spanish architect Lluís Sert constructed a museum of Mediterranean light that attracts roughly 200 000 visitors a year.

F

40 Fondation Francès
Contemporary photography in the service of discussion

Collectors:
Estelle & Hervé Francès

Address:
27 Rue Saint-Pierre
60300 Senlis
France
www.fondationfrances.com

Opening Hours:
Tues–Sat: 11am–1pm,
2–7pm

For Estelle and Hervé Francès, the collector's mission is not just to pile up works of art, but rather to be creative in bringing diverse art positions together in order to foster dialogue. In 2009 the head of a cultural communication office and her husband, an ad agency boss, opened their collection in Senlis, a small city outside of Paris. The 300-square-meter space in an eighteenth-century building offers enough room for thematic exhibitions every half year. There are also guest studios, where artists can spend a summer. The Francès' collection aims to provoke viewers into discussion, to foster new interactions, and to unsettle the emotions. Exhibiting photographs of vulnerable or sexually charged human bodies—works by Andres Serrano, Vanessa Beecroft, Dash Snow, or Larry Clark—often does the trick.

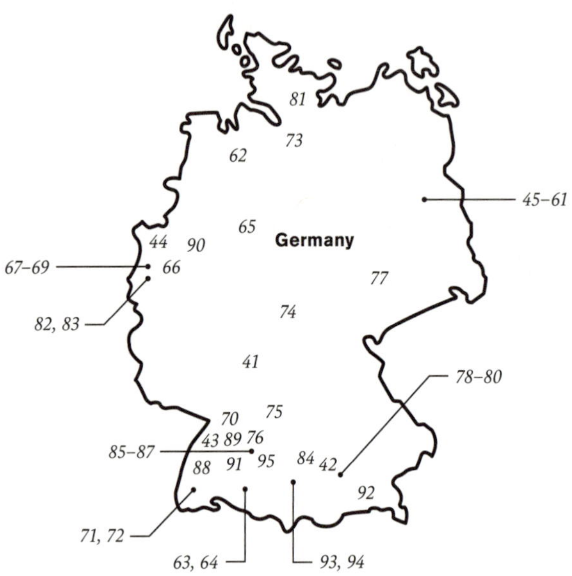

G

41 Sammlung Fiede
Young contemporary art in a carefully renovated former slaughterhouse

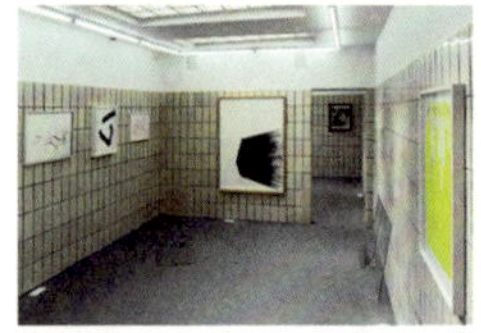

When Friedrich Gräfling was fifteen years old, in 2003, he was faced with the decision to buy a PlayStation or the work of a graffiti artist. He opted for the latter, and thereby laid the foundation for this impressive collection of contemporary art. Today, the architecture student lives in London but he continues to show his art in his hometown of Aschaffenburg, where he has converted a former slaughterhouse into an unconventional 600-square-meter venue, featuring one new exhibition annually. "I am interested in the idea of sharing these works with people who otherwise might not have the opportunity to see artists from abroad or even this kind of art," said the collector, who proved early on to possess a good sense for rising international stars, acquiring works by Marc Quinn, Gregor Hildebrandt, and Alicja Kwade.

Collector:
Friedrich Gräfling

Address:
Frohsinnstrasse 21 (rear building)
63739 Aschaffenburg
Germany
info@sammlung-fiede.com
www.sammlung-fiede.de

Opening hours vary. Please check the website for most current information.

42 Kunstmuseum Walter
Former East meets West in a remodeled industrial monument

Collector:
Ignaz Walter

Address:
Im Glaspalast
86153 Augsburg
Germany
Tel +49 821 8151163
office@kunstmuseumwalter.com
www.kunstmuseumwalter.com

Opening Hours:
Fri–Sun: 11am–6pm
And by appointment.

His motto: *Don't understand art the way others tell you to.* The Augsburg developer Ignaz Walter has been collecting modern and contemporary art since the early 1970s—mainly painting and sculpture, but also the less-than-popular glass art. Big names of the early twentieth century like Otto Dix, Lyonel Feininger, or August Macke find space in Walter's collection, as does art from East and West Germany. Painters from the former East Germany—Bernhard Heisig, Wolfgang Mattheuer, or Werner Tübke—are represented as prominently as Georg Baselitz, Sigmar Polke, or Gerhard Richter, who were all born in East Germany but began their careers in the West. Walter exhibits his roughly 1 600 works in a 6 000-square-meter glass palace, a remodeled industrial landmark in Augsburg's garment district.

G

43 Museum Frieder Burda
Classical modernism and luxury-class international contemporary art

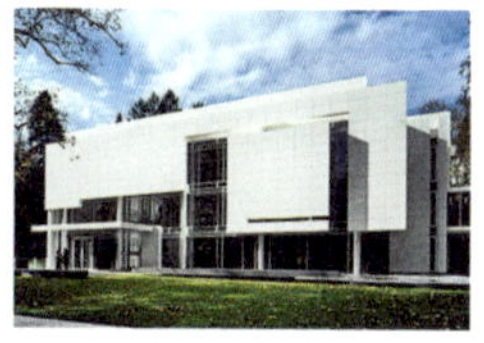

Collector:
Frieder Burda

Address:
Lichtentaler Allee 8B
76530 Baden-Baden
Germany
Tel +49 7221 398980
office@museum-frieder-burda.de
www.museum-frieder-burda.de

Opening Hours:
Tues–Sun: 10am–6pm

For Frieder Burda, art is the elixir of life. The son of a publisher, Burda had proved to have good instincts already in his early thirties: the first artwork he bought was by Lucio Fontana. Now he owns more than 850 works: classics of German Expressionism, as well as representatives of Abstract Expressionism, like Jackson Pollock or Mark Rothko. His Picasso collection ranks among the most important in Germany, as does his collection of German postwar art, with numerous works by Georg Baselitz, Eugen Schönebeck, or Gerhard Richter. Driven by his lust for painting, Burda also buys current positions like Corinne Wasmuht or Karin Kneffel. This extraordinary assembly of works demanded a suitable home: in 2004 the collector opened his private museum in the posh city of Baden-Baden—a snow-white building designed by the American star architect Richard Meier. It has already drawn over two million visitors.

44   Stiftung Museum Schloss Moyland
*An extensive collection of Joseph Beuys's life
and work meets contemporaries*

The art-enthusiast brothers Hans and Franz Joseph van der Grinten had a lifelong friendship with Joseph Beuys. This resulted in a vast collection of nearly 6 000 works and roughly 100 000 letters, photos, and notes by the action artist, as well as numerous works by other artists. The Schloss Moyland collection was made public in 1997, and under director Bettina Paust it has undertaken a new conceptual turn: international research on Beuys has taken center stage since 2009, and the number of exhibited works was reduced by 90 percent. Furthermore, the house has shined anew since a 2011 renovation. Special exhibits featuring young artists or Beuys's students, such as Katharina Sieverding, should certainly sustain visitors to this idyllic moated castle on the Lower Rhine.

G

Collectors:
Hans & Franz Joseph
van der Grinten

Address:
Am Schloss 4
47551 Bedburg-Hau
Germany
Tel +49 2824 951060
info@moyland.de
www.moyland.de

Opening Hours:
April–September
Tues–Fri: 11am–6pm
Sat–Sun: 10am–6pm
October–March
Tues–Sun: 11am–5pm

45   Ausstellungsraum
Céline & Heiner Bastian
*Top figures and new positions in a Berlin
"townhouse for art"*

The corner building across from the Neues Museum is a good address: Heiner Bastian bought the prime property at the Kupfergraben in 2000 and initiated an international architectural competition to build on it. David Chipperfield offered the most convincing pitch, an elegant contemporary building adapted to the historical context that peers onto the street through large plate-glass windows. Bastian, a former assistant to Joseph Beuys, financed the entire project, which he calls a "townhouse for art." The two lower levels are rented to the blue-chip gallery Contemporary Fine Arts, and part of Bastian's own collection inhabits a second-floor showroom, where the work of Beuys and Damien Hirst mingle with that of younger artists. Bastian was a curator at the Hamburger Bahnhof until 2007, and he aims now to show artists he was not able to show then.

Collectors:
Céline & Heiner Bastian

Address:
Am Kupfergraben 10
10117 Berlin
Germany
Tel +49 30 20673840
info@heinerbastian.com

Opening Hours:
Thurs–Fri: 11am–5pm
Sat: 11am–4pm

46   Sammlung Boros

*Roughly 700 works of contemporary art
in an extensively refurbished bunker*

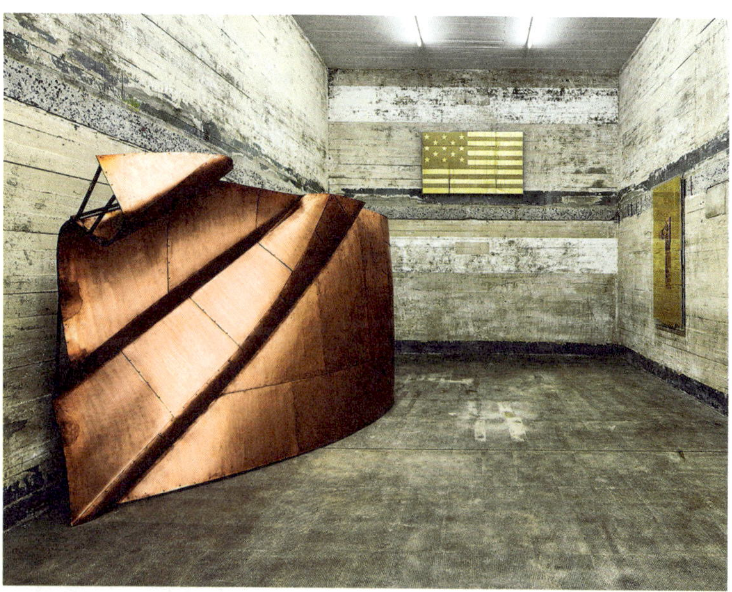

Collectors:
Christian & Karen Boros

Address:
Bunker, Reinhardtstrasse 20
10117 Berlin
Germany
Tel +49 30 27594065
info@sammlung-boros.de
www.sammlung-boros.de

Opening Hours:
Thurs: 4–7:30pm
Fri–Sun: 10am–4:30pm
Only guided tours with prior online
registration. Special tours available
by e-mail appointment.

This is one of the most spectacular places for a private collection of zeitgeisty art. It took Karen and Christian Boros four years to transform a former air-raid bunker, a historic monument in Berlin-Mitte, into their private museum. On top of this colossus they built a luxurious penthouse. Ad-man Boros, who has offices in Wuppertal and Berlin, has been collecting contemporary art since the 1990s. Since 2008 the collection has exhibited groups of works by twenty contemporary artists, who have operated within a given space. Many of them, like Olafur Eliasson, Cosima von Bonin, or Tomás Saraceno, created very tailored site-specific works. The remodeling of the Boros bunker—which was used in East Germany as a warehouse for exotic fruits, and then as a techno club after the Wall came down—took both time and money. Architect Jens Casper had to remove a number of walls to transform 120 small rooms into 80 larger ones that take up 3 000 square meters.

47   Salon Dahlmann
*A Finnish collector and the revival of the
salon tradition in Berlin*

You simply can't ignore Berlin. The Finnish collector
Timo Miettinen is convinced of this. In 2010 he acquired,
together with his three sisters, an impressive historical
building in Berlin-Charlottenburg. The technology company owner initiated a salon with rotating exhibitions
on the building's first floor. Since 2004 he has collected—
together with his wife, the architect Iiris Ulin—international contemporary art with a focus on Germany and Finland. At the Marburger Strasse 3 address he also presents
works from his collection, ranging from Albert Oehlen
and Björn Dahlem to Marianna Uutinen. At the center
of his interest, however, is his Salon Dahlmann—named
after the home's previous owner—which hosts openings
that are always well attended. Miettinen also regularly
invites young curators to have a fresh look at other scenes
and collectors.

Collectors:
Timo Miettinen & Iiris Ulin

Address:
Marburger Strasse 3
10789 Berlin
Germany
Tel +49 30 21909830
info@marburger3.de
www.marburger3.de

Opening hours vary. Please
check the website for most
current information.

48   Sammlung Arthur de Ganay
*Architectural, city, and landscape photography
in an extraordinary Berlin loft*

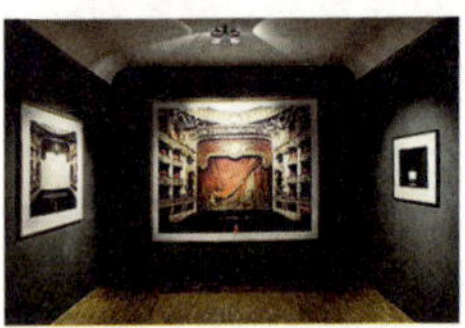

Once a month, on an entire floor of a spacious loft converted in 2006 from an old jelly factory in Berlin-Kreuzberg,
photography fans swarm to hear Arthur de Ganay lead
a tour through his remarkable collection overlooking the
river Spree. The collection's nucleus is comprised of works
by Becher students like Candida Höfer, Thomas Ruff, and
Thomas Struth. But conceptual photographers also play a
role—Lewis Baltz or Hiroshi Sugimoto, for example—and
younger positions are given ample room. When de Ganay,
a Paris-born architect, moved to Berlin, in 2001, he had
been collecting for eight years. Now he's not just interested in bringing together works of art and making them
publicly accessible; he also wants to push the medium of
photography into equal standing with painting. Considering the immense caliber of his collection, photography
stands quite the chance.

Collector:
Arthur de Ganay

Address:
Köpenicker Strasse 10A
10997 Berlin
Germany
info@collectionarthurdeganay.com
www.collectionarthurdeganay.com

Only guided tours with prior e-mail
registration. Every first Saturday of
the month, 2–4pm.

49   Sammlung Barbara and Axel Haubrok— Haubrokprojects
Contemporary avant-garde instead of government vehicles in Berlin-Lichtenberg

Collectors:
Barbara & Axel Haubrok

Address:
Herzbergstrasse 40–43
10365 Berlin
Germany
Tel +49 172 2109525
info@haubrok.org
www.haubrok.org

By appointment only.

Barbara and Axel Haubrok like art they don't immediately get. Perhaps this is why the Berlin couple, who moved from the Rhineland, has managed since 1988 to compile one of the most progressive collections of contemporary art in all of Germany. Their focus is clearly on contemporary minimalist and concept art, with works by exactly thirty international artists, including Christopher Williams, Carol Bove, and Wade Guyton. Understatement instead of extravagance: Since 2005, the Haubroks have been organizing sophisticated exhibitions in their showroom at Strausbergerplatz. Looking for a new challenge, in April 2013 they started to show their collection in rooms on the premises of a 20 000-square-meter compound of a former car-dispatch garage in Berlin-Lichtenberg. Where official vehicles of the former GDR ministries once stood will soon stand a new cultural center with workshops, warehouses, and exhibit spaces.

G

50   Sammlung Hoffmann
International contemporary art in a collector's private residence

Collectors:
Erika & Rolf Hoffmann

Address:
Sophie-Gips-Höfe, Staircase C
Sophienstrasse 21
10178 Berlin
Germany
Tel +49 30 28499120
info@sammlung-hoffmann.de
www.sammlung-hoffmann.de

Only guided tours with prior registration, every Saturday from 11am–4pm.

They were among the first to head to Berlin after the Fall of the Wall to make their personal collection of art available to the public. Erika and Rolf Hoffmann, from Mönchengladbach, had been collecting German and American artists such as Günther Uecker, Frank Stella, or Bruce Nauman for some time. When they moved to Berlin, in the mid-1990s, they had long since sold their textile company. They acquired a former sewing-machine factory in Berlin-Mitte, entirely renovated it, and then moved into two of its floors. And now they have created something of a ritual in the German capital: every Saturday small groups of visitors in grey felt slippers push through the spacious private rooms, led by young, laid-back guides. Once a year the rooms are switched out with new works. Fresh acquisitions from Poland, Japan, or China have shifted the collection's focus ever more eastward. Since her husband's death, in 2001, Erika Hoffmann has been actively leading the project herself.

51   Jarla Partilager
*In-depth mid-career exhibitions by known
contemporaries*

Who knows what the word *partilager* means? People familiar with Swedish, that's who: it means "outlet sale." But what
does that have to do with art? The Swedish financial advisor
Gerard De Geer collects high-quality, expensive contemporary works, like that of British video artist Phil Collins,
Dutch installation artist Mark Manders, or Danish superstar Olafur Eliasson. Back in Stockholm, De Geer used to
display works in his collection in a former warehouse outlet, before inaugurating a showroom in Berlin under the
same name, with a Thomas Scheibitz retrospective, in fall
2011. The Berlin location, a bright, sky-lit room on the
fourth floor of a gallery building on Lindenstrasse, is well
chosen. De Geer wants to slow down the hype by presenting just one artist a year. Following the Scheibitz show:
Thomas Schütte.

Collector:
Gerard De Geer

Address:
Lindenstrasse 34, 4th Floor
10969 Berlin
Germany
Tel +49 30 20188543
visit@jarlapartilager.org
www.jarlapartilager.org

E-mail appointment only.

52   Kienzle Art Foundation
Exciting rediscoveries far from the mainstream

Even in the Berlin art scene he is seen as an individualist,
which says a lot. Jochen Kienzle collects and displays
non-mainstream works of art, like those by painter Klaus
Merkel, who in the 1980s worked exclusively in a limited
gray palette. Or work by Josef Kramhöller, a painter and
performance artist who committed suicide in London in
2000 at age 31. Acknowledged as a talent by fellow artists,
Kramhöller was pretty much ignored by the art market.
Jochen Kienzle's parents collected modernist works, and
already as a high-school student he purchased his first work
of art at Art Basel, and went on to study art history. In 2010
the former gallerist opened the Kienzle Art Foundation,
and his engagement in the Berlin scene has earned him
much credit. The Kienzle Art Foundation works closely
with curators organizing temporary exhibitions, film
screenings, and discussion forums.

Collector:
Jochen Kienzle

Address:
Bleibtreustrasse 54
10623 Berlin
Germany
Tel +49 30 89627605
office@kienzleartfoundation.de
www.kienzleartfoundation.de

Opening Hours:
Thurs–Fri: 2–7pm
Sat: 11am–4pm

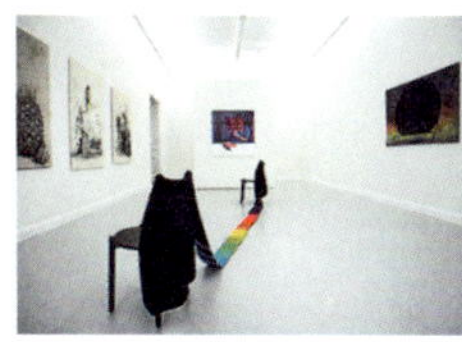

Collectors:
Geraldine Michalke &
Stefan Oehmen

Address:
Bülowstrasse 90
10783 Berlin
Germany
Tel +49 30 81801868
info@kunstsaele.de
www.kunstsaele.de

Opening Hours:
Wed–Sat: 11am–6pm
And by appointment.

53   Kunstsaele Berlin
Two exciting private collections and a gallery
together on one bel étage

Typical Berlin: two non-Berlin art collectors split a space with a new gallery and a hip platform for cultural events. Since the beginning of 2010 this renovated apartment hosts works from the Bergmeier and Oehmen collections. The Halle-born Geraldine Michalke, born Bergmeier, has amassed her collection over twenty-five years. The broad spectrum encompasses German Informel and young Leipzig photographers. Stephan Oehmen, an anesthetist **G** from the Rhineland, started his collection with Dieter Krieg, a painter of the New Figuration movement. He now complements his existing collection with works by artists like Bogomir Ecker or Gert & Uwe Tobias. Bergmeier and Oehmen also show treasured finds of fellow collectors. With the enterprising concept-art gallery Aanant & Zoo and their event program as an added extra, the Kunstsaele has since long become a hip meeting place in western Berlin.

Collector:
Thomas Olbricht

Address:
Auguststrasse 68
10117 Berlin
Germany
Tel +49 30 86008510
info@me-berlin.com
www.me-berlin.com

Opening Hours:
Tues–Sun: 12–6pm

54   ME Collectors Room
Berlin/Olbricht Foundation
A curiosity cabinet of existential themes from the
Renaissance to now

The body, eros, and transitoriness: existential topics at the center of the collection owned by Thomas Olbricht, a physician and heir to the Wella fortune. Olbricht was influenced by his great-uncle Karl Ströher's passion for collecting. Moreover, he loves extremities: Cindy Sherman meets the grand-style painter Jonas Burgert; Marlene Dumas meets Andres Serrano. Since 2010 the collection has been on display at a Düttmann & Kleymann-designed building on Auguststrasse in Berlin-Mitte. The ground floor houses a café, a shop, and a lounge; the remaining 1 300 square meters are reserved for exhibition space. The core of Olbricht's subjective *Wunderkammer* is formed by over 200 objects, dating back to the Renaissance and Baroque periods. The ME Collectors Room quickly became a space for dialogue with other collections and discourse over art in general. The "me," by the way, is an acronym for "moving energies."

55   Collection Regard

*Overlooked photography of the twentieth century
with Berlin in the "Mitte"*

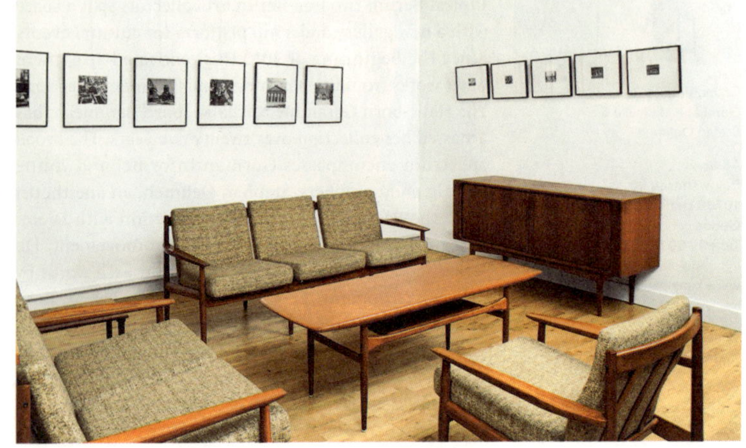

It all began with a fortuitous discovery: A few years ago French photography collector Marc Barbey found a suitcase full of negatives by the German photographer Hein Gorny (1904–1967). Since then he has administered the estate of the underappreciated photojournalist and commercial photographer. In 2011 Barbey showed the first part of the collection, Gorny's images of war-ravaged Berlin, accompanied by art historical research. Connoisseurs of photography were impressed. Since 2005, Barbey, a software entrepreneur and nephew of the Magnum photographer Bruno Barbey, has been focused on growing the Collection Regard. He is endowed with a sharp instinct for other overlooked twentieth-century talents. Stylish vintage furniture from Scandinavia provides for a relaxed atmosphere in his Berlin-Mitte apartment.

Collector:
Marc Barbey

Address:
Steinstrasse 12
10119 Berlin
Germany
Tel +49 30 84711947
info@collectionregard.com
www.collectionregard.com

Opening Hours:
Fri: 2–6pm (closed on holidays)
And by appointment.

56   Rocca Stiftung
*A thematically structured collection
of contemporary art in a villa*

Collector:
Joëlle & Eric Romba

Address:
Berlin, Germany
Tel +49 30 89398917
info@rocca-stiftung.de
www.rocca-stiftung.de

Visitation permitted only
occasionally. Please inquire
by e-mail.

Joëlle Romba brings the best possible conditions to building her own art collection. The art historian, curator, collection consultant, and art dealer garnered experience in a Berlin gallery and as the Berlin representative of the auction house Sotheby's. For the past ten years she and her husband, Eric, a lawyer, have acquired around 150 works of contemporary art, ranging from Gregor Hildebrandt, Thilo Heinzmann, and Wolfgang Tillmans, to Matti Braun and Charlotte Posenenske. The thematic foci of the collection—photorealistic painting, architecture in art, and the rethinking of art historical models—lends the collection structure and conceptual clarity. The Rombas present their treasures in a villa dating back to the turn of the century in Berlin-Nikolassee. Visitors are welcome by appointment.

G

57   Sammlung Schürmann
Art and antagonism in a collection growing since 1972

Collectors:
Gaby & Wilhelm Schürmann

Address:
Berlin, Germany
visit@schuermann-berlin.de

Visitation permitted only
occasionally. Please inquire
by e-mail.

Gaby and Wilhelm Schürmann's collection has been part of their lives for four decades. Wilhelm Schürmann, a photographer, describes the moment of confronting a new artwork as being like "sudden enlightenment." For the collector couple, this is where the value of art truly lies: in asking us to continuously modify our own set of values. They find this kind of edginess in the works of renowned artists like Martin Kippenberger or Cady Noland, as well as in the unsettling works of Monika Baer or Michael E. Smith. Continuously expanding since 1972, the Schürmann's collection is housed in a private Berlin apartment and shown to interested parties occasionally upon request.

58   Sammlung Christian Schwarm
*New art on a factory floor in Berlin-Kreuzberg—
and around the clock on the Web*

For Christian Schwarm, when it comes to collecting, two things are of the utmost importance: intuition and confrontation. For over eight years, the founder of the online platform Independent Collectors (IC) has been interested primarily in concept art, often that with a social or political connection. He owns major works by the art collective Slavs and Tatars, which pursues socio-historical investigations of Eurasia, and by the internationally established artist Fiona Banner. Schwarm has also assembled extensive groups of works by photo artist Peter Piller. While he regularly shows works from his collection in an old factory floor in Kreuzberg, which doubles as an office, part of his collection can also be seen on Independent Collectors' website, around the clock.

Collector:
Christian Schwarm

Address:
Berlin, Germany
sammlung@christianschwarm.com

Visitation permitted only occasionally. Please inquire by e-mail.

59   Sammlung Springmeier
*International contemporary art on an entire storey
of a Berlin building*

Giovanni Springmeier lives with his collection on an apartment floor in Berlin-Moabit. Since the 1990s the doctor has been purchasing contemporary art, ranging from Valérie Favre to Liam Gillick, and from Clemens von Wedemeyer to Claire Fontaine. When Springmeier occasionally opens his private rooms for visitors, they immediately get a sense of his enthusiasm for artistic positions and for the elaborate staging of his comprehensive collection of all media, which is summed up under the general theme *Man and His Complexities*. The holy alliance between art and life has long been passed down to his teenage children: in their rooms you'll not find standard teenager posters, but rather works by Karin Sander, John Baldessari, and Jonathan Monk. A guest will walk some fifty meters from the entrance to the back bedrooms—a course peppered with international art and design objects.

Collector:
Giovanni Springmeier

Address:
Berlin, Germany
homecollection@springmeier.eu
www.springmeier.eu

Visitation permitted only occasionally. Please inquire by e-mail.

Everyone is drawn to **Berlin**: the art student from Frankfurt or New York; the gallerist from the Rhineland who wants to open a capital-city branch; the foreign collector who can still find affordable rooms with provisional charm for his private showroom. A bustling and broadly branched international art scene gathers in Berlin. They meet at openings in the galleries of Berlin-Mitte, Charlottenburg, Kreuzberg, and Wedding. The current focal point is the area around Potsdamer Strasse, but in a few years, the caravan will surely move on. Institutional contemporary art exhibitions can be found at the Kunst-Werke Berlin (KW), on Auguststrasse, and at the Hamburger Bahnhof. The Martin-Gropius-Bau always offers exciting exhibitions, especially of classical photography. And whoever drives a bit further south of the city center will find the Haus am Waldsee, in Zehlendorf, which offers exciting exhibitions of international artists living in Berlin.
Since 1998, the Berlin Biennale has been enriching contemporary discourse with new artistic positions. But one need not wait two years; new ideas can always be found. Almost every evening, art enthusiasts can participate in intellectually stimulating events like artist talks, performances, or video screenings. Well-stocked art bookstores, such as Pro qm, or the cool newspaper shop Do You Read Me?, both in the city center, or Motto, in the Kreuzberg district, all invite visitors to linger for hours. And the art market? Since 2004, Gallery Weekend, which takes place the last weekend in April, attracts hundreds of international collectors to the city. Via VIP shuttle or bike, visitors can hit about fifty galleries. And at the start of the new art season, in September, there's the Art Berlin Contemporary (ABC), which is the nontraditional successor to the Art Forum Berlin, which concluded in 2011. All in all, there are a thousand good reasons to keep coming back to Berlin.

Nicole Büsing & Heiko Klaas

More Information: www.bmw-art-guide.com

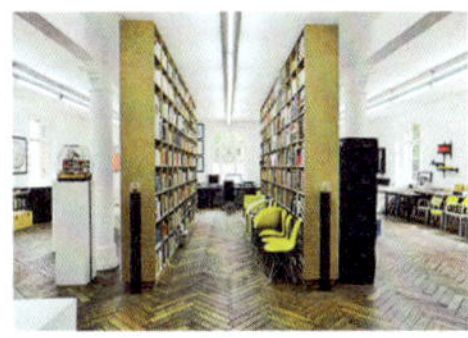

Collector:
Ivo Wessel

Address:
Berlin, Germany
email@ivo-wessel.de

Visitation permitted only
occasionally. Please inquire
by e-mail.

60   Sammlung Ivo Wessel
*Profound and humorous German and international
video and concept art*

Ivo Wessel is a fixture of the Berlin art scene. He's a frequent guest at podium discussions, a favorite interview partner when the topic is private collections, and, together with Olaf Stüber, an organizer of the successful monthly film-screening series *Videoart at Midnight*, at Kino Babylon. This all makes sense, as the main focus of the software developer's collection is video art. Wessel owns work by artists of his generation, such as Bjørn Melhus, Stefan Panhans, or Tracey Moffatt, all of which lean toward the dreamily surreal. He also collects works of concept art by the likes of Karin Sander, Via Lewandowsky, or Sven Johne. For Wessel, how the work is shown is not important. His private rooms, located on a former military property, have more of a "warehouse feel than exhibit space." If you want to visit, arrange a personal tour with Ivo Wessel himself.

G

Collector:
Thomas Rusche

Address:
Berlin, Germany
m.kuehn@kleidungskultur-soer.de
www.kleidungskultur-soer.de

Visitation permitted only
occasionally. Please inquire
by e-mail.

61   Sør Rusche Sammlung
*A traditional collection of Old Masters meets
contemporary art*

Thomas Rusche is a fourth-generation collector. The textile entrepreneur's great-grandfather drove a horse and carriage through the Münster region buying antiques from farmers. His grandfather collected old paintings, and his father focused on Old Masters of the seventeenth century. He took his son to auctions and museums, and at age fourteen Thomas Rusche acquired his first work of art. Today, the collection boasts over 2 500 works from over 500 artists, located at the family estate in the Westphalian city of Oelde, and, at a second location, in an Art Nouveau apartment in Berlin-Charlottenburg. The focus of the collection is now on contemporary painting, with works by Marlene Dumas, Daniel Richter, Matthias Weischer, or Martin Eder, among others. Rusche bought their pictures early and often—and before they were well known, a fact of which he remains proud. "It's a mistake to collect names," he warns.

62   Karin und Uwe Hollweg Stiftung
*Fluxus, Informel, and Pop live in discreet
Hanseatic ambience*

Businessman Uwe Hollweg and his wife, Karin, a painter, have been collectors since the early 1970s. They are known in Bremen as patrons and supporters of the local Kunsthalle. That the private collectors only sometimes open their collection to visitors is a bit of Hanseatic understatement. But whoever does manage to nab one of the very rare appointments will discover a fine collection in a historic trading house not far from the Kunsthalle. The collection bears the strong imprint of the collector couple's eclectic tastes, with works ranging from British Pop-Art pioneer Richard Hamilton to those by Dieter Roth and Wols and the melancholic paintings of Bremen's local art hero, Norbert Schwontkowski. The couple also owns an impressive collection of artist's books. Chairs and sofas add to the cozy ambience. "I find it very important that our guests have the opportunity to sit down and be comfortable," says Karin Hollweg.

Collectors:
Karin & Uwe Hollweg

Address:
Altenwall 6
28195 Bremen
Germany
office@hollweg-stiftung.de

By appointment only.

63   Museum Biedermann
*International contemporary art from the Neue Wilde
to the present*

When she was eighteen years old, Margit Biedermann traded a pack of cigarettes and a watch for her first artwork. By the end of the 1970s, she had started to collect more seriously: the Neue Wilde for example, which today comprises a large part of her collection, as well as abstract and figurative painting, prints, and sculpture from roughly 150 contemporary artists. The medical-technology businesswoman also collects works by artists who investigate the dialectic between materiality and surface, most prominently the British sculptor David Nash. The Museum Biedermann opened in 2009 in a former movie theater in the town of Donaueschingen. The structure was painstakingly renovated, and to it was added an elegant minimalist extension—room enough for Biedermann to present groupings of her collection at regular intervals.

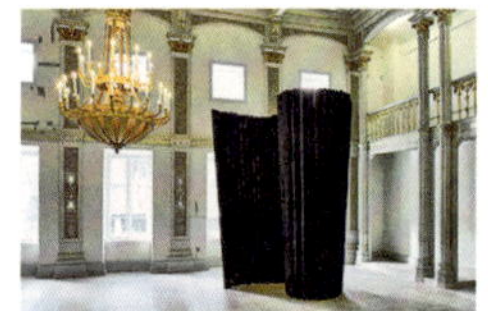

Collector:
Margit Biedermann

Address:
Museumsweg 1
78166 Donaueschingen
Germany
Tel +49 771 8966890
info@museum-biedermann.de
www.museum-biedermann.de

Opening Hours:
Tues–Sun: 11am–5pm

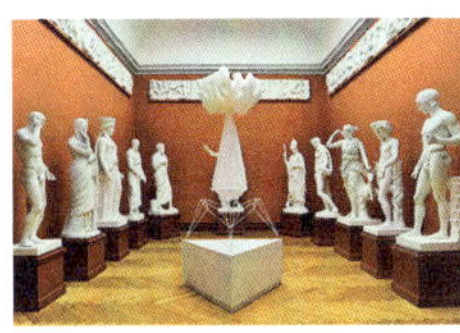

Collectors:
Christian & Jeannette
zu Fürstenberg

Address:
Am Karlsplatz 7
78166 Donaueschingen
Germany
Tel +49 771 229677563
info@fuerstenberg-
zeitgenoessisch.com
www.fuerstenberg-
zeitgenoessisch.com

Opening Hours:
April–November
Tues–Sat: 10am–1pm,
2–5pm
Sundays and holidays: 10am–7pm

64   Fürstenberg Zeitgenössisch
Innovative young art infiltrates princely pomp

Expectations are high: The aristocratic couple Christian and Jeannette zu Fürstenberg are creating a collection by seeking "young, emerging artists who have distinguished themselves in recent years by new formal languages and concepts, and in so doing have influenced the international discourse." Moritz Wesseler, a well-connected young curator from Düsseldorf, advises the couple. Since 2011 contemporary art has gradually been replacing the hunting trophies, goblets, and uniforms normally seen in a princely setting. Rising stars like Dirk Bell, Julian Göthe, or Kris Martin are already represented with their own artist rooms or interventions. The collection features regular thematic exhibitions of current positions.

G

Collectors:
Elisabeth & Joachim von Reden

Address:
Schloss & Gut Wendlinghausen
32694 Dörentrup
Germany
Tel +49 5265 8909
info@schloss-wendlinghausen.de
www.schloss-wendlinghausen.de

By appointment only.

65   Schloss Wendlinghausen
Contemporary art in the stately rooms and surrounding park of a moated castle

This is the place where the legendary liar Baron von Münchhausen visited his cousin Hilmar von Münchhausen: a grand, moated castle that the Westphalian nobleman built in the Weser Renaissance style in the early seventeenth century. Since the mid-eighteenth century, the castle and estate have been owned by the von Reden family. Current owners Elizabeth and Joachim von Reden operate an organic vegetable business and are avid collectors and supporters of contemporary art. Since the early 1980s they have presented a portion of their collection and work by guest artists in the castle itself. Since 1988 they have also utilized the property's vast park and its collection of rare botanicals. Visitors are invited to linger at works like Christoph Keller's *Regenmaschine* (Rain Machine), a red living-unit by Atelier van Lieshout, or—a new acquisition—a pavilion by the artist duo Heike Mutter and Ulrich Genth.

66   Museum DKM
An eclectic collection from antiquity to the present

G

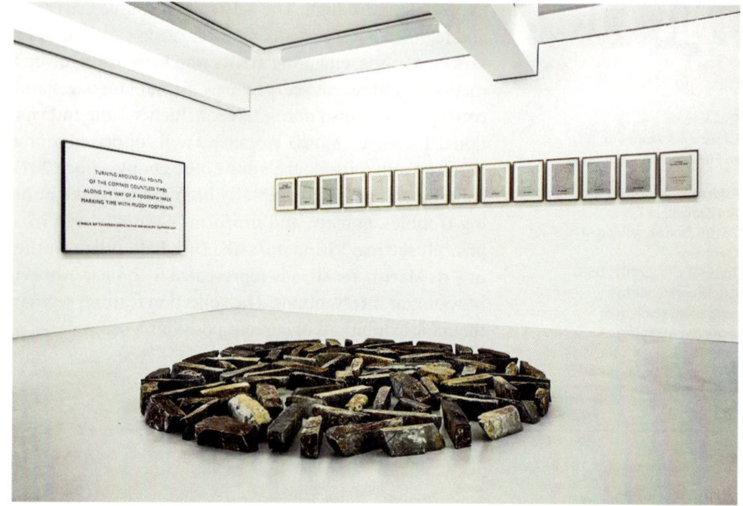

Germany is becoming a nation of non-profiteers, with over 350 new foundations established each year. Dirk Krämer and Klaus Maas include their own Museum DKM under this motto. The two collectors have been involved with art for over twenty years, along the way encouraging the responsible behavior of private collectors vis-à-vis the public. They established their foundation in 1999, and ten years later they opened a private museum designed by Swiss architect Hans Rohr. Their collection covers a wide array of areas: from ancient art through classical photography to contemporary art—particularly Concrete and Conceptual positions like Jan J. Schoonhoven or Ai Weiwei. Krämer and Maas also administer the estate of the German sculptor Ernst Hermanns, an important representative of Concrete Art.

Collectors:
Dirk Krämer & Klaus Maas

Address:
Güntherstrasse 13–15
47051 Duisburg
Germany
Tel +49 203 93555470
mail@museum-dkm.de
www.museum-dkm.de

Opening Hours:
Fri–Mon: 12–6pm
Tue–Thurs: by appointment

67   JaLiMa Collection
Young contemporary art at a new collectors hotspot in Düsseldorf

Collectors:
Jan-Holger & Mariam Arndt

Address:
Walzwerkstrasse 14
40599 Düsseldorf
Germany
info@jalimacollection.com
www.jalimacollection.com

Opening Hours:
Sat: 2–5:30pm
Sun: 2–4pm
And by appointment.

That a good neighborhood creates productive synergy is not only true in economics. In September 2012 Jan-Holger Arndt and his wife, Mariam, opened their Düsseldorf exhibition space not only in the same building, but even on the same floor as Gil Bronner's collection Philara. This allows for joint openings. Arndt, a lawyer from Hamburg and his German-Persian wife, a doctor, from Oldenburg, set out in their inaugural exhibition, *Life in the Woods – Aspects of Escapism*, the standards of what JaLiMa hopes to achieve in the future: exhibitions of young contemporary art drawn from the collection, supplemented by—where it makes sense—loans from other collectors and galleries. What remains is the question of the collection's unusual name, JaLiMa. It's an endearing compression of the German phrase "Jan liebt Mariam": Jan loves Mariam.

G

68   Philara—Sammlung zeitgenössischer Kunst
A dynamically growing collection of young art in all media

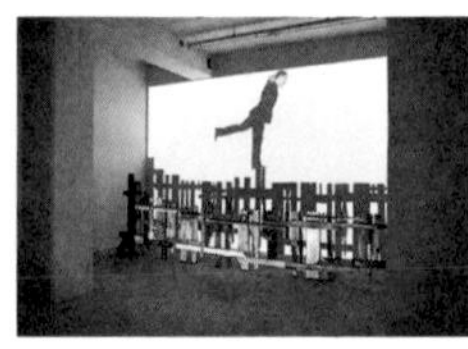

Collector:
Gil Bronner

Address:
Walzwerkstrasse 14
40599 Düsseldorf
Germany
info@philara.de
www.philara.de

By appointment only.

Art instead of file folders: the former Leitz factory in Düsseldorf-Reisholz retains the charming atmosphere of historical industrial architecture. It has been the center of Gil Bronner's activities since 2007. The busy real-estate developer from Düsseldorf feels bound to art on several levels: he owns a building containing seventy artist studios, the largest in the city; he organizes exhibitions four times a year; he endows artist stipends; and he adds to his collection, Philara, seemingly without pause. His showroom offers space enough for parts of his collection. Here one can find trendy installations by Terence Koh or Björn Dahlem, next to works from young Leipzig painters like Tilo Baumgärtel. The collection is comprised of around 800 works—and growing. Bronner buys works that capture him emotionally and aesthetically. One of them was the first sculpture ever made by Neo Rauch, in 2010.

69 Julia Stoschek Collection
An ambitious young collector lasered-in on media art

For the young collector Julia Stoschek, opening a private museum in 2007 was the climax of her rapid collecting career: one day while taking a walk, the 1975-born heiress came across a historic landmark factory building. Today it holds one of the most extensive private collections of media art in Germany. After undergoing complex modifications by the Berlin-based architecture firm Kuehn Malvezzi, the reinforced-concrete building shows a smattering of videos, **G** installations, and photographs spread across its multiple floors. The 2 500 square meters represent a veritable Who's Who of the international media-art scene, with annual exhibits that include Douglas Gordon through Thomas Demand to Pipilotti Rist or Andreas Gursky. Stoschek is also devoted to up-and-coming stars, like the Frenchman Cyprien Gaillard, or the Hawaii-born Paul Pfeiffer.

Collector:
Julia Stoschek

Address:
Schanzenstrasse 54
40549 Düsseldorf
Germany
Tel +49 211 5858840
besuch@julia-stoschek-collection.net
www.julia-stoschek-collection.net

Opening hours vary depending on exhibition. Please check the website for most current information.

70 Kunstwerk—Sammlung Alison & Peter W. Klein
Contemporary and Aboriginal art in a remodeled factory

They don't follow art market trends. Alison and Peter W. Klein, who live just outside Stuttgart, buy what they like: photography of the Helsinki school, paintings by Karin Kneffel, works of the American photo-artist Gregory Crewdson, but also works by younger, emerging artists. Over nearly thirty years, the Swabian and his American wife have brought together 1 500 works of contemporary painting and photography. They regularly travel to Australia, which is why contemporary Aboriginal art constitutes a second pillar of their collection. Klein sold his company, which made clutch systems, in 2007, and a year later opened this private museum, which occupies a spacious 1 000 square meters in Nussdorf—the town where Klein was once the largest employer.

Collectors:
Alison & Peter W. Klein

Address:
Siemensstrasse 40
71735 Eberdingen-Nussdorf
Germany
Tel +49 7042 3769566
kunstwerk@sammlung-klein.de
www.sammlung-klein.de

Opening Hours:
Wed–Sun: 11am–5pm

71   Kunstraum Alexander Bürkle
*Monochrome painting and Minimal art in dialogue
with younger artists*

Collector:
Paul Ege

Address:
Robert-Bunsen-Strasse 5
79108 Freiburg
Germany
Tel +49 761 5106606
kunstraum@alexander-buerkle.de
www.kunstraum-alexander-
buerkle.de

Opening Hours:
Tues–Fri: 11am–5pm
Sundays and holidays: 11am–5pm

Established in 2004, the Kunstraum Alexander Bürkle is located in northern Freiburg on the premises of the electronics wholesale company Alexander Bürkle. The collector, Paul Ege, the third-generation head of the company, founded in 1900, has a clear guideline: "A collection should not be a mere accumulation. I think the strength of a collection lies in its unique focus." Based on this principle, three to four internationally staffed exhibitions are shown annually in the nearly 1 000-square-meter art space, which is committed to the neutrality of the white cube. Classics of Minimalism like Fred Sandback, Donald Judd, or—in the electronics industry, almost a must—light artist Dan Flavin, meet younger artists like the Swiss painter Adrian Schiess, known for his radical monochrome art.

G

72   Morat-Institut für Kunst & Kunstwissenschaft
*An excellent print collection, African tribal art,
and an extensive library*

Collector:
Franz Armin Morat

Address:
Lörracher Strasse 31
79115 Freiburg
Germany
Tel +49 761 4765916
eva.morat@morat-institut.de
www.morat-institut.de

Opening Hours:
Sat: 11am–6pm
And by appointment.

At the Morat-Institut für Kunst und Kunstwissenschaft, in Freiburg, the focus is on research. The institute organizes symposiums, publishes catalogue raisonnés, and oversees a library with around 50 000 volumes. The institute boasts the largest collection of works by the Viennese painter Carl Schuch, and earns additional points with an extensive print collection featuring work by Giorgio Morandi, Max Beckmann, and Albrecht Dürer. Treasures like a complete set of prints by Francisco de Goya, or high-quality West African sculptures are often requested on loan by other museums. The foundation resides in a 1950s light-flooded shed-roof hall. Since early 2010 the institute has tried to streamline and decelerate, focusing exclusively on its own collection rather than cultivating special exhibitions.

G

73   Deichtorhallen Hamburg—
       Sammlung Falckenberg
*Positions of social criticism in German and American
contemporary art*

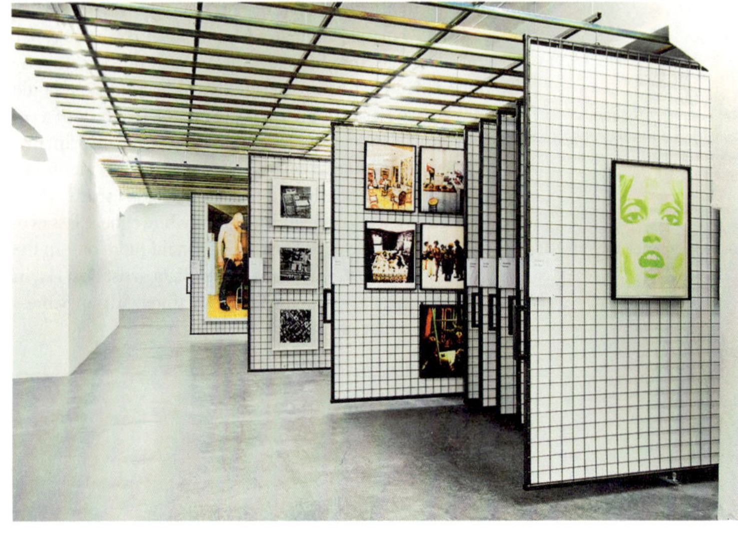

Irony, social criticism, and the grotesque: Harald Falckenberg's art collection is essentially about resistance. Over the past twenty years, the Hamburg-based businessman has assembled around 2 000 works of art, mainly by German and American contemporary artists who use biting sarcasm to hold a mirror up to society's ills. Paul McCarthy, Andreas Slominski, Martin Kippenberger, and Paul Thek are just some of his favorites. Since 2001 Falckenberg has shown his collection on some 6 000 square meters of a former rubber factory in Hamburg-Harburg, called the Phoenix Hallen, cleverly altered by the architect Roger Bundschuh. Unconventional temporary exhibitions and guest appearances by other private collections makes it one of the most important spaces for contemporary art. Starting in 2011 the Sammlung Falckenberg has cooperated closely with the Deichtorhallen Hamburg, which is now in charge of overall business operations.

Collector:
Harald Falckenberg

Address:
Phoenix-Hallen
Wilstorfer Strasse 71, Gate 2
21073 Hamburg
Germany
Tel +49 40 32506762
besuch@sammlung-falckenberg.de
www.sammlung-falckenberg.de

Opening Hours:
Wed–Thurs: 6pm
Fri: 5pm
Sat–Sun: 11am and 3pm
Only guided tours with prior registration.

It doesn't have to be the big-star architects. But many private collectors pay a lot of attention to the right architectural frame for their collections. Some have historical buildings renovated to house their art. Like Carl-Jürgen Schroth, for example, who converted a former school building in Soest, Germany, to accommodate his works. The young collector Friedrich Gräfling, who was born in Aschaffenburg, Germany, and now studies architecture in London, likes things a bit more rough around the edges. His Fiede Collection is presented in the tiled rooms of a former slaughterhouse. And the Norwegian collector-couple Hoff discovered a former caviar factory, enveloped in ocean mist at the Lofoten, for their collection. They commissioned the Oslo architecture firm Element, which has an affinity for art, for their striking remodeling.

Some collectors open their private homes and apartments by appointment. For visitors, it's interesting to see how the living environment engages in a dialogue with art. Munich-based collector Karsten Schmitz, of Stiftung Federkiel, commissioned the artist group Famed to transform the former working-class apartment on the grounds of the famed Leipzig *Baumwollspinnerei* into a habitable *Gesamtkunstwerk*—and with minimal intervention.

Art collectors frequently have a clear preference for good design. Berliner Giovanni Springmeier, for example, combines art and select design pieces in his generously sized apartment. And Rotterdam-based collector Alexander Ramselaar lives with his avant-garde furniture collection in a historic townhouse. Well-stocked bookshelves serve as a room divider, as they do in the space belonging to art collector and book lover Ivo Wessel in Berlin.

The ideal situation is **when collectors are able to commission their favorite architects** to create new spaces for their works. Wiel Arets, for example, designed the modern pavilion The Hedge House, in the Dutch province of Limburg, for the collectors Jo and Marlies Eyck, which blends perfectly into the natural surroundings of this castle park.

Nicole Büsing & Heiko Klaas

74   Museum Modern Art Hünfeld—
       Sammlung Jürgen Blum
*Over 4 000 works of Concrete, Constructivist,
and Conceptual Art*

Collector:
Jürgen Blum

Address:
Hersfelder Strasse 25
36088 Hünfeld
Germany
Tel +49 6652 72433
museum.modern.art@huenfeld.de
www.museum-modern-art.de

Opening Hours:
Tues–Sun: 3–5pm
And by appointment.

It's not an outpost of the Museum of Modern Art in New
York City, but the Museum Modern Art Hünfeld is well
worth the detour. Thanks to the German-Polish artist and
collector Jürgen Blum, the small Hessian city near Fulda
has a stellar private museum. Blum opened the museum
in 1990 and remains its director. Inside the historic landmark building, a former gas plant, Blum's collection of
over 4 000 works brings together the East and the West,
Concrete Art and conceptual thought, starkly reduced
forms and intellect. Highlights include works by the Polish
avant-garde. The exhibit entirely changes once a year, and
a marvelous sculpture garden pulls the curious museum
visitor—and collection—into the outdoors.

G

75   Sammlung Würth
*From the Middle Ages to the present:
art at fifteen sites in Europe*

Collector:
Reinhold Würth

Address:
Würth Museum
Reinhold-Würth-Strasse 15
74653 Künzelsau-Gaisbach
Germany
Tel +49 7940 152200
museum@wuerth.com
www.kunst.wuerth.com

Opening Hours:
Daily: 11am–6pm
Opening hours vary depending on
exhibition. Please check the website for most current information.

"Art at Würth should not take place in an ivory tower, but
in everyday life; it should be experienced close to the work-
place," says company president Reinhold Würth. Since the
1960s, the owner of a wholesaler for assembly and fasten-
ing materials has amassed a comprehensive collection of
art—from the Middle Ages through the modern period to
the present—comprised of roughly 15 000 works. In 1991
the Museum Würth opened at the company's headquarters
in Künzelsau. Then, in 2001, the Kunsthalle Würth was
opened in Schwäbisch Hall. Today, fifteen exhibition spaces inside innovative architectural structures are located
at various European locations of the Würth Group, from
Norway to Spain. The temporary exhibitions shown here
are drawn from the collection. Works from Pablo Picasso
to Gerhard Richter, from Paul Gauguin to Alex Katz—and
the largest compilation of works by Christo and Jeanne-
Claude in central Europe—mark the impressive range of
the Würth Collection.

76   Sammlung Froehlich
*An impressive group of works by German
and American art stars*

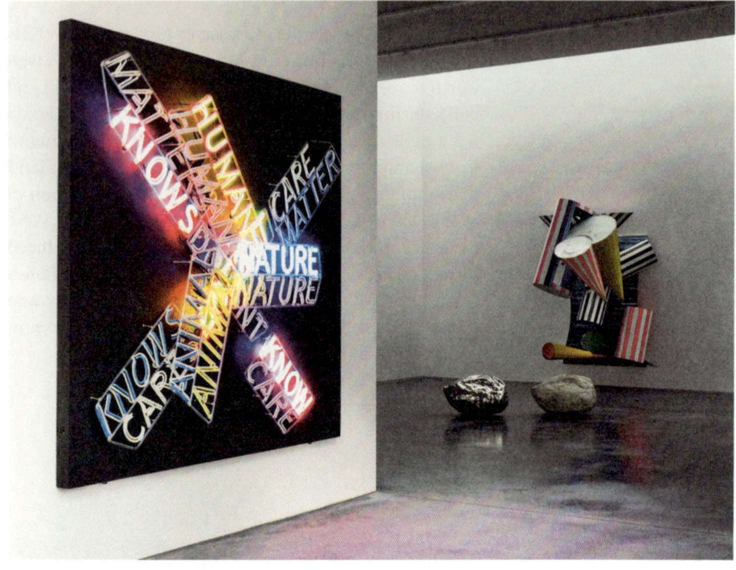

G

He was a blood-brother to Joseph Beuys. He was a regular at Andy Warhol's Factory. He met with Donald Judd at the artist's Texas studio. Josef Froehlich, a Stuttgart industrialist originally from Austria, does not just buy art; he also cultivates close relationships with artists. His life as a collector began with a run-in with Joseph Beuys at Documenta 7 in 1982. There, Froehlich helped the art shaman with his action *7000 Eichen*. Beuys thanked him with a work of art. A variety of important German and American artists—Gerhard Richter, Rosemarie Trockel, or Bruce Nauman—have since all found their way into the collection. Sammlung Froehlich comprises around 300 works and has been shown at the Tate Modern in London and the Museum of Modern Art in New York City. Since 2009 it has been housed in the architecturally adventurous building on the premises of Froehlich's Stuttgart firm.

Collectors:
Josef & Anna Froehlich

Address:
Kohlhammerstrasse 20
70771 Leinfelden-Echterdingen
Germany
Tel +49 711 753944
froehlich@sammlung-froehlich.de
www.sammlung-froehlich.de

By appointment only.

77 Arbeitswohnung Federkiel
A former working-class apartment as subtly ironic Gesamtkunstwerk

Collector:
Karsten Schmitz

Address:
Leipziger Baumwollspinnerei
Spinnereistrasse 7
04179 Leipzig
Germany
sammlung@federkiel.org
www.federkiel.org/sammlung

Visitation permitted only
occasionally. Please inquire
by e-mail.

The Munich economist Karsten Schmitz is no stranger to Leipzig. As an art collector and founder of the Stiftung Federkiel—whose mission is the preservation of Leipzig's *Baumwollspinnerei* as a location for galleries, studios, and institutional exhibition—Schmitz is among the most important private sponsors of this Leipzig art center. His own apartment, a former working-class home on the premises, is for the collector both a place to generate ideas and an exhibition space. But he also uses it regularly to accommodate collector friends, artists, or scholars. He invited the three-member Leipzig artist-group Famed to use the apartment and its furniture as artistic material to create a permanent intervention. The result is an ironic narrative installation that runs through all of the rooms, providing a cheeky visual link between them.

G

78 Museum Brandhorst
Art stars of the late twentieth century housed in a dazzling new space

Collectors:
Udo & Anette Brandhorst

Address:
Kunstareal München
Theresienstrasse 35A
80333 Munich
Germany
Tel +49 89 238052286
presse@museum-brandhorst.de
www.museum-brandhorst.de

Opening Hours:
Tue–Wed: 10am–6pm
Thurs: 10am–8pm
Fri–Sun: 10am–6pm

The vibrant, shimmering façade of 36 000 ceramic rods in twenty-three varying shades has a magnetic effect on people. Nearly 350 000 visitors were attracted to the Museum Brandhorst in 2009, the year it opened. But perhaps its success also lies on what is inside: nowhere in Europe will you find more works by Andy Warhol—represented by no less than one hundred pieces. Among the other highlights are works by Gerhard Richter, Ed Ruscha, and Cy Twombly, to name just a few. Located in the heart of Munich's art quarter, this distinctive building—designed by Sauerbruch Hutton—quickly became one of the most popular exhibition spaces in all of Germany. The 700-work collection belongs to Henkel heiress Anette Brandhorst and her husband, Udo, who began assembling it in the 1970s. They found a comfortable home for the collection in Munich, and the state of Bavaria covers building-maintenance costs. The Brandhorsts' foundation is endowed with 120 million euros, which guarantees a deep source of funds for purchasing new work at the highest level.

G

79   Sammlung Goetz
*Impressive architecture for international
contemporary art*

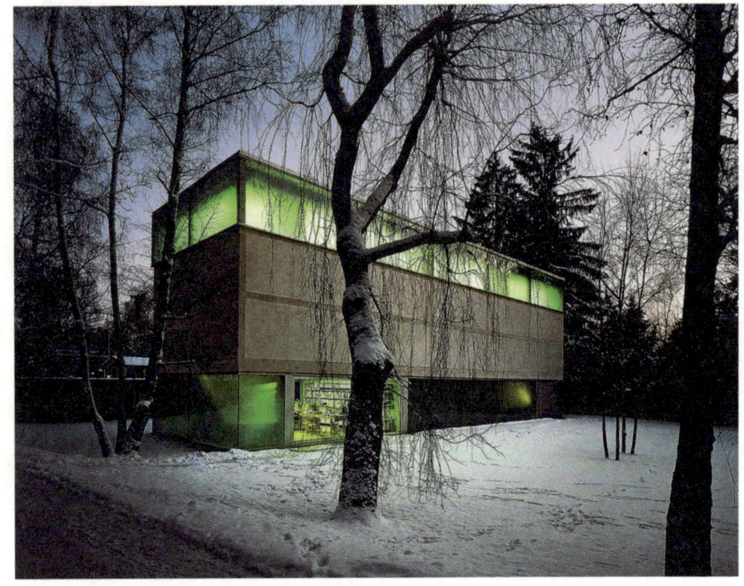

Before she began concentrating on her own private collection, in 1984, Ingvild Goetz had been a gallerist for fifteen years. With around 5 000 works by over 300 artists, she now ranks among the most important private collectors of contemporary art in Germany. She started out with Arte Povera. Then came works by American artists of the 1980s and the Young British Artists of the 1990s, as well as some German stars. Names like Richard Prince, Tracey Emin, or Rosemarie Trockel are represented prominently. Since 1993 the collection has been housed in a cube constructed of frosted glass and birchwood—a stylish private museum that counts among the most successful buildings made by the Swiss architects Herzog & de Meuron. Exhibitions are curated regularly from the collection. Media works, a focus of the collection, have also been presented in Munich's Haus der Kunst since 2011.

Collector:
Ingvild Goetz

Address:
Oberföhringer Strasse 103
81925 Munich
Germany
Tel +49 89 95939690
info@sammlung-goetz.de
www.sammlung-goetz.de

Opening Hours:
Thurs–Fri: 2–6pm
Sat: 11am–4pm
By telephone appointment only.

80   Alexander Tutsek-Stiftung
The use of glass in international contemporary art

Collectors:
Alexander Tutsek &
Eva-Maria Fahrner-Tutsek

Address:
Karl-Theodor-Strasse 27
80803 Munich
Germany
Tel +49 89 343856
info@atutsek-stiftung.de
www.atutsek-stiftung.de

Opening hours vary depending on
exhibition. Please check the website for most current information.

The challenging goal of the Alexander Tutsek-Stiftung, founded in 2000, is to move the fascinating material of glass out of the niche of "applied art." The collection and exhibition space endeavors to focus on the deployment of this fragile material in international contemporary art. The foundation's home, a national landmark Art Deco mansion in Munich-Schwabing, was once the private residence and studio of the German sculptor Georg Albertshofer. His former studio is now used for annual exhibits of glass art. Since 2008 the program has been supplemented by positions in contemporary photography. Alexander Tutsek, who died in 2011, had a company that produced fireproof materials for industrial use. This professional engagement with glass also sparked the interest of his wife, Eva-Maria, who is heavily involved in the foundation.

G

81   The Walther Collection
*Highbrow contemporary photographic art
in the midst of the Swabian provinces*

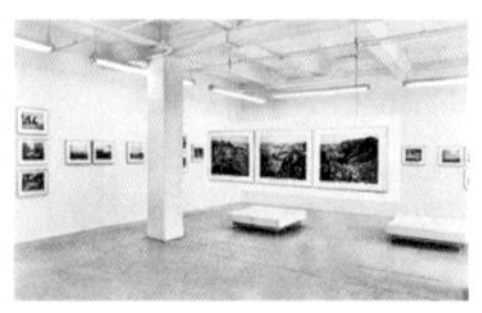

Collector:
Artur Walther

Address:
Reichenauer Strasse 21
89233 Neu-Ulm/Burlafingen
Germany
Tel +49 731 1769143
info@walthercollection.com
www.walthercollection.com

Opening Hours:
Thurs–Sun: 11am–5pm
Only guided tours with prior
registration.

Additional exhibition locations:
New York, United States of
America, p. 182

This is the tale of a man who went out to discover the world and returned to his hometown with a museum. Artur Walther worked as an investment banker on Wall Street. But in 1994 the then forty-five year old made a clean break and began to focus on art. More specifically, on photography. He went on African journeys with the former Documenta director Okwui Enwezor to gather his extensive collection of African photographic art. Positions from Asia and Western artists, such as August Sander or Bernd and Hilla Becher, complete the collection. After all this, Walther returned, and on his parents' property he erected a clear white cube with a 500-square-meter main gallery to display his finds. Two regional-specific houses also serve as exhibition spaces. The grand opening in Neu-Ulm was in 2010; an outpost in New York City was launched a year later.

82   Herbert-Gerisch-Stiftung
*Contemporary sculpture in the park, current art
in the villa*

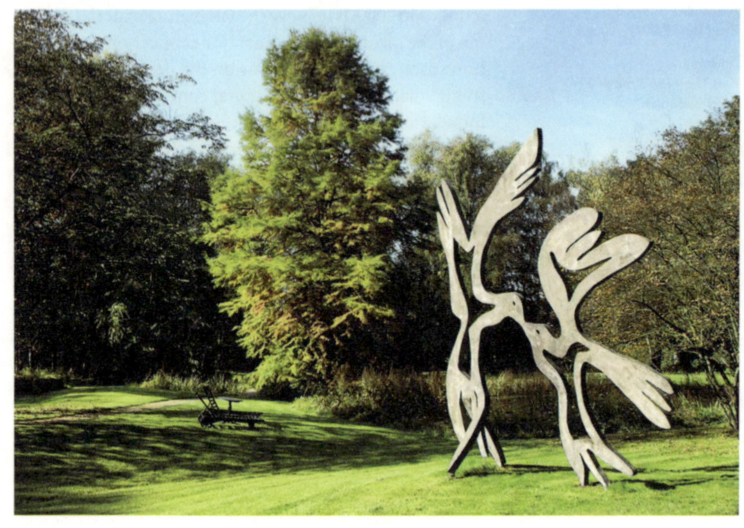

The mythical land of Arcadia apparently lies in the middle
of Schleswig-Holstein, in the city of Neumünster. There
you'll find a dreamy sculpture park founded by Brigitte
and Herbert Gerisch. There, among the property's series
of intricate paths, ponds of water lilies, and fields of forget-
me-not flowers, you discover contemporary sculptures by
Bogomir Ecker, Olaf Nicolai, or Ian Hamilton Finlay. The
foundation was established in 2001 with the mission of
transforming a once overgrown park into an international
sculpture garden of high repute. The founders have lived
in the modern mansion on the adjacent property since the
1960s, when they bought the run-down Villa Wachholtz
and renovated it back to splendor. In 2007 both the mansion and the park opened their doors to the public. Since
then, temporary exhibitions by artists like Carsten Höller
or Yehudit Sasportas have taken place in Villa Wachholtz
and in the former swim hall of Villa Gerisch.

Collectors:
Brigitte & Herbert Gerisch

Address:
Brachenfelder Strasse 69
24536 Neumünster
Germany
Tel +49 4321 555120
kontakt@gerisch-stiftung.de
www.herbert-gerisch-stiftung.de

Opening Hours:
Wed–Sun: 11am–6pm
And by appointment.

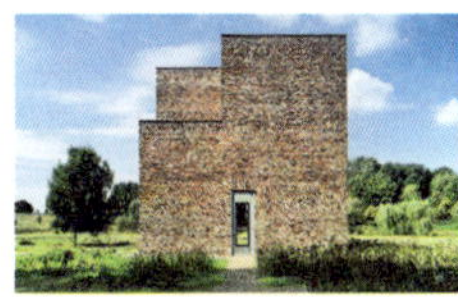

Collector:
Karl-Heinrich Müller

Address:
Minkel 2
41472 Neuss
Germany
Tel +49 2182 8874003
presse@inselhombroich.de
www.inselhombroich.de

Opening Hours:
April–September
Mon–Sun: 10am–7pm
October
Mon–Sun: 10am–6pm
November–March
Mon–Sun: 10am–5pm

Collectors:
Marianne & Viktor Langen

Address:
Raketenstation
Hombroich 1
41472 Neuss
Deutschland
Tel +49 2182 570115
info@langenfoundation.de
www.langenfoundation.de

Opening Hours:
Mon–Sun: 10am–6pm

83   Museum Insel Hombroich
Two thousand years of art in harmony with nature and the landscape

The idyllic Museum Insel Hombroich, today operated by the city of Neuss and the state of North Rhine-Westphalia, was founded by a Düsseldorf real estate agent and arts patron. In 1982 Karl-Heinrich Müller (1936–2007) bought twenty-five hectares of wild meadow snaking alongside the river Erft. In 1994 he acquired an adjacent former NATO missile base. Today, visitors to the Museum Insel Hombroich stroll through this vast terrain, passing along the way sculptures by Per Kirkeby or Eduardo Chillida, eventually running into Erwin Heerich's modest brick pavilions. Müller assembled his collection based solely on his personal tastes, thus one also discovers African fetishes and centuries-old Chinese artifacts alongside works by Lovis Corinth, Yves Klein, or Gotthard Graubner.

G

84   Langen Foundation
European and Asian art presented in a fascinating building by Tadao Ando

A highlight for architecture fans: the Langen Foundation fits perfectly into the spaciousness of the former NATO missile base on the island of Hombroich. For founder Marianne Langen, who died in 2004, the minimalist building, made of exposed concrete by the Japanese architect Tadao Ando, is the most important work of art she ever acquired. Together with her husband, Viktor Langen, she began to compile a collection of modernist work at the beginning of the 1950s, now numbering roughly 300 works of art from Max Ernst and Paul Klee to Pablo Picasso. The second focus is on a collection of Japanese artworks quite unique to Europe: nearly 500 scrolls, Shoji screens, and sculptures from across eight centuries. The collectors' motto: *Art is not luxury; it is necessity.* The 1 300-square-meter exhibition space is used to show contemporary art in dialogue with the permanent collection.

85   Gratianusstiftung
*Plentiful space for artifacts from the Paleolithic
to the present*

A comprehensive view of the world: the Reutlingen-based collector couple Hanns-Gerhard Rösch and Gabriele Straub offer a concise overview of the world's art history in a modernized mansion from 1904. The collectors mix epochs and genres in thirteen rooms on two floors. The spectrum runs from Paleolithic tools through African tribal art, and from Columbian shamanic figures to precious East Asian artifacts and works by modernists like Henri Matisse, Giorgio Morandi, or Paul Klee. The collectors are brave enough to leave their shows up for a longer duration. The current exhibition, with works by Raimer Jochims, a Städel School professor emeritus, runs until 2015. With his abstract works on board and paper, Jochims offers a contemporary interpretation of the collection's motto: *Color as the substance of painting, of visible reality, and of sight itself.*

G

Collectors:
Hanns-Gerhard Rösch &
Gabriele Straub

Address:
Gratianusstrasse 11
72766 Reutlingen
Germany
Tel +49 7121 490177
info@gratianusstiftung.de
www.gratianusstiftung.de

Opening Hours:
Mon: 2–6pm
Thurs: 6–8pm (only every first
Thursday per month)
And by appointment.

86   Stiftung für konkrete Kunst
*Concrete Art by over one hundred artists
in a former factory building*

The Stiftung für konkrete Kunst, in Reutlingen, is not a place that rushes masses of people through its halls. Instead, personalized art education is the foundation's core mission. Each visitor is guided individually through the exhibition by either the collector, Manfred Wandel, or by the director, Gabriele Kübler. Theo van Doesburg's 1924 definition of Concrete Art supplies the collection's motto: *There is nothing more concrete or more real than a line, a color, or a plane.* Wandel's private collection forms the foundation's core, joined by additional bodies of work and archives. The three floors in a former cheesecloth factory are straightforwardly designed for an industrial feel. But Concrete Art is not a dogma: in special exhibitions these works are placed in relation to Bauhaus furniture or Russian icons.

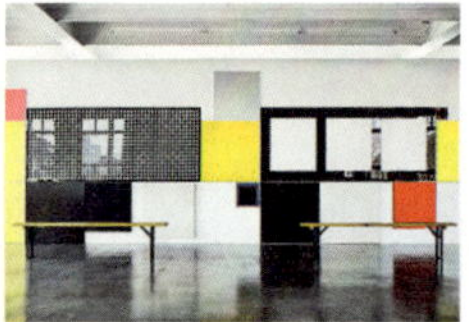

Collector:
Manfred Wandel

Address:
Eberhardstrasse 14
72764 Reutlingen
Germany
Tel +49 7121 370328
skk.kuebler@t-online.de
www.stiftungkonkretekunst.de

Opening Hours:
Wed: 2–6pm
Sat: 2–6pm
And by appointment.

87 Sammlung Siegfried Seiz
*Figurative painting from the last decade
of East Germany*

Collector:
Siegfried Seiz

Address:
Reutlingen, Germany
info@sieger-seiz.de

Visitation permitted only
occasionally. Please inquire
by e-mail.

As soon you hear the phrase "painting in East Germany," Socialist Realism comes to mind—and you head for the door. But business executive Siegfried Seiz's Reutlingen-based collection shows that there was another, non-official kind of figurative painting in East Germany. Sixty-six primarily large-format paintings by twenty-three artists have found a comfortable home in his 600-square-meter exhibition space, built out of a former factory. The art historian Gisold Lammel pointed Seiz to artist studios in Berlin, Dresden, Leipzig, and Halle, which he visited during the last decade of the GDR. Alongside early pictures by Neo Rauch, Seiz's collection holds unexpected works, like some wildly expressive paintings by Klaus Killisch, or the realist punk portraits by Clemens Gröszer.

G

88 Messmer Foundation/ Kunsthalle Messmer
*Concrete and Constructivist Art, plus the estate
of Swiss painter André Evard*

Collector:
Jürgen A. Messmer

Address:
Großherzog-Leopold-Platz 1
79359 Riegel am Kaiserstuhl
Germany
Tel +49 7642 9201620
info@messmerfoundation.com
www.messmerfoundation.com

Opening Hours:
Tues–Sun: 10am–5pm

His life is defined by art and design. In 2003 Jürgen A. Messmer, a former manufacturer of premium writing utensils, established the Messmer Foundation in memory of his deceased daughter, Petra. Six years later he opened the Kunsthalle Messmer in a former brewery in Riegel am Kaiserstuhl. Across 900 square meters he exhibits works from his trove of 800 pieces in thematic and monographic groupings in up to three shows a year: classics like Paul Klee and Otto Freundlich, inspiring figures of Concrete Art like Max Bill or Victor Vasarely, as well as numerous younger positions. Loans from other art institutions broaden the exhibitions' scope. A central pillar of the Messmer collection is the nearly complete estate of the little-known Swiss painter André Evard (1876–1972), which Messmer acquired in 1978 and has shown regularly ever since.

89 Schauwerk Sindelfingen
*A cool, remodeled factory with first-class
international contemporary art*

For him, beauty has a lot to do with purity and the harmony of form and color, says the Swabian businessman Peter Schaufler. His company, Bitzer, which makes refrigerator compressors, is among the world's market leaders. Schaufler and his wife, Christiane Schaufler-Münch, are known as reserved people. In fact, until the opening of their private museum, Schauwerk Sindelfingen, in summer 2010, only a few people had even known that they had started to build their private collection, one of the largest in Germany, as early as the late 1970s. The surprise was thus all the more: a 6 500-square-meter exhibition space where visitors can see top-quality works by artists like Donald Judd, Frank Stella, Imi Knoebel, John Armleder, or Sylvie Fleury, and an equally impressive collection of photography, which boasts works by the most important of the Becher students, as well as international giants like Nobuyoshi Araki or Vanessa Beecroft.

G

Collectors:
Peter Schaufler &
Christiane Schaufler-Münch

Address:
Eschenbrünnlestrasse 15/1
71065 Sindelfingen
Germany
Tel +49 7031 9324900
fuehrungen@schauwerk-
sindelfingen.de
contact@schauwerk-sindelfingen.de
www.schauwerk-sindelfingen.de

Opening Hours:
Sat–Sun: 11am–5pm
Tues, Thurs: 3–4:30pm (guided
tours)

90 Sammlung Schroth
Concrete and Minimalist Art in a former school

Carl-Jürgen Schroth discovered his interest in Constructivism in art class. But first he got a degree in mechanical engineering and then he focused on expanding the family business in the city of Arnsberg, in Sauerland. Schroth devoted his entire professional career to the development of better safety belts, but in his free time he was drawn ever closer to art. He began building a collection in the 1980s, with a focus on Concrete Art and Post-Minimalism: artists that were interested in scientific and mathematical investigations like light, space, and perception: Daniel Buren, Francois Morellet, or Victor Vasarely, in addition to younger positions. Periodically throughout the year Schroth opens the collection to the public in his private home—a former school building erected around 1900 in the city of Soest, in North Rhine-Westphalia.

Collector:
Carl-Jürgen Schroth

Address:
Filzenstrasse 6
59494 Soest
Germany
Tel +49 2921 14177
info@sammlungschroth.org
www.sammlungschroth.org

Opening hours vary depending on exhibition. Please check the website for most current information.

91   Sammlung Grässlin—
      Kunstraum Grässlin & Räume für Kunst
*An extraordinary collection with
a Black Forest backdrop*

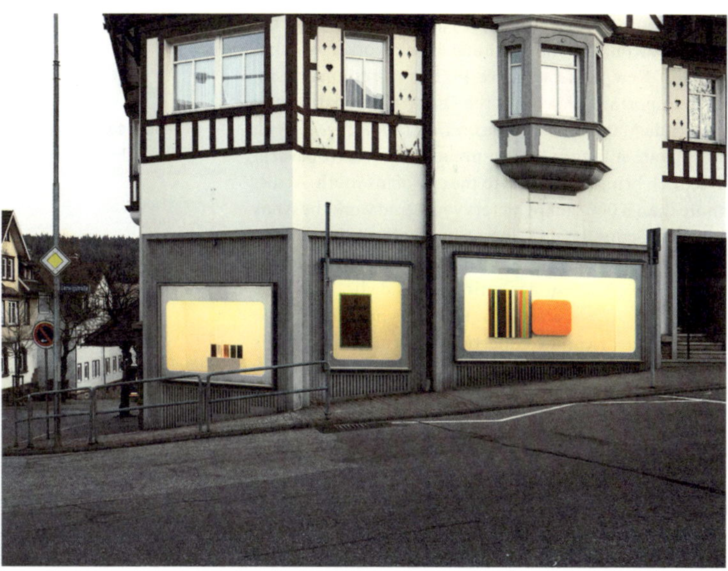

G

Collector:
Grässlin Family

Address:
Museumstrasse 2
78112 St. Georgen
Germany
Tel +49 7724 9161805
info@sammlung-graesslin.eu
www.sammlung-graesslin.eu

Opening Hours:
Thurs–Sun by appointment.
Early registration recommended.

Ever since the Grässlin family established the Räume für Kunst, in 1995, the city of St. Georgen has become obsessed with art. Every weekend the art-going crowd streaks through the vacant shops and factory floors elected to temporarily house artworks by figures like Albert Oehlen, Reinhard Mucha, Isa Genzken, or Cosima von Bonin. A tour of the impressive collection starts at the Kunstraum Grässlin, opened in 2006, and leads through the long-faded economic miracle of the 1960s, which is when the previous Grässlin generation began collecting Art Informel. Since the 1980s, their children have been adding contemporary works to the collection. Artist Martin Kippenberger also knew that St. Georgen breathed art, ever since he began coming to the Black Forest to recuperate from his excesses. Today, the Grässlins are among the largest holders of Kippenberger's works.

92   Das Maximum—KunstGegenwart
An attractive permanent exhibition of seven German
and American artists

"It was always important for me to be in a dialogue with artists," says Heiner Friedrich. The former gallerist, collector, patron, and international art networker, who has lived in New York City since 1971, is co-responsible for such important projects as the Dia Art Foundation and Walter de Maria's Land-Art icon *The Lightning Field*. With his private museum in Traunreut, in southern Bavaria, Friedrich brings top artists to the city of his youth. Across more than 3 000 square meters you'll find works by Andy Warhol, Georg Baselitz, John Chamberlain, Dan Flavin, Imi Knoebel, Walter de Maria, and the nearly forgotten painter Uwe Lausen. An entire hall is dedicated to the early work of light artist Dan Flavin. Typical for the pioneering Friedrich: the collection is permanently on display, but opening hours change according to the shifting seasonal light.

Collector:
Heiner Friedrich

Address:
Fridtjof-Nansen-Strasse 16
83301 Traunreut
Germany
Tel +49 8669 1203713
mail@dasmaximum.com
www.dasmaximum.com

Opening Hours:
April–October
Sat–Sun: 12–6pm
November–March
Sat–Sun: 11am–4pm
Closed in December

93   Sammlung FER Collection
Minimal and Conceptual Art since the 1960s
as an intellectual challenge

Friedrich E. Rentschler collects art that inspires thought, whether it's American Minimalism by Carl Andre or Sol LeWitt, Conceptual work by Robert Barry, or Italian Arte Povera by Giulio Paolini. Younger artists like Sylvie Fleury or Mathieu Mercier also find their way into the collection of this pharmaceutical entrepreneur—which has been growing constantly since 1960. This Ulm-based collection could be characterized by its discerning selectivity and its collector's subsequent courage for early purchase. Since 2009 Rentschler has shown his treasures at the award-winning Ulmer Stadtregal, a former factory building turned into lofts, workshops, and cultural institutions in the western part of the city. With a little luck, you can catch a tour by Rentschler himself, who will explain why he doesn't just collect with his eye but also with his brain.

Collectors:
Friedrich E. Rentschler &
Maria Schlumberger

Address:
Magirus-Deutz-Strasse 16
89077 Ulm
Germany
Tel +49 731 3885478
maria.schlumberger@
fer-collection.de
www.fer-collection.de

Only guided tours with prior online registration.

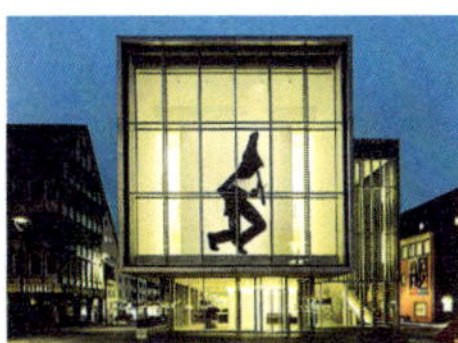

Collectors:
Siegfried & Jutta Weishaupt

Address:
Hans-und-Sophie-Scholl-Platz 1
89073 Ulm
Germany
Tel +49 731 1614360
info@kunsthalle-weishaupt.de
www.kunsthalle-weishaupt.de

Opening Hours:
Tue–Wed: 11am–5pm
Thurs: 11am–8pm
Fri–Sun: 11am–5pm

94   Kunsthalle Weishaupt
Geometric American and European art since the 1960s

Siegfried Weishaupt likes to point out that he collects by instinct. His father, Max, had good contacts in the Ulm School of Design. Like his father, Siegfried was inspired by director Max Bill and interested in the connections between aesthetics and mathematics. In his early acquisitions, in the mid 1960s, the young engineer focused on Concrete and Geometric Art by professors at the Ulm School, such as Josef Albers. Later, travels to the US opened his eyes to Color Field Painting, like the works by Mark Rothko. Under the guidance of his daughter, the art historian Kathrin Weishaupt-Theopold, the Kunsthalle Weishaupt has acquired some more contemporary positions, like Markus Oehlen, Robert Longo, or Liam Gillick. Works from the collection are regularly shown in a transparent glass building in the center of Ulm.

G

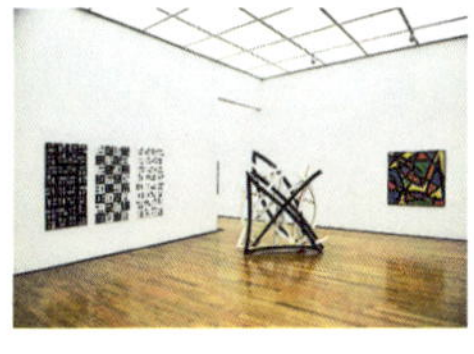

Collector:
Marli Hoppe-Ritter

Address:
Alfred-Ritter-Strasse 27
71111 Waldenbuch
Germany
Tel +49 7157 535110
besucherservice@museum-ritter.de
www.museum-ritter.de

Opening Hours:
Tues–Sun: 11am–6pm

95   Museum Ritter—Sammlung Marli Hoppe-Ritter
Square-centered geometric abstraction from the twentieth and twenty-first century

Almost everyone has seen a square-shaped Ritter Sport chocolate bar. Marli Hoppe-Ritter, the grandchild of the company's founder, took this basic form as the starting point for her art collection. Kazimir Malevich defined the square in 1915 as "the first step of pure creation in art"; a small drawing by the Russian Constructivist forms the basis of the collection. Geometric-constructive works from Joseph Albers, Johannes Itten, and the Zurich Concrete artists to the Zero Group form the collection's inner core. Add to this a few younger artists like Gerold Miller or Paola Pivi, and the consistent 800-work collection progresses further into the present. Swiss architect Max Dudler constructed a modernistic limestone cube on the chocolate company's Waldenbuch property. Since its inauguration, in 2005, the Museum Ritter has staged three to four exhibitions annually, derived from the collection.

G

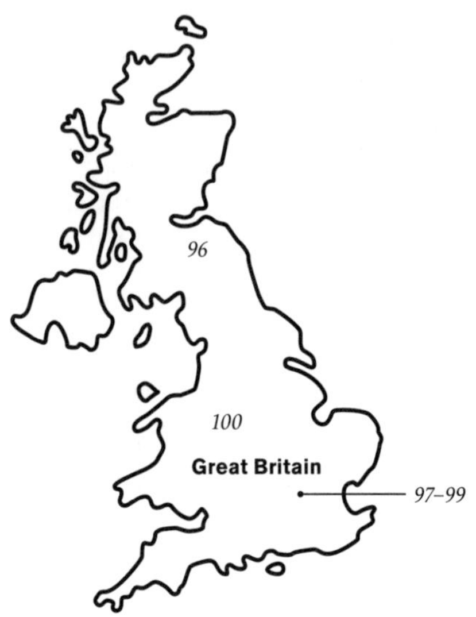

96 Jupiter Artland
A sculpture garden where art is anything but parked and forgotten

In 1999 Robert and Nicky Wilson bought the historic Bonnington House and its surrounding property. Since then, monstrous exotic flowers have begun to bloom, courtesy of *Love Bomb*, by Marc Quinn. And Charles Jenck's *Life Mounds* have transformed part of the grounds into wavy terraces. Such alterations have come about because the couple has engaged internationally acclaimed sculptors and installation artists—Anish Kapoor, Jim Lambie, or Antony Gormley—to build works specifically for their garden. The works fit seamlessly into the landscape; some, like Andy Goldsworthy's *Stone House*, spur an art double take. Jupiter Artland is closed during the winter. The lively dialogue the collectors demand of their art garden cannot flourish when the garden is barren of natural life.

Collectors:
Robert & Nicky Wilson

Address:
Bonnington House Steadings
Wilkieston
Edinburgh EH27 8BB
Great Britain
Tel +44 1506 889900
enquiries@jupiterartland.org
www.jupiterartland.org

Opening Hours:
May 25–September 15
Thurs–Sun: 10am–5pm
Online registration required.

A new and interesting basement opened during the Olympic Games in

London

. In summer 2012, the Tate Modern unbolted its old, underground oil tanks—imposing, impressive spaces—for the presentation of artworks. Not far from there begins the district of Bermondsey, where more and more galleries have been settling down in the shadow of the area's vital art institutions, like the Design Museum. Among the pioneers in London's Southeast is Jay Jopling, whose White Cube Gallery now counts two London branches. There's only one Serpentine Gallery, of course, with its rich program, annual Summer Pavilion in Hyde Park, and Sackler Gallery, which was converted by Zaha Hadid and is still scheduled to open in 2013. With the Gagosian Gallery, Hauser & Wirth, the London branch of Pace, Sadie Coles, David Zwirner, or the Lisson Gallery one can visit all the big players—and still has time for the next generation. Or maybe for one of the classic "hop on, hop off" tours: ride the red double-decker bus through central London that will bring you within walking distance to a few young, exciting galleries. Herald St. is one of them, and then there is Josh Lilley, Rokeby, and Alma Enterprises. In the former working-class borough of Hackney you will find Rivington Place, featuring not only a stellar building by star architect David Adjaye, but also a young institution totally devoted primarily to photography, featuring thematic talks and a multitude of publications. Additional, stimulating reading material is provided by Donlon Books in the Hackney borough. Last but not least, London's museums await a visit. In addition to the National Gallery and the Royal Academy of Arts, of course, there's the Victoria and Albert Museum, and the Tate Gallery. The mandatory cultural program also includes a visit to the Institute of Contemporary Art (ICA), which has been showing art of the present since 1947.

Christiane Meixner

More Information: www.bmw-art-guide.com

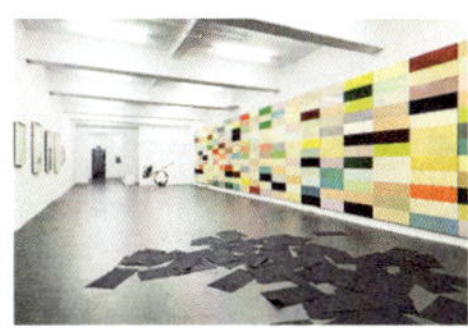

Collector:
David Roberts

Address:
Symes Mews
London NW17JE
Great Britain
Tel + 44 20 73833004
info@davidrobertsartfoundation.com
www.davidrobertsartfoundation.com

Opening Hours:
Thurs–Sat: 12–6pm
Tues–Wed: by appointment

97   The David Roberts Art Foundation
*A foundation with a focus on the avant-garde
from all media*

In 2012 the David Roberts Art Foundation (DRAF) was pulled from the posh West End of London to a former furniture factory in vibrant Camden Town. The Scottish collector acquires art from British and international contemporaries, including photography by Ed Ruscha, paintings by Miriam Cahn, Gerhard Richter, Anselm Kiefer, and Louise Bourgeois, alongside important works by Martin Creed, Thomas Houseago, and Martin Kippenberger. While the collection and its throng of important names occupy part of the premises, the remaining area is charged with a different task: housing current artists' projects. Whether artistic interventions, movie nights, or panel discussions, all is welcome, as long as the platform hosts exciting forays into contemporary art.

Collector:
Charles Saatchi

Address:
Duke of York's HQ
King's Road
London SW3 4RY
Great Britain
www.saatchi-gallery.co.uk

Opening Hours:
Mon–Sun: 10am–6pm

98   Saatchi Gallery
*Whether as collector or gallerist, he puts
Young British Artists first*

Charles Saatchi is known as a man who makes artists. Born in Iraq, he's been collecting for over forty years. The Young British Artists thank him for assisting their stratospheric rise in the 1990s. The founder of Saatchi & Saatchi advertising agency has a second passion as a gallerist. In the beginning, he was interested in artists like Andy Warhol or Donald Judd, whose work has been in Saatchi's private London museum since 1985. A few years later he acquired a cornucopia of works by Damien Hirst, Tracey Emin, or Jake & Dinos Chapman, making the graduates of Goldsmiths College a flourishing brand name. His collection, which since 2008 has been housed in a classically restored building by the architecture firm Alford Hall Monaghan Morris, counts among the world's largest. This remains true, even though he gave part of it to the British government, and over 140 works were destroyed in a 2004 fire.

99   Zabludowicz Collection, London
A collection in the unconventional ambiance of a church

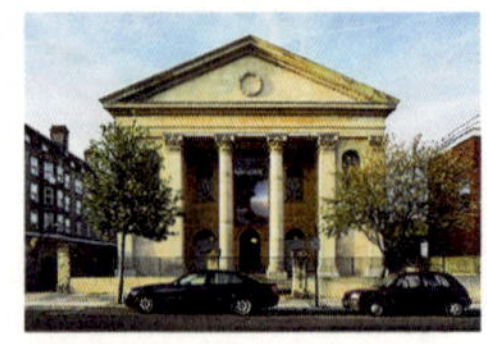

Studying art and learning the ropes in an international auction house have made Anita Zabludowicz fit to be a collector. In 1994 she began amassing her private collection, placing young, international, untested positions at the center. Her husband, Poju Zabludowicz, the Finnish financier, preferred to collect more established names. Given this combination, one finds in the couple's 2 000-work collection of videos, photographs, drawings, and installations stars like Vanessa Beecroft or the Swiss duo Fischli/Weiss—as well as artists whose work is less prevalent: Tom Burr, Ryan Gander, or Rivane Neuenschwander. The London outpost is located in a nineteenth-century Methodist church. Part of the Zabludowicz collection has been shown here—in addition to New York—in alternating exhibitions since 2007.

Collectors:
Anita & Poju Zabludowicz

Address:
176 Prince of Wales Road
London NW5 3PT
Great Britain
info@zabludowiczcollection.com
www.zabludowiczcollection.com/
london

Opening Hours:
Thurs–Sun: 12–6pm
And by appointment.

Additional exhibition locations:
New York, United States of
America, p. 185

100   Initial Access
*Art from around the world in one of Britain's
largest collections*

It's been said that Frank Cohen purchases art once a week. Together with his wife, Cherryl, the retired businessman has amassed one of the largest collections in Great Britain: over 1 500 works, and always with an eye toward Charles Saatchi, a fellow Brit and one of the largest collectors of contemporary art from China and India. Cohen's art fills his private home and, since 2007, an entire industrial hall near Wolverhampton. There one finds pictures by German artists Dirk Skreber or Gregor Hildebrandt; images of teenage fantasies by Gerald Davis, and sculptures by Matt Johnson, both of whom live in Los Angeles. Naturally the big names are also here: Richard Prince, Jason Rhoades, and Takashi Murakami. Cherryl and Frank Cohen also have a soft spot for the work of the Young British Artists.

Collectors:
Frank & Cherryl Cohen

Address:
Units 19 & 20
Calibre Industrial Park
Laches Close
Off Enterprise Drive
Four Ashes
Wolverhampton WV10 7DZ
Great Britain
Tel +44 1902 790419
visit@initialaccess.co.uk
www.initialaccess.co.uk

Opening Hours:
Mon–Fri: 10am–4pm

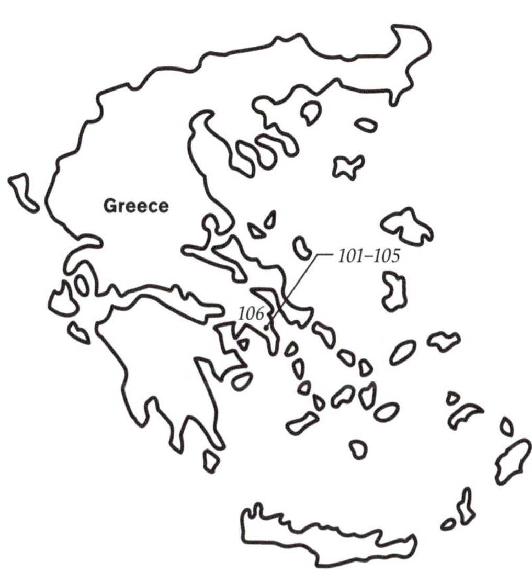

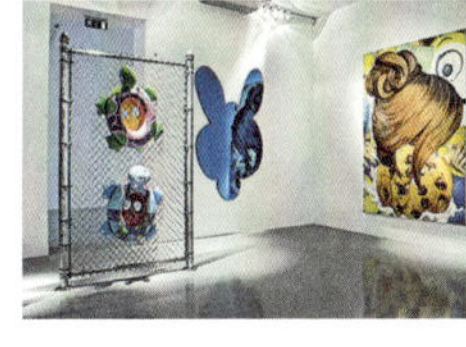

Collector:
Dakis Joannou

Address:
Filellinon 11, Nea Ionia
14234 Athens
Greece
Tel +30 210 2758490
info@deste.gr
www.deste.gr

Opening Hours:
Wed: 12–8pm
Sat: 10am–2pm

101   Deste Foundation for Contemporary Art
*A renowned collection with a flair for color
and provocation*

While walking through New York's East Village in the
1980s, Greek Cypriot industrialist Dakis Joannou passed
by the International With Monument Gallery, saw Jeff
Koons's *One Ball Total Equilibrium Tank*, and bought it. This,
anyway, is the legendary tale of how Joannou began his collection of contemporary art, today acknowledged as one of
the most important in the world and shown in museums
like the Palais de Tokyo, in Paris, and the New Museum, in
New York. Joannou's Deste Foundation, established in 1983,
aims to be a "container" for culture, an idea suggested by
the design of the foundation's main entrance: a giant wood-
en crate similar to those used to transport works of art.
Since 1999 the foundation has been supporting young artists through the bi-annual 10 000 euros Deste prize, whose
recipients include Anastasia Douka and Eirene Efstathiou.

102   The George Economou Collection
German art in Greece

G

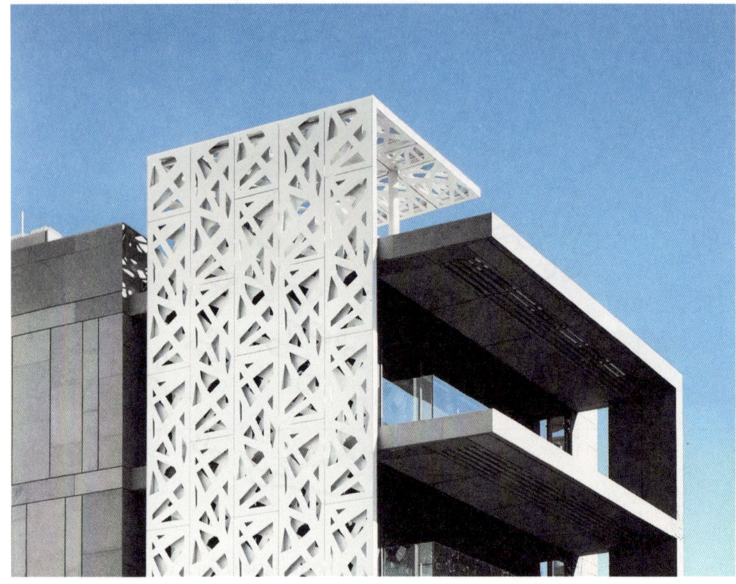

Greek ship-owner George Economou has a penchant for German art. His collection, which has been expanding rapidly since the late 1990s (the *Economist* says at a rate of roughly a new picture every two days), offers in-depth insights into modern art in Germany, with a focus on art movements like Expressionism or Neue Sachlichkeit (New Objectivity). But the coverage does not end with modernism; it also includes artists ranging from Anselm Kiefer and Georg Baselitz, to Neo Rauch and Andreas Gursky. "All my purchases of contemporary art have a strong historic element," says Economou. Alongside his interest in artists like Ellsworth Kelly, Cady Noland, or Jenny Saville, is concept art of the postwar period. Since 2011, two to three exhibitions have been organized annually in his exhibition space in Athens.

Collector:
George Economou

Address:
80, Kifissias Ave.
15125, Marousi
Athens
Greece
Tel +30 210 8090519
info@economoucollection.com
www.thegeorgeeconomoucollection.
com

Opening Hours:
Mon–Wed: 10am–6pm
Thurs: 10am–8pm
Fri: 10am–6pm

In 1980, the British news channel BBC aired a series entitled *The Shock of the New.* The eight episodes documenting the development of modern art are still praised by insiders for their quality and humor. Though the series used the words "the new" to describe the emergence of a whole new era, the little adjective "new" continues to play a crucial role in the art world to this day.

In the context of collecting, "new" has multiple meanings. Buyers often eagerly await new works by their favorite artists. Gallery owners report how difficult it is to excite collectors about works of the same quality, though older. As a rule, collectors are thrilled by the encounter with a new artistic position, with works by an artist hitherto unknown.
But how do art lovers make such discoveries? Where do they find what touches them? In general, the quest for art on which one is willing to actually spend money is like finding a needle in a haystack. Collectors are inspired by gallery or museum exhibitions, by books or magazines, by art fairs or advice from friends. And though the art market now sees tens of thousands of artists vying for purchase, the following still applies: Good art is rare, and good art one must own is even rarer. Seasoned art collectors thus bestow the same advice to beginners: Look at as much art as possible before your first purchase. A hastily acquired work will "fall off the wall" just as fast. Much that is new just loses its appeal once it is not longer new. A neon sculpture by the artist Maurizio Nannucci long mounted on the front of Berlin's Altes Museum curtly illustrates the continuing need for a healthy skepticism towards the dominance of the new. It read: *All art has been contemporary.*

Independent Collectors

103   Frissiras Museum
3 500 contemporary figurative paintings

Collector:
Vlassis Frissiras

Address:
Monis Asteriou 3 & 7, Plaka
10558 Athens
Greece
Tel +30 210 3234678
info@frissirasmuseum.com
www.frissirasmuseum.com

Opening Hours:
Wed–Fri: 10am–5pm
Sat–Sun: 11am–5pm

"In our age, art has a right to pure madness. Assuming a defensive position against the prevailing artistic atmosphere, I made my personal aesthetic choices and embraced contemporary painting with an anthropocentric slant." With his bold statement, Greek lawyer and passionate collector Vlassis Frissiras explains how he became the proud owner of over 3 500 contemporary paintings of the human figure. "Anything else leaves me indifferent," he told the *Athens News*, where he also stated that he has an erotic relationship to all his paintings, adding: "I decided right away that I wanted the paintings to be anthropocentric. That's my character—it is monomaniacal and very focused." The Frissiras Museum includes, of course, a number of Greek artists, such as Yannis Moralis and Diamantis Diamantopoulos, as well as Europeans like David Hockney and Frank Auerbach.

G

104   Herakleidon—Experience in Visual Arts
The perfect place for mathematicians with an eye for art

Collectors:
Paul & Anna-Belinda Firos

Address:
Herakleidon 16, Thissio
11851 Athens
Greece
Tel +30 210 3461981
info@herakleidon-art.gr
www.herakleidon-art.gr

Opening Hours:
Fri: 1–9pm
Sat–Sun: 11am–7pm

Few visual motifs have found the commercial success of Dutch graphic artist M.C. Escher's interlocking patterns of nature and geometry, mathematics and architecture. The consequence of Escher's ubiquity is that almost anyone, no matter how unversed in art, can recognize his work when they see it. Lesser known, however, is exactly where to do so. That one of the largest collections of Escher's work is located in Athens, Greece, in a neoclassical building next to the Acropolis, may come as a surprise. Yet Paul and Anna-Belinda Firos's collection, aside from the impressive gathering of Escher prints, shows a general predilection for mathematical and geometrical patterns: Op Art pioneer Victor Vasarely, and American engraver Carol Wax are both extensively represented. The institution also organizes exhibitions of earlier moderns like Edgar Degas, Edvard Munch, and Henri de Toulouse-Lautrec.

105 Portalakis Collection
International art in the heart of the business district

The typical art lover might not go to the business district to look for art, but, then again, the eighth floor of Zacharias Portalakis's brokerage company, located directly across from the former location of the Athens Exchange, is not your typical location. A self-made broker, Portalakis once told *The National Herald*, "All of the money I made is now colors." He started buying Greek artists at the end of the 1980s and then moved on to expatriated Greeks, such as Jannis Kounellis and Theodoros Stamos, the latter of whom he is the world's foremost collector. It was not always so: when Portalakis first met Stamos, the baffled collector says he did not understand the work. Instead, he let his eight-year-old daughter choose a painting for her father's burgeoning collection, which today counts such international stars as Lucio Fontana, Christopher Wool, and Richard Prince among its highlights.

G

Collector:
Zacharias Portalakis

Address:
Pesmazoglou 8, 8th Floor
10559 Athens
Greece
Tel +30 210 3318933
info@portalakiscollection.gr
www.portalakiscollection.gr

Opening Hours:
Wed: 12–8pm
Sat: 11am–3pm
And by appointment.

106 Vorres Museum
3 000 years of Greek history and postwar Greek art

In the small town of Paiania, just east of Athens, the Vorres Museum strives to preserve Greek national heritage by covering 3 000 years of the nation's history. The nearly 6 000 works in the collection are divided into two sections: an impressive folk art collection, exhibited in four reconstructed village houses, and a museum of contemporary Greek art, featuring paintings and sculptures by Greek artists from the second half of the twentieth century, including Lucas Samaras and Vlassis Kaniaris. The sheer diversity of the collection reflects the personality of its owner, Ian Vorres, a Greek expatriate who lives in Canada and whose notable past endeavors include art critic, liaison between Canada and Greece, biographer of Russian grand duchess Olga Alexandrovna, and even mayor of Paiania.

Collector:
Ian Vorres

Address:
Diadochou Konstantinou 1
19002 Paiania
Greece
Tel +30 210 6642520
mvorres@otenet.gr
www.vorresmuseum.gr

Opening Hours:
Sat–Sun: 10am–2pm
And by appointment.

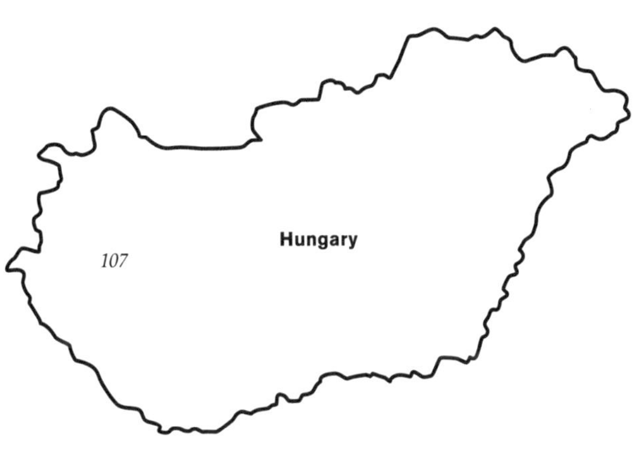

107　Vass Collection
Hungarian and international abstraction,
Constructivist and Concrete Art

Collector:
László Vass

Address:
Vár Utca 3
8200 Veszprém
Hungary
Tel +36 88 561310
info@vasscollection.hu
www.vasscollection.hu

Opening Hours:
May–October
Mo–Sat: 10am–6pm
November–April
Mo–Sat: 10am–5pm

In keeping with the Budapest cordwainer tradition, the name László Vass is known as a hallmark of quality and elegance in men's handmade leather shoes. Less well known—but no less refined—is the Vass art collection, preserved in the castle district of Veszprém, a small town of history and lore located 100 kilometers from Budapest. Incidentally, Veszprém is also known as "the city of queens": for centuries, Hungary's female royals were crowned by the local bishop. Vass began collecting contemporary Hungarian art in the 1970s and, influenced by an encounter with artist Jenö Barcsay, initially focused on native Constructivist Art and abstraction. He then turned to the same positions on an international level, assembling a collection of roughly 600 works by artists like Max Bill, Josef Albers, and Manfred Mohr.

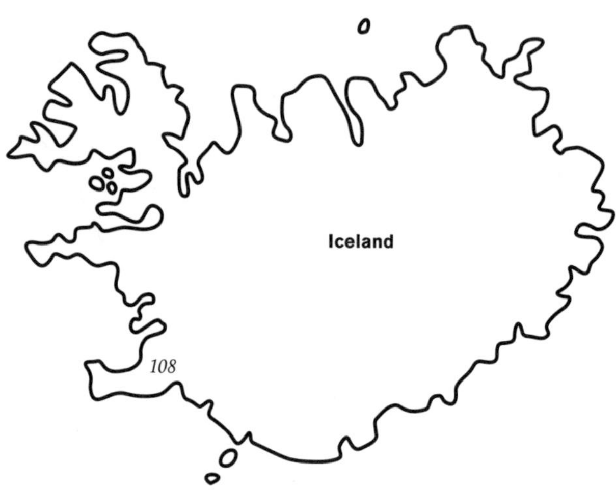

108   Hafnarborg—The Hafnarfjordur Centre
of Culture and Fine Art
Icelandic art of the twentieth century, plus plentiful
special exhibitions

No matter if it's in Berlin, New York, or Venice, Icelandic art has great appeal. And whoever wishes to trace Icelandic art to the homeland of elves and mountain trolls should begin in the Hafnarborg—The Hafnarfjordur Centre of Culture and Fine Art. In 1983 the pharmacist couple Sverrir Magnússon and Ingibjörg Sigurjónsdóttir donated their extensive collection of Icelandic modern art, and their private home, to the small town near to Reykjavik. An extensive cultural center was developed around the building and opened in 1988. Almost every month there is a new special exhibition that focuses mainly on Icelandic art. Today the ever-expanding collection includes 1 400 works. Icelandic artists living outside their home country, such as Ragnar Kjartansson, Egill Saebjörnsson, or Olafur Eliasson, have all had exhibitions there. Eliasson has the home-game advantage: he grew up in Hafnarfjordur.

Collectors:
Sverrir Magnússon &
Ingibjörg Sigurjónsdóttir

Address:
Strandgata 34
220 Hafnarfjordur
Iceland
Tel +354 585 5790
hafnarborg@hafnarfjordur.is
en.hafnarborg.is

Opening Hours:
Wed: 12–5pm
Thurs: 11am–9pm
Fri–Mon: 12–5pm

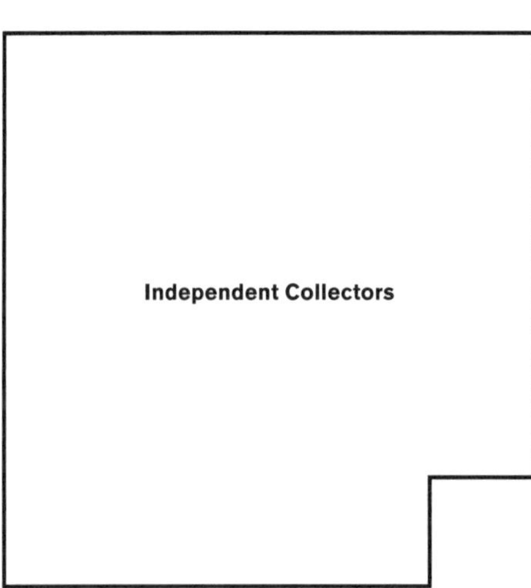

109   Independent Collectors
*International contemporary art accessible
from anywhere, anytime*

Collector:
Independent Collectors

Address:
info@independent-collectors.com
www.independent-collectors.com

Opening Hours:
Mon–Sun: 24 hours

This collection's "country" is a unique case: geographically speaking, it is the smallest; and in terms of the collection's size, it is this guide's largest. Defining this place as a country may seem odd, since it has no cities, houses, streets, or anything else inhabitable. Nevertheless, a broad-based and lively collector community has come to call this place home. The location: Independent Collectors (IC), the first online platform for collectors of contemporary art. Since the beginning of 2008, nearly 5 000 collectors have registered, offering a view into approximately 2 200 private exhibitions. IC's members are able to manage and share their personal art collections and collecting experiences with other collectors across the globe. IC is not only a buzzing network, it is also the largest online presence of privately owned art.

India, Gurgaon

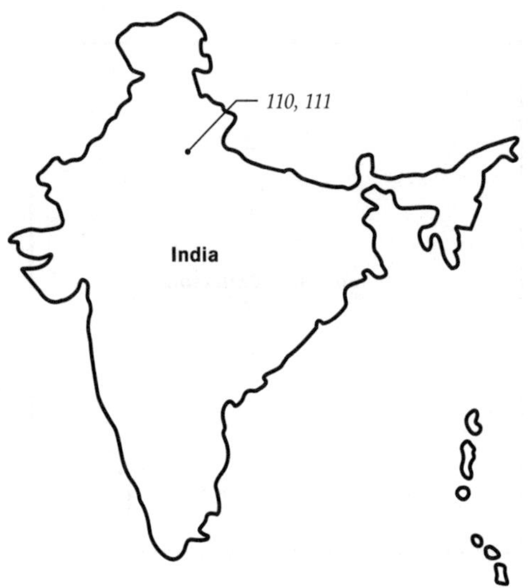

110 Devi Art Foundation
*The spectrum of Indian contemporary art
in one family collection*

Businesswomen Lekha Poddar began collecting art in the 1970s, concentrating on work that highlighted domestic Indian art. Her son Anupam Poddar has since broadened the scope of the family collection by harnessing work from the Asian subcontinent: Pakistan, Bangladesh, and Sri Lanka, as well as from Afghanistan, Tibet, and the Middle East. His main interest is in experimental artists of his own generation whose genre-bending artworks mirror the vision of India. Examples range from Sudarshan Shetty through Subodh Gupta or Jagannath Panda, all the way to Sakshi Gupta. Also represented are the Iranian Golnaz Fathi and Kuwaiti Hamra Abbas. The Devi Art Foundation, in Gurgaon, near New Delhi, displays a large part of its collection in the family's company building, completed in 2008.

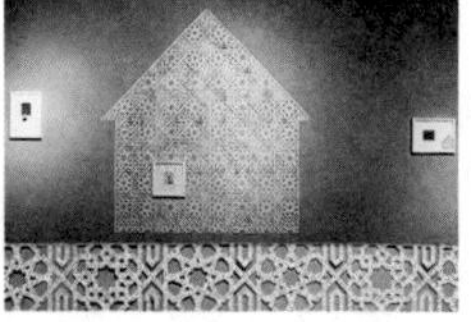

Collectors:
Lekha & Anupam Poddar

Address:
Devi Art Foundation
Sirpur House, Plot 39,
Sector 44, Gurgaon
India
Tel +91 124 4888177
info@deviartfoundation.org
www.deviartfoundation.org

Opening Hours:
Tues–Sun: 11am–7pm

111   The Kiran Nadar Museum of Art
150 years of Indian art from the Kiran Nadar Collection

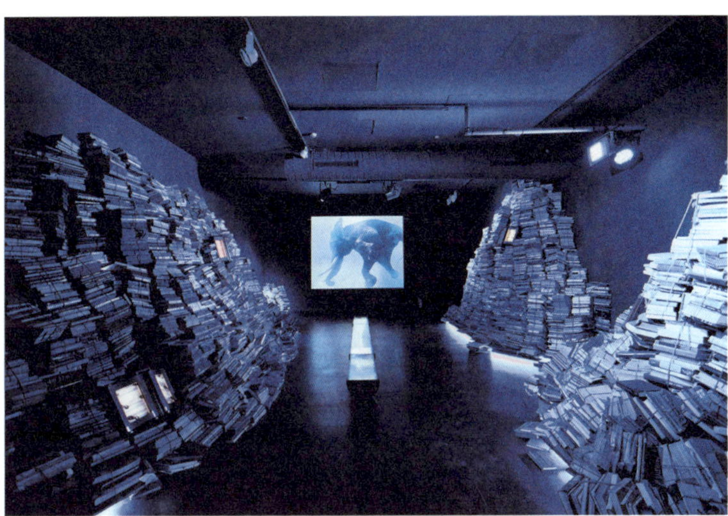

Collector:
Kiran Nadar

Address:
145, DLF South Court Mall, Saket
New Delhi, 110017
India
roobina.karode@hcl.in
www.knma.in

Opening Hours:
Tues–Sun: 10:30am–6:30pm

One of the first private museums in India was opened in New Delhi in 2010. Kiran Nadar not only aims to make her twenty-year collection public, but to increase the quality of India's museum culture while doing so. A large part of Nadar's program is dedicated to education for schoolchildren and university students. Ninety percent of the roughly 450 artworks are from India, while the remainder comes primarily from Pakistanis and from Indian artists who live abroad. In the museum's 1 600 square meters, visitors find key works by well-known Indian modernists, such as Raja Ravi Varma or Maqbul Fida Husain, the "Picasso of India." Alongside these are works by a pioneering group of Bombay artists who worked together in the 1940s, as well as art by contemporaries like Anish Kapoor, Bharti Kher, or Raqib Shaw.

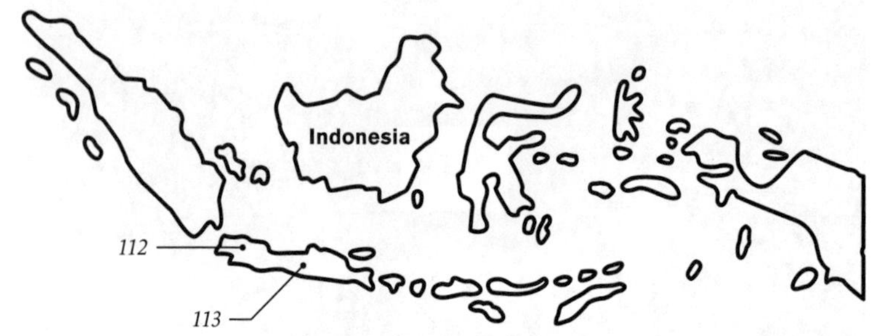

112   Yuz Museum
Asian and Western contemporary art of the influential collector Budi Tek

Budi Tek, a businessman of Chinese-Indonesian heritage, owns a collection of art that reflects his background: in his Yuz Museum, in Jakarta, Tek grants artists a show every three months and often includes part of his collection in their exhibitions. His foundation's office is located in Hong Kong and Shanghai, and his collection boasts a wide-ranging contingent of works by well-known Chinese artists, such as Zeng Fanzhi, Zhang Xiaogang, or Ai Weiwei, often from their early years, between the 1980s and 1990s. The collection also includes large installations by young artists like Sun Yuan & Peng Yu or Li Hui. A new museum in Shanghai, designed by architect Sou Fujimoto, is planned to open in 2013. Along with Asian art, Tek also holds large-format works by some Western stars, among them Maurizio Cattelan, Adel Abdessemed, and Fred Sandback.

Collector:
Budi Tek

Address:
Darmawangsa Square
The City Walk Unit 31-33
Jakarta 12160
Indonesia
Tel +62 21 72788272
www.yuzf.org

Opening Hours:
Mon–Sun: 10am–8pm

113   OHD Museum of Modern & Contemporary Indonesian Art
A private collection with museum-level Indonesian art

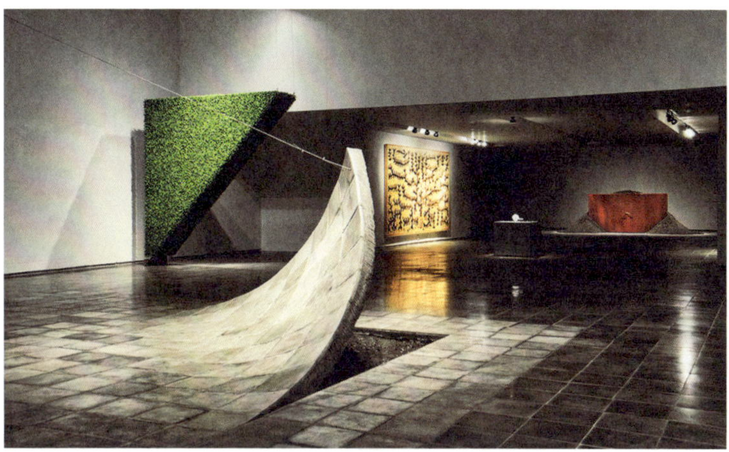

Collector:
Oei Hong Djien

Address:
Jl. Jenggolo 14
Magelang 56122
Central Java
Indonesia
Tel +62 293 362444
info@ohdmuseum.com
www.ohdmuseum.com

Opening Hours:
Wed–Mon: 10am–5pm

Quite an accomplishment: since the 1980s former physician Oei Hong Djien has assembled over 2 500 works of Indonesian art. The result is a stellar overview of abstract and figurative painting, installation, and video art. The collection spans from the European-educated Prince Raden Saleh (1807–1880) to artists of the twentieth century, such as Affandi, S. Sudjojono, and Hendra Gunawan. Notable are European artists like Rudolf Bonnet or Walter Spies, both of who played important roles in Balinese art. Roughly half of the collection is comprised of contemporary artists, among them the 1960s-born Entang Wiharso, Heri Dono, or Nasirun. For some of them, the culture of the Wayang, or "shadow play," has been an important factor in their works. The collection is housed in three beautiful two-storey buildings.

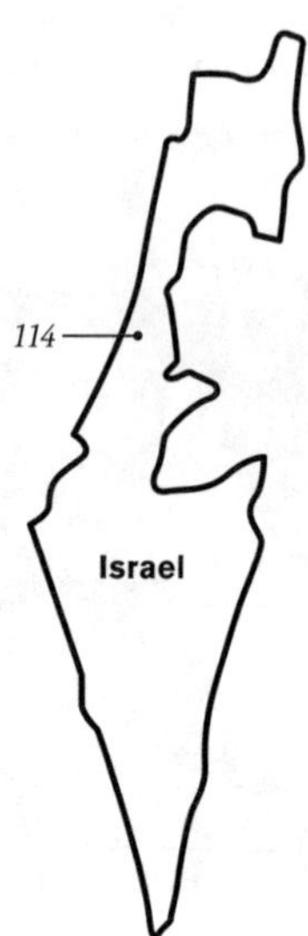

114   SIP Shpilman Institute of Photography

*Highlights from the history of photography from the
Bauhaus to Israeli avant-garde*

A radical step: at the age of sixty the Israeli entrepreneur
Shalom Shpilman sold his company to devote, during the
second part of his life, his "intellectual and financial resources 100 percent to photography." Established in 2010,
the SIP Shpilman Institute of Photography, sprawled across
700 square meters, presents an ever-growing collection that
captures the medium in all its diversity: from the Bauhaus
to Man Ray and Hans Bellmer, all the way to Thomas Ruff,
Hiroshi Sugimoto, and young Israeli photographers like
the rising star Assaf Shaham. Of the works, 65 percent are
by international artists, and the remaining 35 percent are
from Israel. Regularly scheduled artist talks, lectures, and
discussions make SIP an important address for photo fans
from Israel and abroad.

Collector:
Shalom Shpilman

Address:
27 Shoken Street, 3rd Floor
Tel Aviv 66532
Israel
Tel +972 3 7283737
info@thesip.org
www.thesip.org

Opening Hours:
Tues, Thurs: 4–8pm
Fri–Sat: 10am–2pm

Most of them could easily fill their own exhibition halls with art they
have acquired. But collectors like Janelle and Alden Pinnell, in Dallas,
or Ziba Ardalan de Weck, in London, pursue other goals: they fund and
finance spaces and provide them to artists and exceptional projects.
The interests often overlap, of course. Artists that exhibit in Pinnells'
Power Station or at West London Projects, an initiative founded by
Maddalena and Paolo Kind, are often also represented in their private

collections. The real intention of such initiatives is **to offer a
space where artists can work a
bit more freely and playfully** than they
usually do in institutions or galleries.
This is a free space in the art world where most dealers expect an
artist's consistent, recognizable handwriting; the work is otherwise
difficult to sell. This time-out for all sides is often financially supported
by the collectors. The Power Station is a carefully restored factory
building from the 1920s. Parasol Unit in London, founded in 2004 by
Ziba Ardalan de Weck, offers family days alongside philosophical
debates. Participation is also the key in financial matters: the
foundation is always looking for supporting members. Here, the private
project-room has long had the qualities of an art institution. Such
examples point the way forward: now even a super-collector like Frank
Cohen has a newly awaked desire to contribute. In spring of 2013 he
opened the project space Dairy Art Center in London-Bloomsbury
together with the art collector Nicolai Frahm. The concept is to show
works by young or established artists next to those who have found
themselves wrongfully neglected.

Christiane Meixner

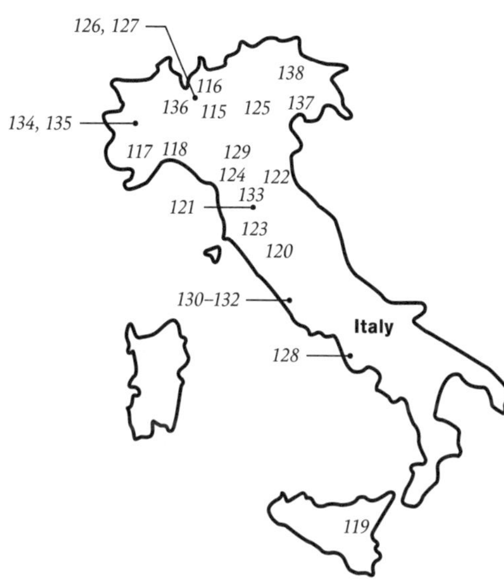

115   ALT Arte Contemporanea
Industrial archeology meets contemporary aesthetics

Collectors:
Tullio Leggeri & Fausto Radici

Address:
Via Gerolamo Acerbis 14
24022 Alzano Lombardo
Italy
Tel +39 035 4536730
info@altartecontemporanea.it
www.altartecontemporanea.it

Opening Hours:
Sun: 3–7pm
Only guided tours by appointment.

The exhibition space ALT, near Bergamo, in northern Italy, is a testimony to the friendship between Tullio Leggeri, an architect and builder, and Fausto Radici, a one-time professional skier and businessman. Radici died in 2002, and the two men had shared a passion for contemporary art; they dreamed of opening their collections to the public. To this end, they bought the former headquarters of Italcementi, a cement factory and site of industrial archeology, and gave it a new lease on life. Opened in 2009 and dedicated to Radici, the ALT exhibition space shows part of the founders' own collections as well as new site-specific projects. Among the artists included are Enrico Castellani, Joseph Beuys, Maurizio Cattelan, Shirin Neshat, Vanessa Beecroft, Wim Delvoye, Carsten Höller, and Paul McCarthy.

116   Fondazione Pietro Rossini
Large-scale sculptures in a landscaped park

Just north of Milan is a park that fuses modern and contemporary sculpture, architecture, and landscape. It is, in fact, an open-air museum, founded in 2010 by entrepreneur Alberto Rossini and his wife, Luisa, in memory of their son Pietro. Alberto Rossini's interest in art began in the 1950s. Several large sculptures are located in the park, some of them developed as site-specific projects. Among the artists are important Italian names of the postwar period, including Fausto Melotti, Pietro Consagra, or Giulio Turcato, as well as international names such as Dennis Oppenheim, César, Erik Dietman, or Nobuho Nagasawa. A pavilion in the park used for exhibitions was designed by James Wines of the New York architecture firm Site—one of the largest agencies in the field of green architecture.

Collector:
Alberto Rossini

Address:
Via Col del Frejus 3
20836 Briosco
Monza and Brianza
Italy
Mobile +39 335 5378472
info@fondazionepietrorossini.it
www.fondazionepietrorossini.it

Opening Hours:
From April to September,
by telephone appointment
only (please call between
10am–12pm, 3–7pm).

117   Collezione La Gaia
*Minimal Art, Conceptual Art, and Arte Povera
in Piedmont*

When Bruna Girodengo and Matteo Viglietta began collecting art, at the end of the 1970s, they did so "on tiptoe and with a big desire to learn." Initially the pair bought modern works—their first acquisition a 1918 collage by Giacomo Balla—but they soon turned their attention to art from the 1960s to the present. Today the collection counts nearly 1 200 pieces, including a significant group by Arte Povera artists like Alighiero Boetti, Giuseppe Penone, and Michelangelo Pistoletto, which are placed in a "conversation" with more contemporary works by Bill Viola, Anish Kapoor, and Tony Cragg, among others. Despite its cool appeal, Girodengo's and Viglietta's taste in contemporary art is not to be confused with what is currently in. Personal preference has always been their guide.

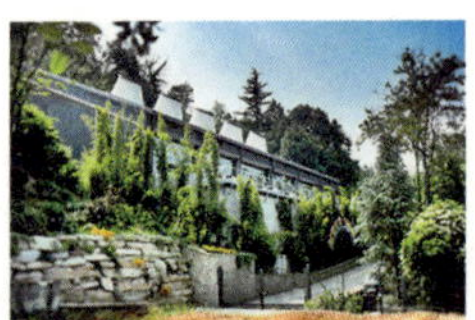

Collectors:
Bruna Girodengo &
Matteo Viglietta

Address:
Strada di Montegaudio 13
12022 Busca
Italy
Tel +39 0171 945900
info@collezionelagaia.it
www.collezionelagaia.it

E-mail appointment only.

118   Fondazione Pier Luigi e
Natalina Remotti

*A marriage in the name of art, and a collection
in a former church*

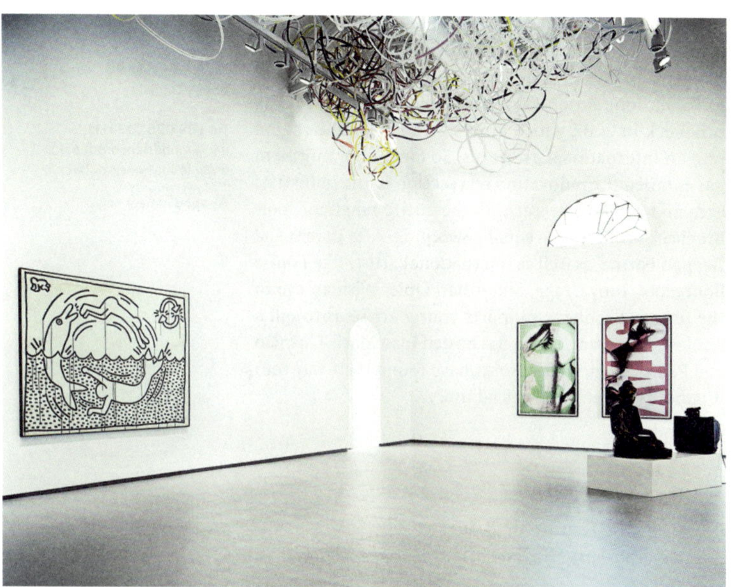

Collectors:
Pier Luigi & Natalina Remotti

Address:
Via Castagneto 52
16032 Camogli, Genoa
Italy
Tel +39 0185 772137
info@fondazioneremotti.it
www.fondazioneremotti.it

Opening Hours:
Sat–Sun: 3–7pm
And by appointment.

Since their wedding nuptials, at the end of the 1960s, Pier Luigi and Natalina Remotti have been collecting contemporary art. "We have always looked for artists who are experimenting with a new language but who do not yet command exorbitant prices," says Natalina Remotti. "A collector must recognize an artist before the market does." Their collection includes works by Francesco Vezzoli, Vanessa Beecroft, and Nico Vascellari and has a special slant toward photography. Their foundation was opened in 2008 in a former church renovated by the artist Alberto Garutti. There they present their collection and organize exhibitions with additional artists they appreciate. "Our collection has grown quite nicely because my husband and I agree on things," Remotti says. "It's often happened that I've shown him a work of art at a fair and he says, 'I just bought that.'"

119   Fondazione Brodbeck
*Contemporary art in a post-industrial complex—
in the shadow of a volcano*

The 6 000-square-meter industrial complex in the neighbor-hood of San Cristoforo, in Catania, used to be a factory for producing licorice and processing nuts. It has also served as a garrison, a storage facility, and joinery. Now it is home to Fondazione Brodbeck, founded by industrialist Paolo Brodbeck in 2007, which aims to transform the region into an international art nexus. So far the commitment has entailed the renovation of a section of the industrial area and a chance to rethink the entire neighborhood. Brodbeck's collecting is equally sweeping: Arte Povera and Gruppo Forma, as well as international artists like Louise Bourgeois, Tony Cragg, and Julian Opie. With an eye to the future, Brodbeck supports young artists through a residency program, which has hosted João Maria Gusmão and Pedro Paiva, whose works have found their way into Brodbeck's esteemed compendium.

Collector:
Paolo Brodbeck

Address:
Via Gramignani 93
95121 Catania
Italy
Tel +39 095 7233111
info@fondazionebrodbeck.it
www.fondazionebrodbeck.it

By appointment only.

120   Il Giardino dei Lauri
Contemporary blue chips in the Umbrian countryside

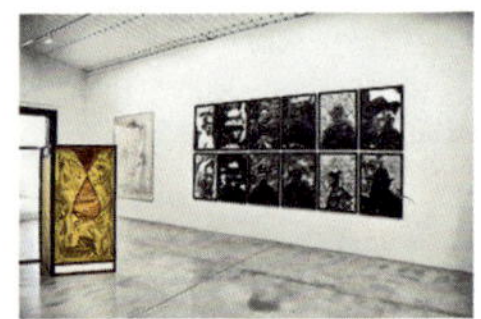

Born into a family of art collectors, Massimo Lauro came in contact with art at a young age. He was love-struck by his parents' enthusiasm and eventually began collecting. Knowing he could not compete with his parents' stately compilation, he began, in the 1990s, garnering the work of a younger generation. Today the collection Massimo Lauro and his wife, Angela, have amassed in their Umbrian countryside residence boasts more than 300 works of established contemporary artists like Urs Fischer, Jeff Koons, Allora & Calzadilla, Takashi Murakami, and Fischli/Weiss. Some sculptures are installed in the garden: a hulking metallic hand by Piotr Uklanski, and an unsettling sculpture of a hanged child by Maurizio Cattelan, which shocked some of Milan's city dwellers in 2004. A neon rainbow by Ugo Rondinone glows over wandering garden visitors, asking, *Where Do We Go from Here?*

Collectors:
Massimo & Angela Lauro

Address:
Località San Litardo
ss Umbro Casentinese Km 79
06062 Città della Pieve
Italy
Tel +39 3409669052
info@ilgiardinodeilauri.it
www.ilgiardinodeilauri.it

Opening Hours:
Fri–Sat: 10am–1pm,
3:30–6:30pm
And by appointment.

121 Sensus—Luoghi per l'Arte
Contemporanea
Space as leitmotif in a 1960s building

Collector:
Claudio Cosma

Address:
Viale Gramsci 42
50132 Florence
Italy
info@sensusstorage.com
www.sensusstorage.com

Opening Hours:
Fri–Sat: 6–8pm

"Collecting has always been a priority for me. As a child I was already collecting things that triggered my imagination. I used them to create my own world." This is how insurance broker Claudio Cosma explains the motivation behind his passion of the last thirty years. "My greatest satisfaction," he says, "is to assist in the creation of works, to exchange ideas with artists to such an extent that these works would not exist without me." This approach is reflected in the name of Cosma's showroom in Florence, which refers to perception: Sensus. Opened in December 2012 on the ground floor of a 1960s building, the collection's overarching theme is the relationship between art and its surrounding space. Aside from Italian artists like Fabrizio Corneli, Angelo Barone, and Maurizio Nannucci are Asian representatives like Maitree Siriboon or Yuki Ichihashi.

122 Fondazione Dino Zoli
*Twentieth-century Italian art in a
multifunctional museum*

Collector:
Dino Zoli

Address:
Viale Bologna 288
47100 Forlì
Italy
Tel +39 0543 755770
info@fondazionedinozoli.com
www.fondazionedinozoli.com

Opening Hours:
Mon–Fri: 10am–1pm,
4–7pm

The Fondazione Dino Zoli, located in the city of Forlì, in the central-north district Emilia-Romagna, calls itself a "dynamic museum." Rightly so: opened by local industrialist Dino Zoli in 2007, the foundation not only houses his exquisite collection of modern art, but also a vibrant series of talks, music events, fashion shows, and book launches, with a particular attention paid to the region. The foundation's connection to the surrounding locale is also evidenced by exhibitions of paintings by Mattia Moreni, an artist in Emilia-Romagna. The collection as a whole lends a visual excursus of twentieth-century Italian art, featuring established names like Alberto Magnelli, Mimmo Paladino, and Fabrizio Plessi, as well as those lesser known internationally but beloved in Italy: Salvatore Fiume and Emilio Scanavino.

123   Castello di Ama per l'Arte Contemporanea
Site-specific installations for a dual passion:
art and wine

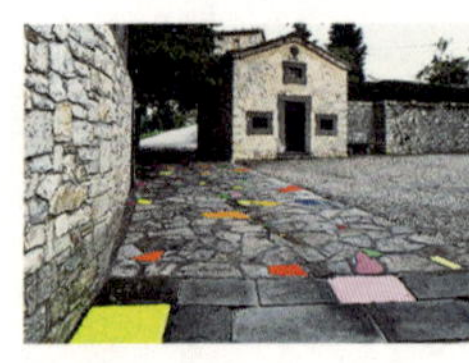

One thing is essential for the vintner couple Marco and Lorenza Pallanti: the uniqueness of place. This is true of their wines, of course, whose uniqueness is owed the soil's inherent qualities, but as well as of their art collection, which is exclusively comprised of site-specific installations. Since 2000 they have invited artists once a year to install work on their vineyard estate. The project was created in collaboration with Lorenzo Fiaschi of the Galleria Continua in San Gimignano. The first artist was Michelangelo Pistoletto, who set up a four-meter-high tree with a mirror hidden inside of it—a trademark of the artist—in the basement of the Villa Pianigiani. After Pistoletto, many other well-known artists, such as Daniel Buren or Ilya and Emilia Kabakov, came and dealt adroitly with this unique space.

Collectors:
Marco & Lorenza Pallanti

Address:
Località Ama
53013 Gaiole in Chianti, Siena
Italy
Tel +39 0577 746031
info@castellodiama.com
arte@castellodiama.com

E-mail appointment only.

124   Collezione Nunzia e Vittorio Gaddi
International contemporary art in the city and country

Tuscan notary Vittorio Gaddi has been collecting contemporary art since the beginning of the 1990s. His first work was the sculpture *The Daughter of the Sun,* by the Italian artist Giò Pomodoro. After this, his attention shifted to more international and emerging art. Today, Gaddi owns around 350 works by artists such as Olafur Eliasson, Carsten Höller, or Wade Guyton. His interest is triggered less by a specific style or medium than by an artist's contemporaneity. From the very outset Gaddi wanted to have his collection publicly accessible. Today it is divided among a 1920s Art Nouveau mansion, in the city of Lucca, and in two old farmhouses nestled in the countryside. One of these adjacent houses was intended as a country chalet but was gradually overrun by art. The other was renovated for the collection in summer 2012.

Collectors:
Nunzia & Vittorio Gaddi

Address:
Viale Carducci 627
55100 Lucca
Italy
Tel +39 0583 587748
info@collezionegaddi.com
www.collezionegaddi.com

By appointment only.

125   La Casabianca
Graphic art from the 1960s to the 1990s

Collector:
Giobatta Meneguzzo

Address:
Largo Morandi 1
36034 Malo
Italy
Tel +39 0445 602474
info@museocasabianca.com
www.museocasabianca.com

Opening Hours:
Sun: 10am–12:30pm,
3–6:30pm
And by appointment.

Aspiring collectors with insufficiently deep pockets can always turn to works on paper for beauty and value. Giobatta Meneguzzo turned to exactly such work in the 1970s, and his decisions have paid off. Today he possesses a distinguished collection of more than 1 200 works by 700 international artists spanning from the 1960s to the 1990s. His collection, in La Casabianca, is housed in a seventeenth-century palace—replete with a library—in a small town in the Veneto region. The collection's artworks are grouped together by movement and, all told, evidence a tight spectrum: Minimalism and Pop, Conceptual Art and Transavanguardia. All the works are hung salon style—and without labels—so that visitors approach the works with an unbiased eye.

126   Fondazione Opera
Contemporary art meets toys and antiques

Collectors:
Guido Galimberti &
Donatella Picenelli

Address:
Piazza San Marco 1
20121 Milan
Italy.
info@operadv.com
www.operadv.com

E-mail appointment only.

If you're the son of a passionate collector who had already purchased works by Lucio Fontana and Piero Manzoni in the 1960s, the probability that you'd fall in love with art in an early age is pretty high. This is precisely what happened to Guido Galimberti. He was twenty years old when he acquired his first work of art: *Flowers*, by Andy Warhol, which he paid for in installments. For years he had worked as a financial consultant but considered art his passion. In 2007 he transformed his hobby into his profession and became an art consultant. Galimberti's handling of art is playful and provocative, combining works of contemporary artists like Nedko Solakov and Pascale Marthine Tayou with Asian antiques or toys. You will find, for example, a top hat by Giulio Paolini next to a Japanese samurai helmet, or a cube by Stuart Arends next to an antique Chinese vase.

Italy, Milan
Italy, Naples

127 Collezione Peruzzi
Prints and multiples from Arte Povera to today

Graphic art is often falsely viewed as a second-class art. But in order to master the praxis of printing, one must precisely control the materials. The results some artists achieve are amazing. When Milanese engineer Vittorio Peruzzi first became interested in prints and multiples, in the 1970s, the reason was primarily economic: these works were usually less expensive than unique works. Today he has put together an extraordinarily coherent collection of some of the best prints and multiples by selected artists. Lucio Fontana's series *Teatrini* was the first work Peruzzi purchased, followed by prints by Enrico Castellani and Alberto Burri, as well as by Arte Povera artists like Gilberto Zorio or Giuseppe Penone. Among contemporary artists, the collector appreciates the work of Maurizio Cattelan and Vanessa Beecroft.

Collector:
Vittorio Peruzzi

Address:
Corso Lodi 78
20139 Milan
Italy
Mobile +39 3484937953
collezioneperuzzi@collezione
peruzzi.it
www.collezioneperuzzi.it

E-mail appointment only.

128 Fondazione Morra Greco
International contemporary art in the historic heart of Naples

The Neapolitan palace that houses the foundation of dentist Maurizio Morra Greco has contained art for centuries. It was used in the seventeenth century as an exhibition hall by the Caracciolos, the royal family of Avellino. Today, works by Italian artists such as Roberto Cuoghi and Diego Perrone are represented, as are those of international names such as Mark Dion or Manfred Pernice. "I started to buy antiques at the age of fourteen," says Morra Greco. "Then I understood that contemporary art is an expression of my time." The artists of Greco's collection not only draw the zeitgeist to Naples, they also provide a connection to the city: the foundation regularly invites artists to create site-specific works. One of the most spectacular was an installation by the German artist Gregor Schneider, who transformed the basement of the palace into a shadowy labyrinth.

Collector:
Maurizio Morra Greco

Address:
Largo Avellino 17
80138 Naples
Italy
Tel +39 081 210690
info@fondazionemorragreco.com
www.fondazionemorragreco.com

Opening Hours:
Mon–Fri: 10am–2pm,
3–7pm
Wed: 10am–2pm
Sat: 11am–7pm

Auction houses like Sotheby's and Christie's are important players in the art world. The sensationally high prices their houses see offered for paintings and sculptures make the most dramatic entrance into the public mind. In 2010, a bronze sculpture by Alberto Giacometti was auctioned for nearly 75 million euros; nearly 100 million euros was paid for a version of Edvard Munch's *The Scream* in 2012. These two record sales at Sotheby's London and New York, respectively, pack a financial punch which contemporary art is simply not yet able to match. Nevertheless, both of these auction houses are considered "kingmakers" in contemporary art. If multiple collectors compete for to the same lot, prices quickly surge. The auction house price can thus signal an immediate increase in value for the entire oeuvre of an artist's work. It also thereby dictates new gallery prices. Indeed, the power of the auction house has solidified in recent years—but not without its critics. "Art auctions were originally a purely intermediate trade, forming the main shopping source for the art market," writes Dirk Boll, European director at Christie's, in his book *Art for Sale*, which recalls the origins of auction houses. The audience has changed completely. Meanwhile, in many cases, the only bidders who can keep up with private collectors are large galleries, often in order to stabilize prices of their artists. When Damien Hirst decided, in 2008, to auction off 223 of his works at once at Sotheby's in London, his gallerist Jay Jopling bid on them. Such a market does not tolerate failures. As a consequence, auction houses sometimes guarantee some sellers fixed sums for works in demand. If the high price deters buyers, the works go into temporary storage. These methods may be contentious, but auction houses provide critical information on the valuation of an artist's work on the market.

Christiane Meixner

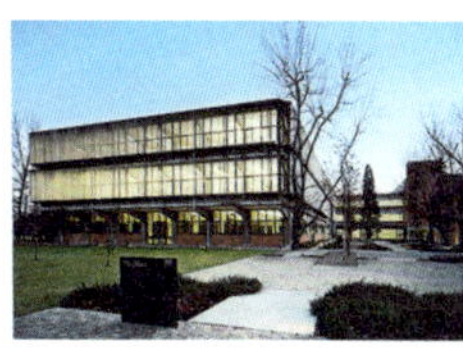

Collector:
Achille Maramotti

Address:
Via Fratelli Cervi 66
42124 Reggio Emilia
Italy
Tel +39 0522 382484
info@collezionemaramotti.org
www.collezionemaramotti.org

Opening Hours:
Thurs–Fri: 2:30–6:30pm
Sat–Sun: 10:30am–6:30pm
By appointment only.

129   Collezione Maramotti
From prêt-à-porter to contemporary art

Achille Maramotti, founder of fashion group Max Mara, was not only the inventor of prêt-à-porter in postwar Italy, he was also an enthusiastic collector of art. His focus was on painting—above all, Transavanguardia, but he also collected works by international stars Julian Schnabel and Alex Katz, of whom he was the first European collector. Sharing Maramotti's collection with the public dates back thirty years: initially it hung in the corridors of the Max Mara factory. When production was moved to accommodate company expansion, the factory was turned into a museum that exhibited 200 of Maramotti's 600-work trove. Though he passed away in 2005, Maramotti's three children have continued to buy and commission works by young artists for their family's collection, such as those by Jacob Kassay and Kara Tanaka.

Collectors:
Giovanni & Valeria Giuliani

Address:
Via Gustavo Bianchi 1
00153 Rome
Italy
Tel +39 06 57301091
info@fondazionegiuliani.org
www.fondazionegiuliani.org

Opening Hours:
Tues–Sat: 3–7:30pm
And by appointment.

130   Fondazione Giuliani
Contemporary flair with blue-collar neighbors

Over the past few years, Rome's contemporary art scene has boomed. Among the most notable events have been the inauguration of a branch of Gagosian Gallery and the opening of Museo Nazionale Della Arti Del XXI Secolo (MAXXI). But beneath all the glitz, Giovanni Giuliani and his wife, Valeria, discreetly opened their impressive private foundation in 2010—a white cube in the basement of a housing project in the neighborhood of Testaccio. The area alone is worth a visit: a working-class district with strong character that offers an attractive nightlife. The Giulianis, who began collecting at the end of the 1980s, now maintain nearly 400 works, primarily sculptures and installations by artists including Cyprien Gaillard, Mona Hatoum, Alicja Kwade, and Nedko Solakov, as well as work by figures of Arte Povera and Conceptual Art.

131   Casa Musumeci Greco
*An historic apartment for contemporary art
in central Rome*

Visiting the Roman house of Ines Musumeci Greco—
a former art writer and gallerist—means not only visiting
a collection of works by contemporary Italian and international artists—Nico Vascellari, Luisa Rabbia, Jonathan
Monk, Pascal Marthine Tayou, or Chen Zhen—but entering a private apartment where life meets art, and where
modernity meets history. Greco's apartment is located
inside Palazzo Bernini, a stately address in the heart of
the historic center, once home to Baroque architect Gian
Lorenzo Bernini and a temporary residence of the Scottish
novelist Sir Walter Scott. Renovated with an eye toward its
idiosyncrasies, the apartment regularly hosts artists' talks
and lectures, evincing Ines Musumeci Greco's preference
for a direct, daily relationship with artists and their work.

Collectors:
Ines & Giuliano Musumeci Greco

Address:
Via Della Mercede 11
00187 Rome
Italy
inesmusumeci@hotmail.com

E-mail appointment only.

132   Nomas Foundation
*Nomadism and otherness against the force
of homogeneity*

The word *nomas* is Latin for "nomad." This is how the
Romans described the Saharan Berbers, who spoke nei-
ther Latin nor Greek and opposed any foreign attempt
to suppress their culture and identity. The Rome-based
collectors Raffaella and Stefano Sciarretta were inspired
by this concept of nomadism and otherness when they
opened their foundation in 2008. Here they present their
expansive collection, complemented by exhibitions, talks,
and seminars. One of their goals is to offer residencies to
support young artists with their projects. The Sciarrettas
began to collect in the 1990s—at first Italian Pop Art, and
then international contemporary works. Today they own
about 700 artworks by 300 artists, among them Rossella
Biscotti, Alexandre Singh, and Ryan Gander.

Collectors:
Raffaella & Stefano Sciarretta

Address:
Viale Somalia 33
00199 Rome
Italy
Tel +39 06 86398381
info@nomasfoundation.com
www.nomasfoundation.com

Opening Hours:
Tues–Fri: 2:30–7pm

133   Collezione Gori—Fattoria di Celle
Site-specific and Land Art nestled in the Tuscan hillside

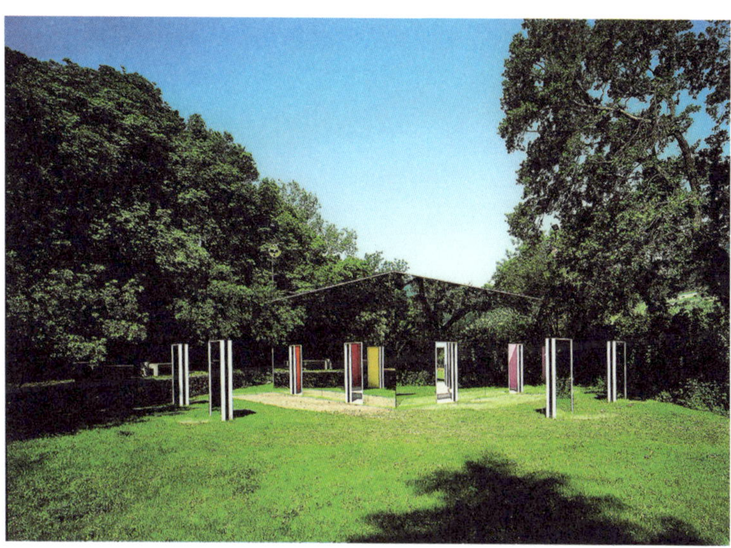

Collector:
Giuliano Gori

Address:
Via Montalese 7
51030 Santomato di Pistoia
Italy
Tel +39 0573 479486
info@goricoll.it
www.goricoll.it

Online registration required.

The beauty of the Tuscan countryside is known the world over. And at Fattoria di Celle, near Pistoia, the region's natural beauty is complemented by the profundity of art. It is here that Giuliano Gori, since the 1980s, has been inviting international stars like Robert Morris, Sol LeWitt, Richard Serra, or Daniel Buren to create site-specific works in the park surrounding his majestic residence. Each artist chose a location after carefully sizing up the local elements and conditions and allowing the local charm and history of the Tuscan region—birthplace of the Renaissance—to win them over. When you visit the Collezione Gori, be sure to bring the right shoes and a genuine interest: more than thirty years of collecting have amassed an extensive collection that can take several hours to visit.

134 Fondazione Sandretto Re Rebaudengo
Not just a collection; a foundation to promote the new

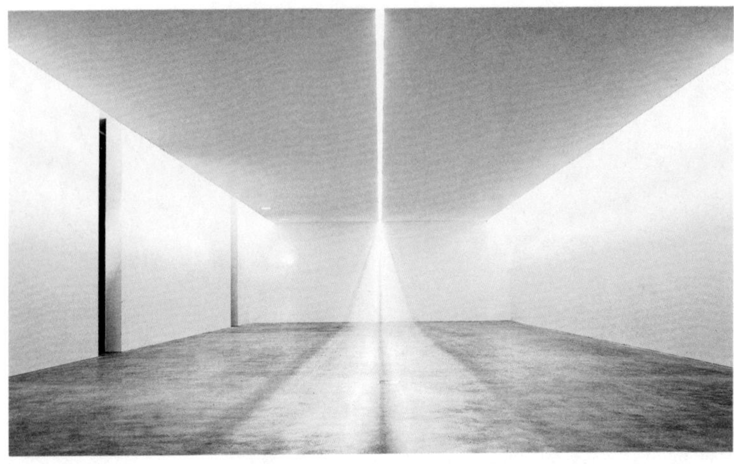

Thanks to a mix of institutional and private initiatives, the region of Piedmont has become an important hub for contemporary art in Italy. And among all the private ventures, perhaps the most well known is Fondazione Sandretto Re Rebaudengo, which was established in 1995 by the Italian grande dame of contemporary collecting, Patrizia Sandretto Re Rebaudengo. The foundation prides itself on the early recognition of talented artists who have achieved international acclaim since the 1990s, like Californian multimedia guru Doug Aitken, for example. Among Rebaudengo's more recent acquisitions are works by Tauba Auerbach and João Onofre. But because the main aim of the foundation is to promote the work of young artists, it not only shows works from Rebaudengo's collection, it also organizes thematic exhibitions and supports the production of work by artists just entering the fray.

Collector:
Patrizia Sandretto Re Rebaudengo

Address:
Via Modane 16
10141 Turin
Italy
Tel +39 011 3797600
info@fsrr.org
www.fsrr.org

Opening Hours:
Thurs: 8–11pm
Fri–Sun: 12–7pm

135   Centro Videoinsight
Art and psychotherapy: a healing combination

Collector:
Rebecca Russo

Address:
Via Ferdinando Bonsignore
10131 Turin
Italy
Tel +39 3472390155
videoinsight@videoinsight.it
www.videoinsight.it

By e-mail or telephone
appointment only.

Art can heal. That's the theory that psychotherapist and art collector Rebecca Russo stands behind and implements at her center Videoinsight. For her, a work must convey universal messages that relate to human needs; this principle has guided her collecting. Ten years ago she started to show art—mostly videos—to her patients. She uses it as a kind of Rorschach test for self-reflection. She also offers this method in the form of group therapy once a week to an interested art audience. One may also visit the monthly rotating exhibitions usually devoted to one artist. The collection includes, among others, Marina Abramović, Vik Muniz, and Thomas Ruff, as well as many artists from Asia, such as Filipino Ronald Ventura or Taiwanese Natee Utarit.

136   Villa & Collezione Panza di Biumo
Minimal Art in a neoclassical villa in dialogue with antique furniture and African art

Collector:
Giuseppe Panza di Biumo

Address:
Piazza Litta 1
21100 Varese
Italy
Tel +39 0332 283960
faibiumo@fondoambiente.it

Opening Hours:
Tues–Sun: 10am–6pm

When Giuseppe Panza di Biumo passed away, in 2010, the *Los Angeles Times* described him as "a Milanese businessman who was the first great international collector of postwar American art." In the mid-1950s, after a trip to America, di Biumo began acquiring art superheroes like Mark Rothko, Bruce Nauman, and Richard Serra. His collection holds a few Europeans but is comprised mostly of American Abstract Expressionist, Pop, Minimal, and Conceptual Art. Large parts of di Biumo's trove are now in museums like the Guggenheim in New York, and the Museum of Contemporary Art in Los Angeles. But an important group of works is still maintained in his neoclassical villa near Varese. One wing boasts light installations by Dan Flavin and James Turrell, and Minimal Art and Monochromes sit next to Renaissance furniture and African and Pre-Colombian art, arrangements decided upon by di Biumo's own keen eye.

137   François Pinault Foundation—
Palazzo Grassi & Punta della Dogana
Big, bigger, Pinault: high art with an even higher profile

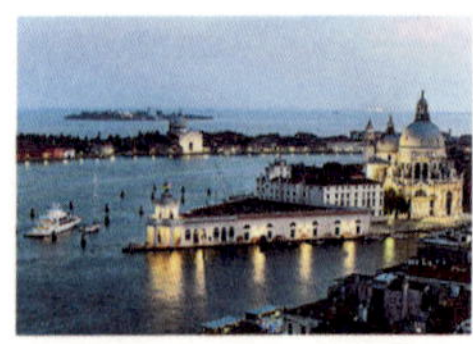

Normally, collecting art takes time. But not in the case of François Pinault, who has managed in just a few years to assemble one of the largest private collections of contemporary art in Europe. Everything is colossal in the two Venetian exhibition buildings maintained by the billionaire owner of the auction house Christie's: the names, the works, and the architecture. While there are variations in the quality of the works by international megastars like Jeff Koons, Sigmar Polke, Cindy Sherman, Takashi Murakami, or Jake & Dinos Chapman, such premium artworks are rare to come by on the art market, and you'll have to be patient to land them. If you want to decide for yourself on the authoritative collector's tastes, head straight to the splendid Palazzo Grassi, at the Canale Grande, or to the 4 500-square-meter address at the Punta della Dogana, renovated into a modern art temple by Tadao Ando.

Collector:
François Pinault

Addresses:
Palazzo Grassi
Campo San Samuele 3231
30124 Venice, Italy

Punta della Dogana
Sestiere Dorsoduro 2
30123 Venice, Italy

Tel +39 041 2719039
www.palazzograssi.it

Opening Hours:
Wed–Mon: 10am–7pm

138   Prato d'Arte Collezione Marzona
Land Art without borders: installations
in the Carnia mountains

It's a truism that many great ideas are conceived in conversation over a glass of wine with good friends on a midsummer's eve. This was surely the case with Art Park, a sculpture garden founded in the late 1980s in the 400-inhabitant town of Verzegnis, in northeastern Italy. The two friends were German art dealer Konrad Fischer—an early supporter of American Minimal and Conceptual artists who was responsible for bringing many of them to Europe—and Egidio Marzona, one of the world's most important collectors of Conceptual, Minimal, Land Art, and Arte Povera, who donated a large part of his collection to Berlin's Hamburger Bahnhof museum in 2002. The sprawling Prato d'Arte Collezione Marzona contains thirteen sculptures by the likes of Bruce Nauman, Richard Long, Dan Graham, and Laurence Weiner, among others, all nestled in the landscape of the mountainous region of Carnia, from whence the Marzona family comes.

Collector:
Egidio Marzona

Address:
Villa di Verzegnis
33020 Verzegnis
Italy
Tel +39 0433 487779
carnia.musei@cmcarnia.regione.fvg.it

Opening Hours:
Mon–Sun: 24 hours

Collecting art is an expression of individuality, and it has been for centuries. But it was only during the Renaissance, when the artist was raised from a craftsman to a genius who created something extraordinary, that the individual work of art was born. While throughout the Middle Ages artworks were assessed and valued according to the amount of precious materials they contained—such as gold or lapis lazuli—the Renaissance valued what part of a painting a master like Sandro Botticelli painted and what part he appointed his apprentices to undertake. Apprentices were usually only responsible for the background and accessories; the master was in charge of the complicated parts, like the face or hands. Increasingly, **as the artwork became something unique, it also became a collector's item.**

But it was not only the work itself with which collectors wished to surround themselves; they aimed also to show their ability to appreciate precious things. The contact, or rather the friendship, with the artist also became important and special. Because an artist did not have to bow to social convention, his genius allowed him to move beyond the rules—this was sometimes even expected of him.

From this history emerged the idea of the twentieth-century bohemian, an individual who was financially poor but artistically gifted. In the best case, the bohemian artist was backed by a patron who both appreciated his art and supported him financially. Some artworks would never have been possible or would not have survived without this constellation of interests. For example, the famous patron Peggy Guggenheim assisted Max Ernst, who immigrated to the United States at the beginning of the 1940s with artworks that the Nazis had defamed as "degenerate."

The delicate balance between giving and taking exists to this day, of course, making art-collecting for the majority of collectors immensely attractive, eternally revealing the uniqueness of the collecting activity.

Independent Collectors

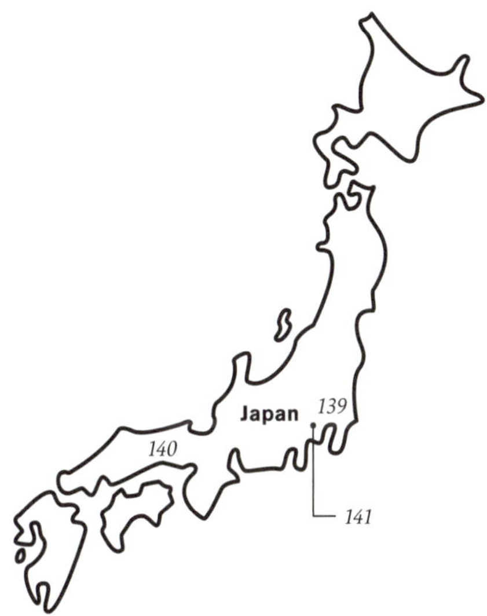

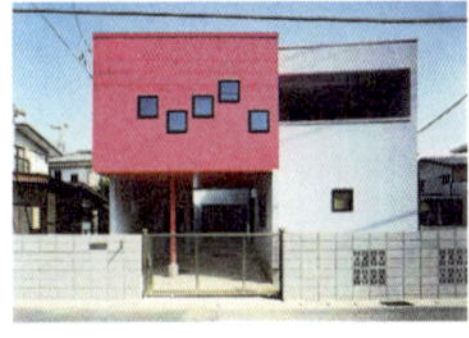

Collector:
Daisuke Miyatsu

Address:
3-3-17 Wakamiya
Ichikawa
Chiba Prefecture 272-0812
Japan
Fax +81 47 3321141

Visitation permitted only
occasionally. Please inquire
by fax or post.

139   Dream House

*High-quality Asian and international art
in an extravagant building*

A house made by an artist for art: Installation artist Domi-nique Gonzalez-Foerster designed a colorful, structurally eye-catching house for the collector Daisuke Miyatsu. In and around the Dream House you'll find works by Asian and international contemporary artists like Yayoi Kusama, Yoshitomo Nara, Yang Jun, Lee Kit, or Olafur Eliasson. Many of the works were designed particularly for the Dream House—where the telecommunications employee lives with his family. Media art is the main focus of this roughly 300-work collection, spanning from Yang Fudong or Cao Fei & Ou Ning, from China, through American Tony Oursler, to Nina Fischer and Maroan el Sani from Germany. Works from the video collection, which began in 1994, are beamed upon request.

140 Benesse Art Site
*Art, nature, and well-being on three small islands
in southern Japan*

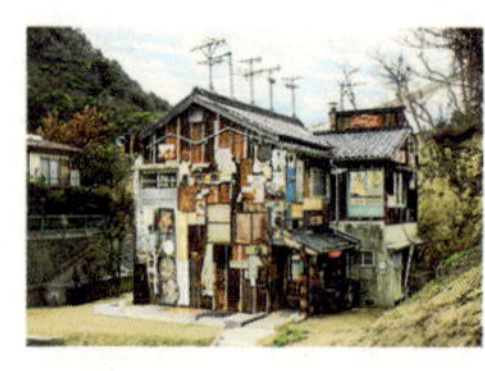

Benesse. The name alone sounds like natural wellness and
relaxation. And this is exactly what is meant. Those who
visit the three islands Naoshima, Teshima, and Inujima,
located in the Seto Inland Sea, far from the hustle and
bustle of Tokyo, are able to dive into a world bathed in contemplative contemporary art. Western visitors meet with
old friends: Bruce Nauman, James Turrell, and Christian
Boltanski are represented with installations that reflect the
dissolution of the individual into pure being. Exhibition
halls by the architect Tadao Ando house works by Japanese artists such as Mariko Mori and Hiroshi Sugimoto.
The bathhouse *I Love Yu*, by Japanese artist Shinro Ohtake,
invites "clothing-optional" relaxation after a long day of
sightseeing. The driving force behind all of this is the
Tokyo publisher Soichiro Fukutake, who describes himself
as a philanthropist rather than a collector.

Collector:
Soichiro Fukutake

Address:
Benesse House Museum
Gotanji, Naoshima
Kagawa 7613110
Japan
Tel +81 87 8923223
naoshima@mail.benesse.co.jp
www.benesse-artsite.jp/en

The twelve venues have different
opening hours. Please check
the website for most current
information.

141 Takahashi Collection
*One of the most important collections of Japanese
contemporary art in Japan*

He's one of the most vital collectors of contemporary art in
Japan. Since 1997 the psychologist Ryutaro Takahashi has
concentrated on gathering together mainly Japanese paintings, drawings, videos, and small sculptures—now numbering more than 1 500 works. He acquired many of these at a
time when Japanese museums no longer could: subsequent
the financial bubble-burst of the 1990s. Prominent older
artists in the collection are Yayoi Kusama—whose works
sparked Takahashi to begin collecting—as well as Katsura
Funakoshi, Yoshitomo Nara, Tomoko Konoike, or Kenji
Yanobe. Among the younger artists in his pool are Ruriko
Murayama and Mika Kato. Since March 2012 the Takahashi
Collection has been exhibited in Tabloid Space, a renovated
industrial hall in Tokyo.

Collector:
Ryutaro Takahashi

Address:
Tabloid Space
Tabloid 1F, 2-6-24 Kaigan
Minato-ku
Tokyo 105-0022
Japan
Tel +81 3 64353173
info@tabloidgallery.com
art@takahashiryutaro.com
www.takahashi-collection.com

Opening Hours:
Tues–Sat: 11:30am–7pm

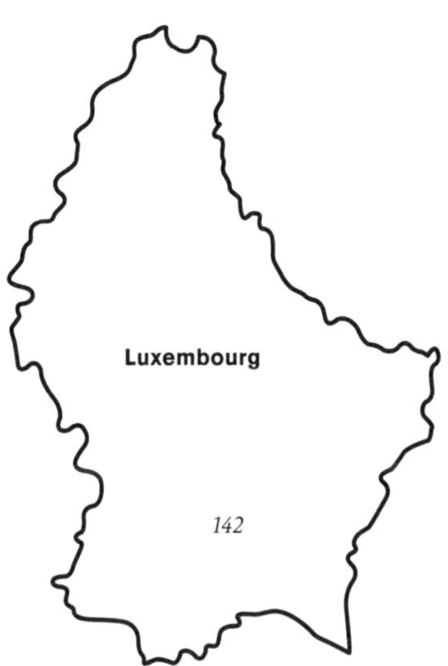

L

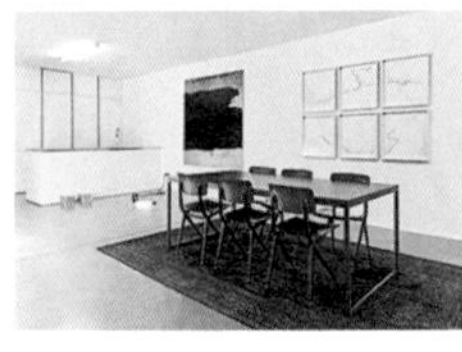

Collector:
Patrick Majerus

Address:
Luxembourg City, Luxembourg
m@jerus.lu

Visitation permitted only
occasionally. Please inquire
by e-mail.

142   Sammlung Patrick Majerus
Pointed contemporary concept art with critical potential

"Either you're a collector or you aren't," says Patrick Majerus, perhaps the only officer in the Luxembourg army with a distinct interest in contemporary concept art, primarily from Berlin. His collection attained international attention in 2010, when it was shown at the Kunstsaele Berlin. Majerus collects entire groups of works from just a few select artists of his generation. He is convinced that it is more important to collect deeply than broadly. Around ten artists between thirty and forty years old, including Alicja Kwade, Tim Berresheim, and Sven Johne, share the walls in Majerus's remodeled private home, which, as one might guess, does not keep fixed opening hours. Instead, he likes to personally guide like-minded art enthusiasts through his collection from time to time.

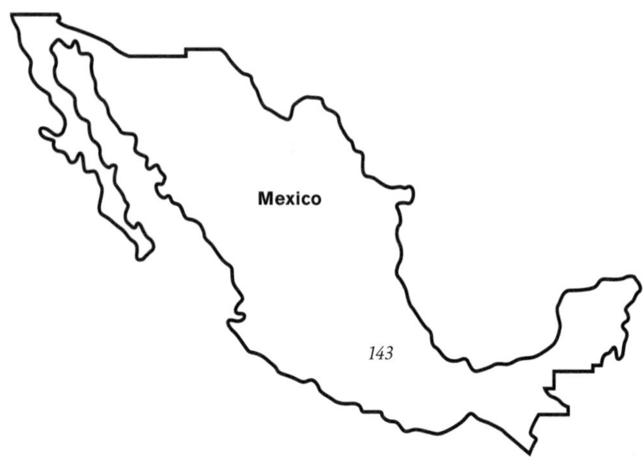

M

143   La Colección Júmex
Young Latin-American and international
contemporary art at the apex

Viva México! Once a year, everyone comes. During the art fair Zona Maco the international art scene jet-set permits itself a few Tequila-soaked days in Mexico City. One highlight is the party at the Colección Júmex. Eugenio López Alonso, the flamboyant, lone heir of Júmex, Mexico's largest juice company, presents his collection of contemporary and international art—more than 2 000 works inhabiting the company property on the outskirts of the city. The artwork is safe there, but any person who wishes to visit the 3 000-square-meter private museum has to first pass two armed guards. "If in a decade only two or three of these artists become famous, I'll know I did something significant," Alonso said in a 2004 interview. Less than a decade later, he's already done something significant: Carlos Amorales, Gabriel Orozco, and Minerva Cuevas have all broken through internationally.

Collector:
Eugenio López Alonso

Address:
Via Morelos 272
Colonia Santa María Tulpetlac
Ecatepec
C.P. 55400
Mexico
Tel +52 55 57758188
info@lacoleccionjumex.org
www.lacoleccionjumex.org

Opening Hours:
Mon–Fri: 10am–5pm

Once upon the time, in the late 1960s, there were three Swiss art dealers who founded an art fair in Basel. Trudl Bruckner, Balz Hilt, and Ernst Beyeler went into direct competition with Art Cologne, the first contemporary art fair, which had just been founded in Cologne, Germany. "Now, the art markets chase the exhibitors," read the headline of a German newspaper in 1971.

This attitude now seems outdated. For the past ten years, the number of art fairs has increased with the growing global interest in contemporary art. Now an art fair is held somewhere in the world almost every week.

Some of these **fairs have become essential events,** participation in which is important for the reputation of a gallery. Among these is the Frieze Art Fair in London, which expanded into New York in 2012 to compete with the traditional Armory Show. Art Basel has also extended its influence to the United States, establishing Art Basel Miami Beach in 2002. Its most recent expansion is in Asia: Art Basel in Hong Kong takes place for the first time in 2013. In the Middle East, Art Dubai still dominates, while in South America the Art Rio has come into gallery owners' increasing focus, attracted as they are by the purchasing power of local collectors. There are also, of course, the countless satellite fairs that occur around all of these main events.

The question is, who benefits? The many fair dates pressure artists to continuously produce more works. For the gallery, an art fair is an enormous investment with an uncertain result. And for visitors and collectors, they can be exhaustive. Nevertheless, art fairs remain the best way to learn about the latest developments in the art world, to meet gallery owners from abroad, and to discover new artists and trends.

Silvia Anna Barrilà

144   Collectors House
*Cooperation between international collectors
and a city museum*

Collector:
Albert Groot

Address:
Raadhuisplein 19
6411 Heerlen
Netherlands
Tel +31 45 5711525
info@collectorshouse.eu
www.collectorshouse.eu

Opening Hours:
Thurs–Sun: 1–5pm

"Strength in unity," goes the saying. This is also the principle of the Collectors House, in Heerlen, a collaboration between the city museum Schunck, the Dutch collector Albert Groot, and several international collectors. Their shared goal is to show works of contemporary art that are otherwise rarely seen in public. The exhibitions at the Collectors House bring together works currently residing in different places—in the Netherlands, Hong Kong, or Romania—and put them in a constructive dialogue with each other. Among the artists shown have been Marina Abramović, Mircea Cantor, Hans Op de Beeck, and Cao Fei. At a time when culture and museums are experiencing drastic cutbacks, initiatives that combine public and private certainly offer an alternative solution.

145   Concordia Collection
*Local and international artists in an historic house
in Rotterdam*

In one of the most beautiful streets of Rotterdam, between the lively Witte de Withstraat and the Boijmans
Van Beuningen Museum, sits the home of Julian Oggel,
a lawyer and the CEO of an investment firm. The house
alone is worth a visit: built in 1860, it survived even the
brutality of World War II. Oggel's collection, which he
has been amassing since 2002, is eclectic and yet retains
a strong connection to the city. This has much to do with
the presence of local artists like Ron van der Ende and
Marin de Jong, and of international artists who have produced work while here, such as Keith Haring and Ivan
Chermayeff. Oggel has a preference for Pop Art but also
owns works of Hyperrealism and Conceptual Art. Once
the neighboring house is turned into luxury apartments,
part of his collection will also be shown there.

Collector:
Julian Oggel

Address:
Eendrachtsweg 57A
3012 LE Rotterdam
Netherlands
Tel +31 10 2409715
Mobile +31 653 771561
julian.oggel@xs4all.nl

E-mail appointment only.

N

146   Alexander Ramselaar Collection
*A townhouse of young talent from Rotterdam,
the Netherlands, and around the world*

Rotterdam collector Alexander Ramselaar discovered his
first artwork in a gallery on the way to work. He was immediately transfixed. After a longer period of collecting
modern design, the real estate specialist, who now advises
arts and cultural institutions, began to specialize in contemporary art. In his cozy townhouse, the hospitable collector presents art in his living room and bedrooms, in
the stairwell, and even in the bathroom. Ramselaar, an
avid traveler, collected first in the Rotterdam art scene and
now does so internationally: Yael Bartana, Hans Op de
Beeck, Guy Tillim, or Rossella Biscotti are just some of the
talented artists in his collection. Moreover, after becoming
frustrated by the massive cuts in the Dutch cultural budget, Ramselaar and a few other collectors established the
Foundation C.o.C.A. to support young artists.

Collector:
Alexander Ramselaar

Address:
Rotterdam, Netherlands
art@alexander-ramselaar.com
www.alexander-ramselaar.com

Visitation permitted only
occasionally. Please inquire
by e-mail.

147   Museum Beelden aan Zee
*Modern and contemporary sculpture nestled
in the Netherlands' pristine dunes*

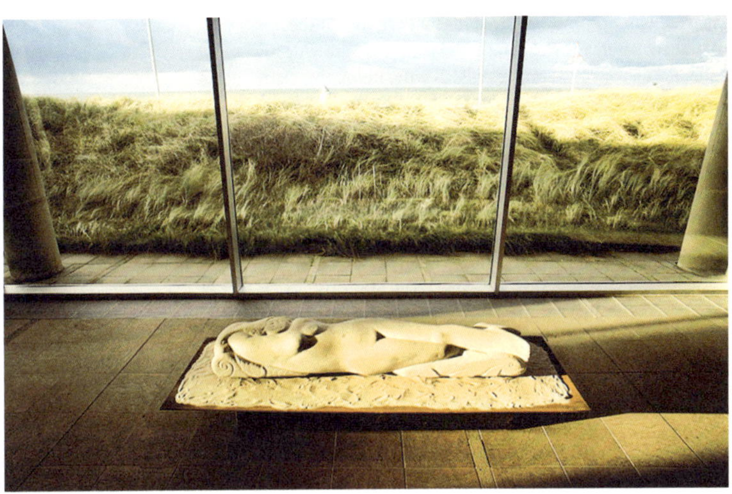

Collectors:
Theo & Lida Scholten

Address:
Harteveltstraat 1
2586 EL
The Hague/Scheveningen
Netherlands
info@beeldenaanzee.nl
www.beeldenaanzee.nl

Opening Hours:
Tues–Sun: 11am–5pm

The Museum Beelden aan Zee is camouflaged so perfectly, **N**
you almost walk right past it. Located in the middle of sand
dunes of the swanky seaside resort of Scheveningen, the
entrance to the most important collection of sculptures
in the Netherlands hides behind an exposed concrete façade. Though highly frequented tourist attractions—the
spa hotel, the pier, or the casino—are right around the
corner, the inside of the house that opened in 1994 is quiet.
Under the leitmotif "man—the human image," Theo and
Lida Scholten began in 1966 to bring together nearly 1 000
sculptures from all major art centers of the world. The
spectrum ranges from Armando to Marc Quinn, all the
way to Berlinde de Bruyckere. Every year three to four
thematic and monographic exhibitions are curated from
the collection.

148   Museum van Bommel van Dam
An enthusiastic Dutch couple and
their personalized collection

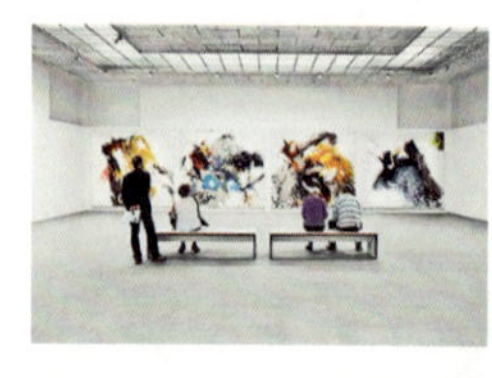

Maarten van Bommel acquired his first artwork at the age
of sixteen. Later, as a stock trader, he continued growing his
collection. From 1944 on, he and his wife, Reina van Dam,
both now deceased, collected unsystematically: abstract
Dutch painting of the Informel and CoBrA, but also African
masks and Japanese woodcuts. After extensively seeking a
suitable location to house their 1 000 works, they found it
in 1969 in the city of Venlo: an ideal museum for their art
and, next door, a residential bungalow. Through a connect-
ing door, they could move freely between the two. Over the
years, the collection has been added to by other collectors,
and under the current director, Rick Vercauteren, it has
become more contemporary and international.

Collectors:
Maarten & Reina
van Bommel van Dam

Address:
Deken van Oppensingel 6
5911 AD Venlo
Netherlands
Tel +31 77 3513457
info@vanbommelvandam.nl
www.vanbommelvandam.nl

Opening Hours:
Tues–Sun: 11am–5pm

N

149   KRC Collection
Dutch and international artists with
a critical-political approach

Curiosity aroused Rattan Chadha's enthusiasm for contemporary art. In the mid-1980s, he came across one
of Andy Warhol's Campbell's Soup paintings and was
shocked at the price: 50 000 dollars for an image of soup
cans? Chadha wanted to understand the valuation, so for
six months he studied Warhol. He became convinced of
Warhol's artistic strategy, and bought the work. Born in
India in 1949, the entrepreneur had founded—and then
sold—the fashion label Mexx. His collection, one of the
largest in the Netherlands, is located in spacious modern
rooms behind the historic façade of an old silver factory
near Leiden. It includes works by Candice Breitz, Thomas
Hirschhorn, Erik van Lieshout, and Marc Bijl—all artists
who have taken a critical stance towards contemporary
politics and society.

Collector:
Rattan Chadha

Address:
Voorschoten, Netherlands
info@krccapital.com
www.krccollection.com

Visitation permitted only
occasionally. Please inquire
by e-mail.

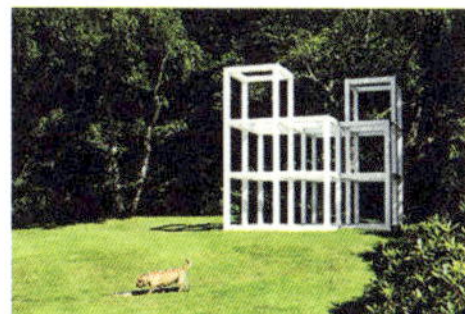

Collector:
Joop N.A. van Caldenborgh

Address:
Buurtweg 90
2244 AG Wassenaar
Netherlands
Tel +31 70 5121660
voorlinden@caldic.nl

Guided tours of the sculpture
garden each Thursday from
May to October. All visits by
appointment only.

150 Caldic Collectie
*Masterpieces of contemporary sculpture
in harmony with nature*

An estate in Wassenaar, near The Hague, is home to sixty-
five sculptures in a park overflowing with natural abun-
dance. The industrialist Joop van Caldenborgh, who acquired his first work of art as a teenager, is considered one
of the most important art collectors in the Netherlands.
His impressive sculpture garden, established in 1995, hosts
major works by Anish Kapoor, Sylvie Fleury, Sol LeWitt,
and Antony Gormley. Visits can be arranged via written
appointment; visitors will be accompanied by an art historian. A visit offers a double experience: "The combination of art and nature sharpens the perception," Joop van
Caldenborgh says. "One begins to look more consciously at
both the artwork and at nature." In the coming years, the
Caldic Collectie plans to realize a museum for its extensive
collection of paintings, photography, video art, and installations in Wassenaar.

N

Collectors:
Jo & Marlies Eyck

Address:
Kasteel Wijlreweg 1
6321 PP Wijlre
Netherlands
Tel +31 43 4502616
info@hedgehouse.eu
www.hedgehouse.eu/nl

Opening Hours:
Thurs–Fri: 11am–5pm
Open only during exhibitions.
Please check the website
for most current information.

151 Bonnefanten Hedge House Foundation
Art from the 1960s to the present in a modern pavilion

Over the past few decades, the collectors Jo and Marlies
Eyck have filled their castle Wijlre, in Limburg, which they
acquired in 1981, with something of a *Gesamtkunstwerk*.
The owners of a paint wholesale company began collecting
abstract painting in the late 1960s. Over time they added
other kinds of art. Today, their collection includes artists
from Donald Judd and René Daniëls to Marlene Dumas.
Sculptural works, mainly site-specific, can be found in the
palace garden, such as a fallen tree by Giuseppe Penone. In
1999 the architect Wiel Arets designed a modern exhibi-
tion-pavilion of concrete, glass, and steel called The Hedge
House. In 2011, Jo and Marlies Eyck entrusted the castle,
the gardens, and the pavilion to the Bonnefantenmuseum
in Maastricht, which organizes two annual exhibitions in
the idyllic castle and guarantees the collection's endurance
into the future.

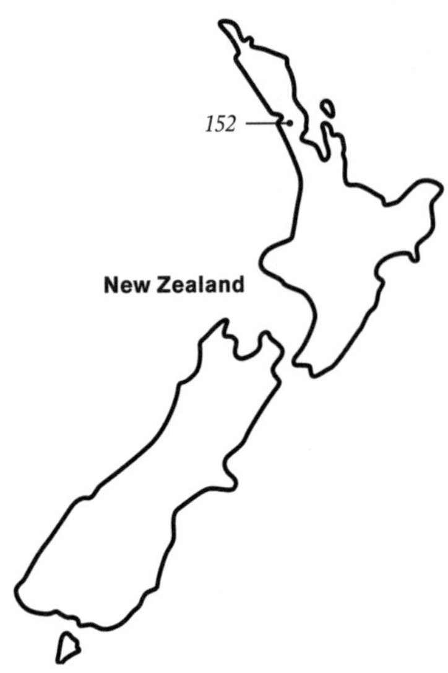

N

152   Gibbs Farm

*A sculpture park in XXL format with monumental art
in the grandness of nature*

It's as if giants had dropped their toys on green grass hills.
At the Gibbs Farm sculpture park, opened in 1991, on the
coast of New Zealand, art and nature correspond in a way
that emphasizes the monumentality of both. Since the
1960s, entrepreneur Alan Gibbs has collected works by
Richard Serra, Sol LeWitt, Andy Goldsworthy, George
Rickey, and Daniel Buren—all artists known for grand
outdoor gestures. But even art aficionados are amazed by
the dimensions of these site-specific sculptures, some of
which extend—in the case of Goldsworthy's *Arches*—into
the water. It's not surprising that the park has become a
visitor magnet. If you're looking to be one of them, however, book a tour as early as possible: Gibbs Farm is open
to the public only one day a month.

Collector:
Alan Gibbs

Address:
Kaipara Harbour
North Auckland Peninsula
New Zealand
www.gibbsfarm.org.nz

Visitation permitted only
occasionally. Please inquire
via website.

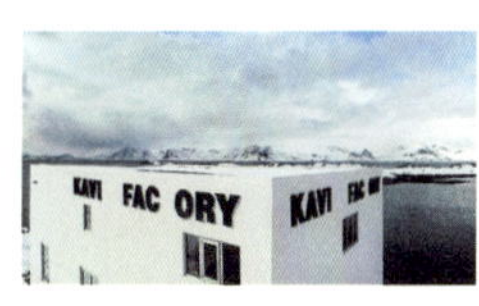

Collectors:
Venke & Rolf A. Hoff

Address:
Henningsværveien 13
8312 Henningsvær
Norway
ve-hoff@online.no

Visitation permitted only
occasionally. Please inquire
by e-mail.

153   Rolf A. Hoff Collection
*Contemporary art projects on an island
off the northern Norwegian coast*

This exhibition space is as close to the Arctic Circle as it
could be. In the summer of 2013, the Norwegian art collectors Venke and Rolf A. Hoff opened their art space in
a former caviar factory on the Lofoten. The Kaviarfabrik-
ken Galleri is located in the picturesque fishing village
of Henningsvær, the gateway to the northern Norwegian
archipelago. The charming building was renovated by
the Norwegian architecture firm Element. "Many international artists have visited us here," says Rolf A. Hoff,
enthusiastically. "All of them love this place and want to
come back." Equally popular is their Lighthouse, which
the Hoffs offer as guest quarters. The collectors own
works by Norwegian and international artists such as
Bjarne Melgaard, Julieta Aranda, or Jack Goldstein, and
they invite artists from all over the world to realize exhibitions in the 500-square-meter former factory.

154   Henie Onstad Kunstsenter (HOK)
*Modern art and exhibitions with contemporary artists
in spectacular architecture*

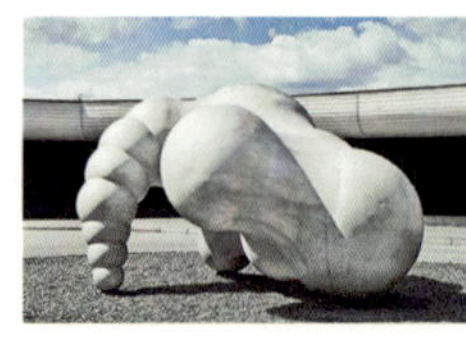

Sonja Henie (1912–1969) is considered one of the most successful figure skaters in history. Together with her third husband, Niels Onstad, a ship owner and art patron, she amassed a collection of modern art. In 1968 they opened the Henie Onstad Kunstsenter (HOK), high over the Oslo Fjord, south of the capital city. Norwegians Jon Eikwar and Sven Erik Engebretsen won the architectural competition, and erected a spectacular neo-expressionist structure that meshes nicely with the surrounding landscape. The building was extended in 1994, and again in 2003, and is now complemented by a sculpture park featuring works by Per Kirkeby and Tony Cragg, among others. Spread across 3 500 square meters, the HOK offers highlights of its collection, from Henri Matisse through Hans Hartung to Fernand Léger, as well as temporary exhibitions with contemporaries such as Ilya Kabakov, Omer Fast, or Olav Christopher Jenssen.

Collectors:
Sonja Henie & Niels Onstad

Address:
Sonja Henie vei 31
1311 Høvikodden
Norway
Tel +47 67 804880
post@hok.no
www.hok.no

Opening Hours:
Tues–Thurs: 11am–7pm
Fri–Sun: 11am–5pm

N

155   Astrup Fearnley Museum
*Major works of contemporary art in a new Renzo Piano
building upon a fjord*

Norwegians seldom complain about strained finances. Oil and gas resources supply an influx of capital, and Oslo has become the most expensive city in the world. Perhaps this is why private museums are somewhat more grandiose in Norway than elsewhere, a fact perfectly illustrated by the brand new building of the Astrup Fearnley Museum, which was founded in 1993. Ship owner and collector Hans Rasmus Astrup commissioned none other than Italian architect Renzo Piano, who, at age 70, remains one of the most in-demand architects in the world. A 4 000-square-meter exhibition space, built in 2012, reflects maritime flair in glass, steel, and wood in an exposed location on a fjord, housing entire work-complexes by well-known blue-chip artists such as Jeff Koons, Takashi Murakami, and Cindy Sherman. The collectors are also interested in young Norwegian art and, more recently, in newcomers from Asia and Latin America.

Collector:
Hans Rasmus Astrup

Address:
Strandpromenaden 2
0252 Oslo
Norway
Tel +47 22 936060
info@fearnleys.no
www.afmuseet.no

Opening Hours:
Tues, Wed, Fri: 12–5pm
Thurs: 12–7pm
Sat–Sun: 11am–5pm

This guide presents over two hundred private collections that are open to the public. Some collections have the character of a museum, accessible only during fixed opening hours. Others exist in strictly private rooms that may be visited by appointment only. Still others place an even higher value on discretion; these spaces are not publicly accessible. The reasons for this are manifold. These collectors have acquired art as an individual passion and want to share it only with an intimate circle of friends and family. Some collectors open their homes for a select group of VIPs during the major art fairs, but others prefer to steer clear entirely from public access. Why? It is understandable that in some South American cities collectors harbor a fear of being robbed and so **conceal their collections from public view.** In São Paulo, for example, there are grand mansions with amazing private collections, but for security reasons they are accessible only to selected visitors. Sometimes the reasons are pragmatic: the video collection of the French collector-couple Isabelle and Jean-Conrad Lemaître takes up very little space; it actually fits in the closet, neatly stacked next to Monsieur Lemaître's shirts. But because the collectors pay enormous attention to the technologically perfect presentation of their treasures, they only work with select art institutions.

One of the most important American private collections is not public. Norman and Irma Braman of Miami Beach have the most comprehensive inventory of works by Alexander Calder outside the museum world, next to key works by Damien Hirst, Mark Rothko, and Andy Warhol. But instead of opening a museum, the elderly billionaires decided in 2011 to posthumously auction off a large part of the collection to benefit breast-cancer research. An understandable and noble gesture.

Nicole Büsing & Heiko Klaas

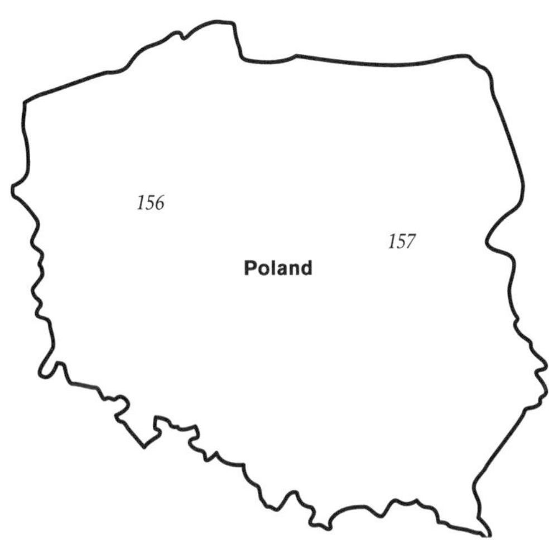

156   Art Stations Foundation
*Polish and international art trends
in a consumer temple*

Collector:
Grażyna Kulczyk

Address:
Półwiejska 42
61-888 Poznań
Poland
Tel +48 61 8596122
office@artstationsfoundation
5050.com
www.artstationsfoundation
5050.com

Opening Hours:
Mon–Sun: 12–7pm

P

Art and business are often seen as separate things. But this isn't the case for Polish businesswoman Grażyna Kulczyk, who says, "I have always known that I would not be satisfied by the division into being an entrepreneur by day, and an 'after-hours' collector. So I married the two, adopting the 50/50 philosophy." To this end, Kulczyk turned an old brewery, the Stary Browar in Poznań, into a complex comprising a shopping mall and an exhibition hall: the Art Stations Gallery. Her collection vaults more than 400 works, including pieces by key Polish artists of the twentieth century, like Jacek Malczewski and Tadeusz Kantor; international names like Victor Vasarely and Sam Francis; and a smattering of contemporary photography. Kulczyk is also fascinated by artists who explore the coexistence of art, science, and technology, as seen in works by Olafur Eliasson or Loris Gréaud.

157   Michał Borowik Collection
Young Polish art melding aesthetics and content

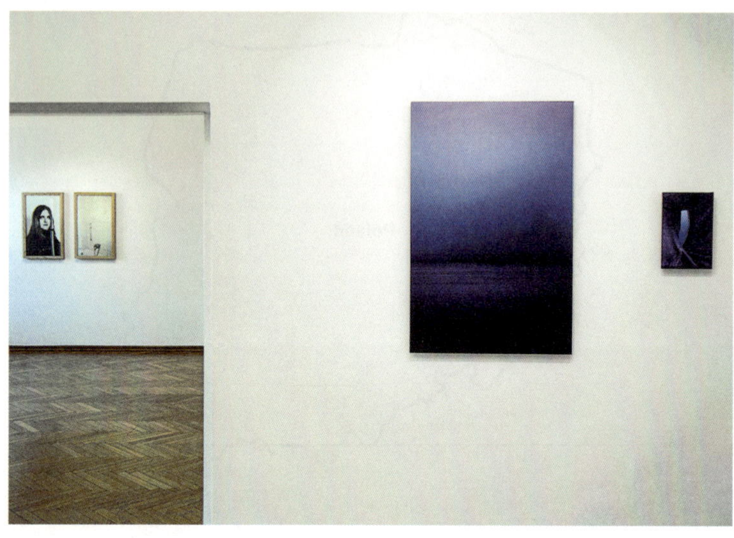

"I collect artworks by young Polish artists in a variety of media. It gives me great pleasure to live with objects that reflect our times." This is how Michał Borowik describes

P his approach. When he chooses a piece to include in his discerning collection, he does so with an eye toward artworks that inject aesthetics with meaning. "I really dislike empty shells," he says, insisting at the same time that the artist's medium fit that message. This attitude has earned Borowik a place on the list of the world's fifty most interesting collections assembled by people under fifty years old, a list drawn up by American magazine *Modern Painters* in 2011. Among other artists, Michał Gayer, Magdalena Starska, and Michał Smandek are some of the young Polish artists one finds in Borowik's stunning assembly.

Collector:
Michał Borowik

Address:
Warsaw, Poland
contact@borowikcollection.com
www.borowikcollection.com

By appointment only.

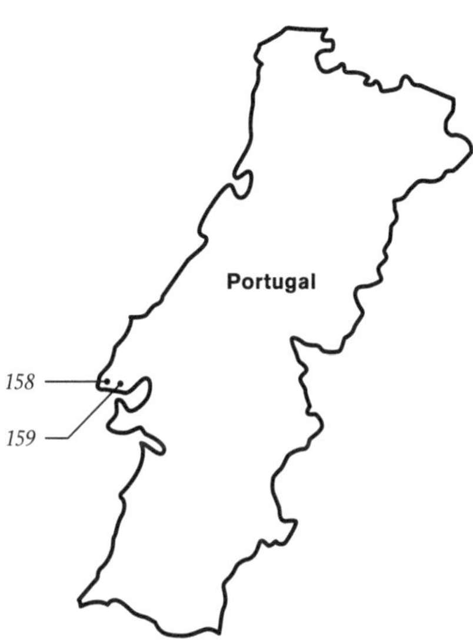

158   Ellipse Foundation
*Trendsetters and big names from all over the world
in a former warehouse*

Collector:
João Oliveira-Rendeiro

Address:
Rua das Fisgas
Pedra Furada
2645-117 Alcoitão
Cascais
Portugal
Tel +351 21 4691806
info@ellipsefoundation.com
www.ellipsefoundation.com

Opening Hours:
Fri–Sun: 11am–6pm

The mission: a budget of 25 million dollars, two years, and a 3 500-square-meter exhibition hall that must be filled with contemporary art. For the three curators of the Ellipse Foundation, this must have been a dream job, albeit an exhausting one. They were encouraged to travel around the world to find both established and emerging positions, which is how the 900 works came together under one roof. In 2006, the initiator of the collection, banker João Oliveira-Rendeiro, opened the collection in a former warehouse transformed by the Lisbon architect Pedro Gadanho into a series of black boxes, white cubes, and colorful mediating spaces. There the international collection presents superstars like Francis Alÿs, Shirin Neshat, and Jeff Wall along with younger positions, dominated mainly by Portuguese and Brazilian artists.

159   Museu Colecção Berardo
*One of Portugal's largest private collections
in a public art center*

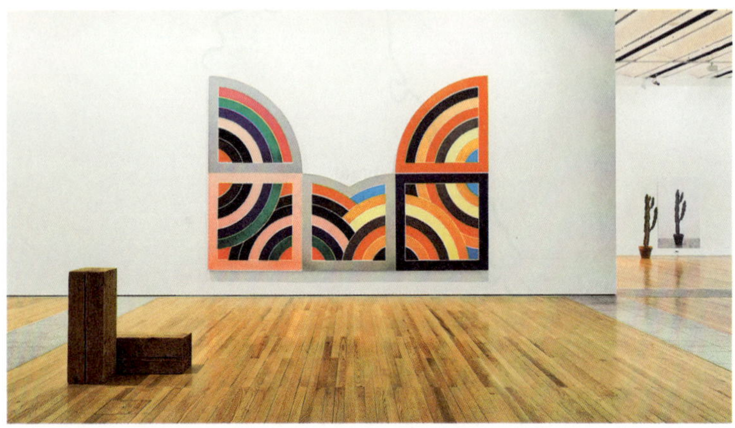

Think big! José Berardo has achieved a lot. The son of farm workers, he had to leave school at age thirteen to work as an unskilled vineyard laborer. At age eighteen he immigrated to South Africa, and what followed was the ascent from fruit picker to owner of gold and diamond mines. Berardo went back to Portugal in 1986 and began his rule over a multinational consortium of companies. His museum-quality and thoroughgoing art collection mirrors his entre-preneurial self-confidence. From Cubism to the Becher School, nearly every art movement is represented. Special attention is paid to Portuguese artists like Helena Almeida or Pedro Cabrita Reis. Since 2007 the roughly 900 works are permanently exhibited at the public art center of Belém.

Collector:
José Berardo

Address:
Praça do Império
1449-003 Lisbon
Portugal
Tel +351 213 612878
museuberardo@museuberardo.pt
www.museuberardo.com

Opening Hours:
Mon–Sun: 10am–7pm

Excessiveness is the latent danger of collecting art. Quite a few

collectors throw a wink and call their buying behavior "an addiction."
But not to worry: the negative side-effects of such an addiction are
slight—apart, of course, from losing your invested money. Most
collectors fight battles on two fronts: too little space and too little
organization. The space at home is limited, in most cases, and it is
rarely sufficient for installing all one's cherished works. Some even say
that one is only a "true collector" when your own four walls no longer
provide enough space for all the works you own. This leads to a choice
between compressing one's collection or expanding into outside
storage. When the works are no longer at your fingertips is exactly
when unexpectedly complicated questions arise about their proper
registration, correct documentation, and the best methods for
packaging and storing—all issues that have nothing to do with why one
began collecting art. This is why, even for large collections, the sword
of Damocles seems to be hanging overhead, ready to unleash chaos.
The only reason it doesn't fall is because no one looks more closely or
requires additional, precise information. Many collectors, for example,
do not maintain invoices or certificates for artworks they purchased a
decade or more ago. In such cases, specialized art historians can
assist with professional analysis and organization. On the other hand,
it is exactly the privilege of private collectors to not fulfill the
requirements a public institution is bound to. Unlike a museum, their
focus is not necessarily the optimal preservation of art, but on living
with it. This appeals, of course, to many artists.

Independent Collectors

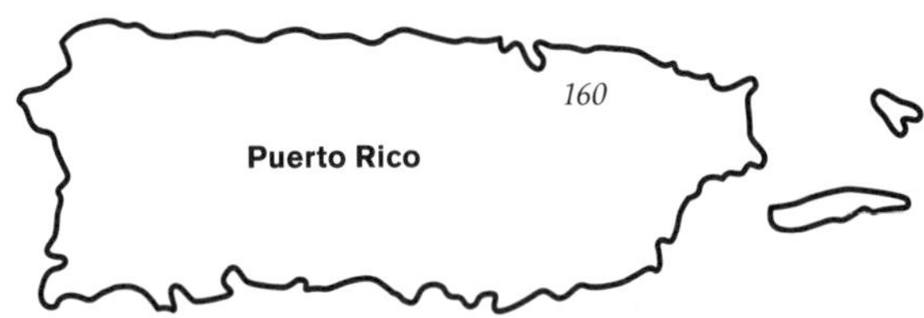

160   Berezdivin Collection—Espacio 1414
Latin American and international avant-garde
in the middle of the Caribbean

P

Collectors:
Diana & Moisés Berezdivin

Address:
1414 Avenida Fernández Juncos
Santurce
San Juan, PR 00909
Puerto Rico
Tel +1 787 7253899
info@berezdivincollection.com
www.espacio1414.org

By appointment only.

They were actually just looking for somewhere to store their art. Then Diana and Moisés Berezdivin came across a former wholesale tire store, which was far too big for just storage. They decided to buy the multifunctional building, alter it, and then make their collection public. There, in a cool ambiance with stark white walls, gray steel steps, and polished concrete floors, they unveil at least two exhibitions a year. Conceptual and socially critical art from Latin America dominates the collection, paired with primarily US and European positions. Originally from Cuba, the Berezdivins, owners of a chain of textile stores, evidence aesthetically honed sensibilities: work by David Lamelas, Julieta Aranda, and Arturo Herrera, to that of David Shrigley and Claire Fontaine, positions that place the Puerto Rican collection far forward in contemporary international art.

Qatar
Qatar, Doha

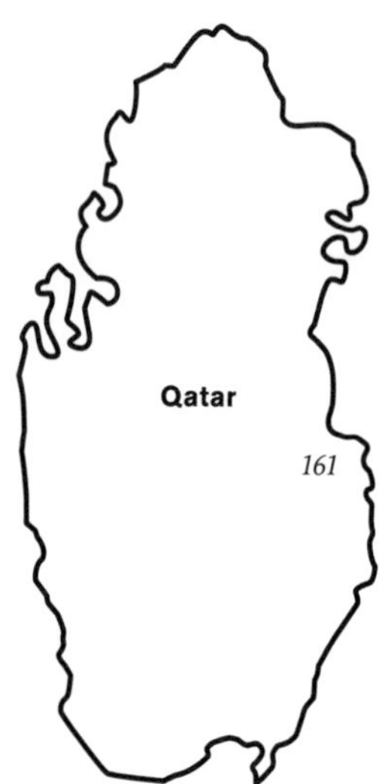

161   Mathaf—Arab Museum of Modern Art
A royal collection spanning 200 years of Arab art

The Art Newspaper once reported that Qatar is the world's biggest art buyer and that it has been behind some of the most important purchases of modern and contemporary art over the last few decades. Indeed Qatar's royal family has played an active role in acquisitions, with the aim of building a top-class collection for Qatar's growing network of museums. The latest of them is Mathaf, which is dedicated solely to Arab art. It opened in December 2010 thanks to the commitment of the Emir's son, Sheikh Hassan bin Mohamed bin Ali Al Thani, and thanks to the support of museum officials. The Sheikh began collecting in the 1980s and has amassed some 6 000 works, including pieces by artists throughout the Middle East, North Africa, and the Arab Diaspora, from 1840 to today.

Collector:
Sheikh Hassan bin Mohamed bin Ali Al Thani

Address:
Education City Student Center
Al-Luqta Street
Doha
Qatar
Tel +974 4402 8855
mathaf_info@qma.org.qa
www.mathaf.org.qa

Opening Hours:
Tues–Thurs: 11am–6pm
Fri: 3–9pm
Sat–Sun: 11am–6pm

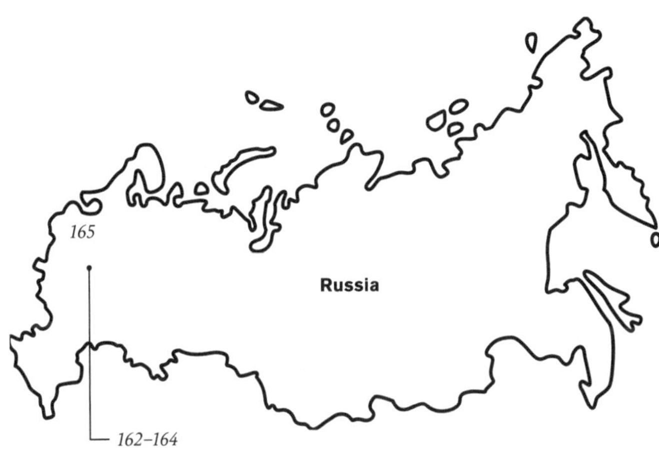

162   Art4.ru

*An exciting display of Russian modern
and contemporary art*

Collector:
Igor Markin

Address:
Hlinovsky Tupik, 4
125009 Moscow
Russia
Tel +7 499 1365656
art@art4.ru
www.art4.ru

By appointment only.

Moscow's Art4.ru museum of contemporary art is a rather
unconventional place. For one, forget everything you ever
learned about museum display, and don't expect to go
tiptoeing around the works. And while we're at it, forget
about hanging systems. In multimillionaire Igor Markin's
private museum, art proliferates everywhere, covering the
walls, windows, and floors. Markin's enormous collection
is a virtual Who's Who of the former Soviet Union's unofficial art scene, boasting names like Ilya Kabakov, Komar &
Melamid, Viktor Pivovarov, and many more. But Art4.ru
is also home to Russia's young art scene, from the famed
Oleg Kulik to a number of artists less known outside of
Russia. It's a wild ride through the country's art history.
You should take it.

R

163   The Cultural Foundation Ekaterina
*Russian and international contemporary art
in a pioneering private museum*

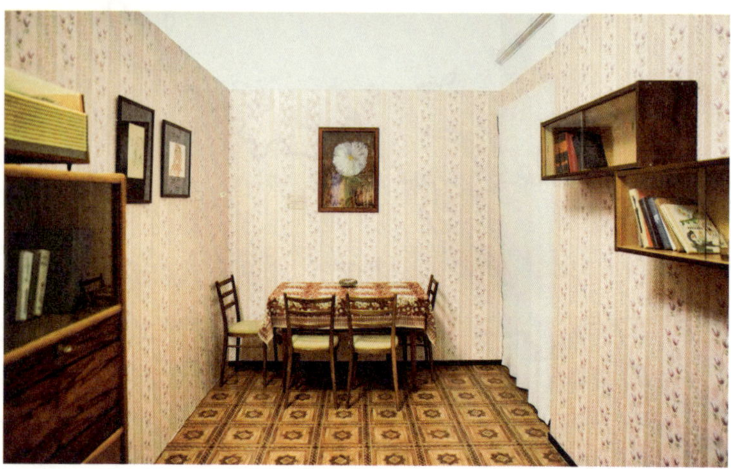

Ekaterina and Vladimir Seminikhin were among the first Russian collectors to open their collection to the public. In the catalogue to their first exhibition, in 2007, the couple wrote: "Those mysterious private collections that were treated with suspicion by both the state and society during Soviet times are now gradually stepping out of the shadows." The Seminikhins have been collecting international contemporary works since 2003, but they were such early supporters of the post-Soviet avant-garde that the *Financial Times* deemed them "pioneers among Russian private collectors" and "the unofficial patron saints of Russia's contemporary arts scene." The Cultural Foundation Ekaterina consists of 800 works of Russian art, from Ivan Shishkin through Komar & Melamid to Dubossarsky & Vinogradov.

Collectors:
Ekaterina & Vladimir Seminikhin

Address:
Kuznetsky Most, 21/5
107996 Moscow
Russia
Tel +7 495 6215522
info@ekaterina-foundation.ru
www.ekaterina-fondation.ru

Opening Hours:
Tues–Sun: 11am–8pm

164   Stella Art Foundation
*Contemporary Russian art waiting to be installed
in a former bus garage*

Collector:
Stella Kesaeva

Address:
Skaryatinsky Pereulok, 7
121069 Moscow
Russia
Tel +7 495 6913407
info@safmuseum.org
en.safmuseum.org

Opening Hours:
Tues–Sun: 10:30am–6pm

Since opening her gallery, in 2003, Stella Kesaeva, art collector and wife of the billionaire Igor Kesaev, has become an influential player on the Russian art scene. She was appointed commissioner for the 2011, 2013, and 2015 Russian Pavilions at the Venice Biennale, and in Moscow she runs a private space with works from her personal collection and elsewhere. The Stella Art Foundation consists of approximately 800 pieces, mainly by contemporary Russian artists like Ilya Kabakov, Andrei Monastyrski, Yuri Albert, and Oleg Kulik. But it also has some famed international types: Andy Warhol, Bill Viola, and Robert Mapplethorpe. Kesaeva is currently planning to open an art museum proper in a former bus garage in Moscow, a seemingly popular thing to do: another Muscovite garage filled with contemporary art is run by Dasha Zhukova, girlfriend to billionaire Roman Abramovich.

165   Novy Muzei
*Soviet nonconformist art: the only alternative
to Socialist Realism*

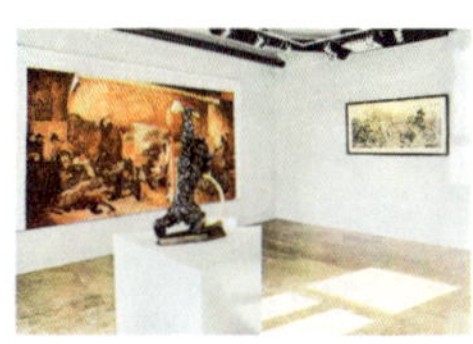

Collector:
Aslan Chekhoyev

Address:
6-ya Liniya, 29
199004 St. Petersburg
Russia
Tel +7 812 3235090
info@novymuseum.ru
www.novymuseum.ru

Opening Hours:
Thurs–Sun: 12–7pm

If you think the only art movement in Russia before the end of the Soviet era was Socialist Realism, you need to visit the Novy Muzei in Saint Petersburg. It holds Aslan Chekhoyev's collection of the unofficial movements of Russian modern art from the postwar era to the end of the twentieth century. After Josef Stalin died, in 1953, there was an underground wave of liberalization in the arts in Russia, and artists began experimenting, even if they could not exhibit. One famous episode of state repression of unsanctioned art was in 1974, when police broke up a show with a bulldozer and water cannons. Chekhoyev's collection is an important effort to direct public attention to works by artists like Lydia Masterkova, Lev Kropivnitsky, and Vladimir Nemukhin. Figures in their contemporary collection are artists like Oleg Kulik and the AES+F group, among others.

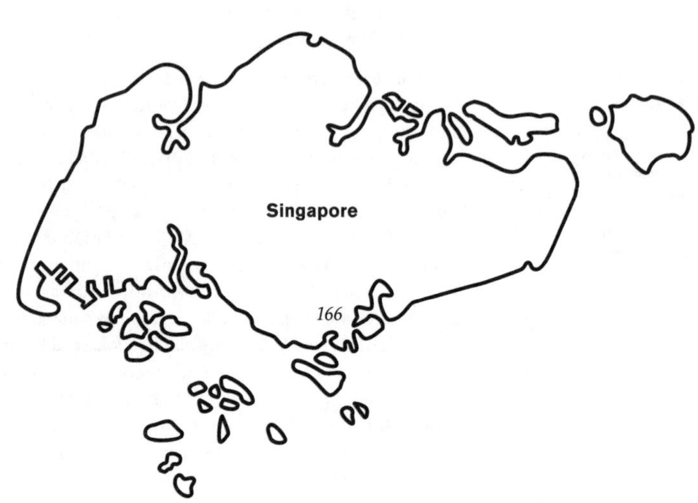

166   The Private Museum
A collector's room—also for other collectors

The architect and real estate developer Daniel Teo began to collect art in the 1990s. His collecting intensified after 1994, when he teamed up with the Swede Björn Wetterling to open the Wetterling Teo Gallery in Singapore, one of the first international art galleries in Southeast Asia. Teo is particularly interested in Pop Art; the first work he acquired was by James Rosenquist. He also collects ink paintings and works by local artists. Alongside images by Roy Lichtenstein, Jim Dine, and Tom Wesselmann are those by Lim Tze Peng, Chua Ek Kay, and Kumari Nahappan. In 2008 he opened the Private Museum, where he exhibits his own collection—and that of fellow collectors. "I have met many collectors," Teo says, "and I would like to encourage more collectors to step forward to showcase their collections. It is an important way to establish relationships between artists, collectors, and the public."

S

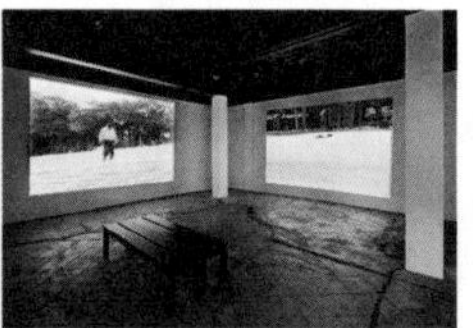

Collector:
Daniel Teo

Address:
51 Waterloo Street, # 02-06
Singapore 187969
Tel +65 6738 2872
mail@theprivatemuseum.org
www.theprivatemuseum.org

Opening Hours:
Mon–Fri: 10am–7pm
Sat–Sun: 11am–5pm

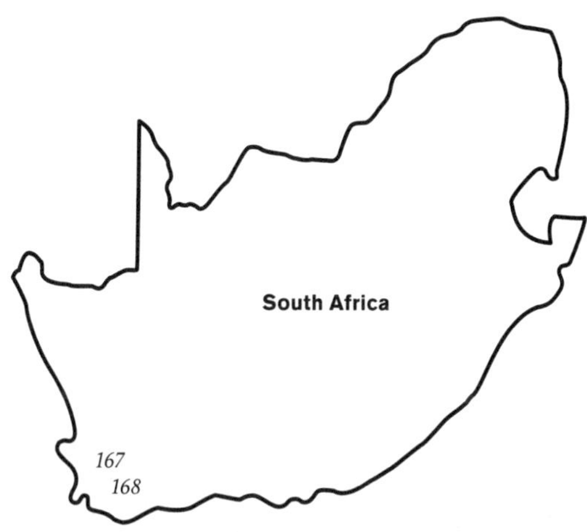

167   The Hess Art Collection, Glen Carlou
*Contemporary art for all and references to historical
and present-day Africa*

Collector:
Donald M. Hess

Address:
Simondium Road
Klapmuts 7625
South Africa
Tel +27 21 8755528
welcome@glencarlou.co.za
www.glencarlou.co.za

Opening Hours:
Mon–Fri: 8:30am–5pm
Sat–Sun: 10am–3pm

Additional exhibition locations:
Salta, Argentina, p. 14
Napa, United States of America,
p. 181

Whether in his vineyards in California's Napa Valley or in the Argentine Andes, cosmopolitan art-and-wine lover Donald M. Hess fuses his passion for wine, contemporary art, and art education in the South African Cape Town region: "I truly believe contemporary art should be made available to the widest possible audience," Hess says, "and that collectors have a responsibility to make their collections accessible to the public to the best of their ability." Everyone is welcome. No entrance fee. At his vineyard Glen Carlou, in Klapmuts, not far from Cape Town, Hess features work by artists like the British Andy Goldsworthy, the South African Deryck Healey, and the Ivory Coast-born painter Ouattara Watts, who lives in New York City. Hess's collection of contemporary art reflects the rich cultural heritage of Africa.

168   Rupert Museum
South African art highlights since 1940
in a region known for its wine

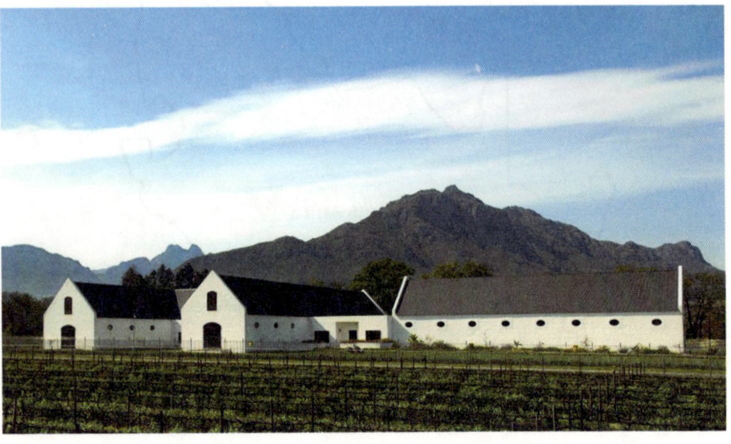

A fire in their private home prompted collectors Huberte and Anton Rupert to build a museum for their extensive art collection. They found the right partner in Hannes Meiring, an artist and architect from Cape Town. Meiring decided upon a contemporary adaption of a simple seventeenth-century farmhouse. In 2003 the Rupert Museum opened in South Africa's famous wine capital, Stellenbosch, and exhibits mainly South African art from 1940 to 1970 in a 2 000-square-meter space. Artists shown include the New Objectivity landscape painter Jacobus Hendrik Pierneef, the sculptor Anton van Wouw and the painter Irma Stern, who was friends with the German Expressionists. Contemporary artists like William Kentridge have also found their way into this 350-work collection.

Collectors:
Huberte & Anton Rupert

Address:
Stellentia Avenue
Stellenbosch 7600
South Africa
Tel +27 21 8883344
saw@remgro.com
www.rupertmuseum.org

Opening Hours:
Mon–Fri: 9:30am–1pm,
2–4pm
Sat: 10am–1pm

Art and nature complement each other well. Thus, for this edition of the *BMW Art Guide by Independent Collectors* we included additional private sculpture parks. After all, works of art in castle gardens and landscaped parks have a long tradition. Noble houses since the Renaissance commissioned artisans to create mythological figures or complex water fountains for their parks, often by the most famous artists of their time. And one can still find fine examples of commissioned works by castle owners today. The von Reden family regularly invites contemporary artists to their castle garden in the Weser Uplands of Germany to create site-specific sculptures. Marika Wachtmeister developed an equally convincing concept for rotating sculpture exhibitions around the area of her Castle Wanås, in southern Sweden.

Exploring these kinds of places is particularly exciting. The visitor ventures, often with map in hand, on a kind of sculptural scavenger hunt. One brushes directly and immediately against nature, an experience often reflected in the works of art themselves. This functions best when artists have engaged with the characteristics of a place over a long period. Such a situation transpires on the grounds of the Basel collector John Schmid, who invites artists to the former convent Schoenthal and offers them time and peace to develop a work of art fitting the place. Or the Brazilian Bernardo Paz, who has created an ideal place of peaceful retreat in his tropical landscape park, Inhotim. He gives artists carte blanche permission to undertake daring aesthetic experiments. In more temperate Europe climes, one finds the sculpture park of Caldic Collectie, in the city of Wassenaar, in the Netherlands. Here Joop van Caldenborgh has forged a convincing harmony of sculptures and landscape on approximately forty acres—a constellation that triggers the joy of discovery for visitors as well as for the collector himself.

Nicole Büsing & Heiko Klaas

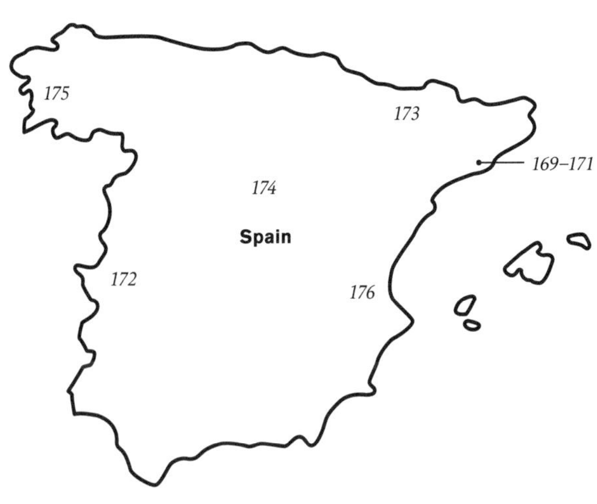

169   Fundación Alorda-Derksen
*International art in an elegant city apartment
in downtown Barcelona*

Collectors:
Manuel Alorda & Hanneke Derksen

Address:
Carrer d'Aragó 314
08009 Barcelona
Spain
Tel +34 93 2726250
www.fundacionad.com

By telephone appointment only.

Manuel Alorda and Hanneke Derksen have been collecting art since 1966. Two years before that, Alorda founded the Kettal company, which has risen from a one-man operation to a leader in the European market for upscale outdoor furniture. The couple is used to working with designers from all over the world. No wonder, then, that their art collection is overwhelmingly international in scope—and with good reason: Alorda and Derksen want to show art in Barcelona that otherwise cannot be seen there. One exception is Catalonian sculptor Jaume Plensa, who sits between British artists like Damien Hirst and Tracey Emin, or Joseph Beuys and his students Imi Knoebel and Anselm Kiefer. The collection, opened in 2008, is hung in a tastefully renovated 200-square-meter fin-de-siècle apartment in the exclusive neighborhood of Eixample.

S

170   Fundació Suñol
Two rooms, two ideas: Spanish classics meet new art

Real estate mogul Josep Suñol's 1 200-work collection, opened in 2007, counts as one of the largest in Catalonia. Represented are the three great Spaniards of the twentieth century—Pablo Picasso, Joan Miró, and Salvador Dalí— as well as artists of the subsequent generation, including Antonio Saura, Antoni Tàpies, and Eduardo Chillida. The collection also holds works from Italy and Switzerland, like those by Giacomo Balla, Lucio Fontana, and Alberto Giacometti, and by the most recent generation of artists, mostly from Catalonia. Two yearly exhibitions permit the public to warm to the collection. Nivell Zero, a second exhibition space with a separate entrance, leans toward to the radically contemporary: events that take place there have a laboratory or workshop feel. Exhibitions and a smattering of film and video screenings deal with current themes.

Collector:
Josep Suñol

Address:
Passeig de Gràcia 98
08008 Barcelona
Spain
www.fundaciosunol.org

Opening Hours:
Mon–Sat: 4–8pm
And by appointment.

171   Fundació Vila Casas
*Three houses, three points of focus: painting,
sculpture, and photography*

The Catalonian pharmaceutical businessman Antoni Vila Casas is fortunate to be able to show his foundation's extensive holdings of modern and contemporary art across three architecturally interesting buildings in Catalonia. The Museo Can Framis, in Barcelona, is located in a former wool factory, replete with a new addition. Its 3 800 square meters are devoted to painting. Over 350 sculptures are housed at the Museo Con Mario, in a renovated cork factory in Palafrugell on the Costa Brava. And not far from there, at the Renaissance-era palace Palau Solterra, in Torroella de Montgrí, is where Vila Casas shows 300 works from his collection of photography. Catalonian art dominates, and you don't find any superstar names. This has been changing since 2010, however, with a rotating exhibition cycle that has brought in the holdings of fellow collectors.

Collector:
Antoni Vila Casas

Addresses:
Museo Can Framis
Carrer Roc Boronat 116-126
08018 Barcelona, Spain
Tel +34 93 3208736

Museo Can Mario
Plaça Can Mario 7
17200 Palafrugell, Spain
Tel +34 972 306246

Museo Palau Solterra
Carrer de l'Església 10
17257 Torroella de Montgrí, Spain
Tel +34 972 761976

www.fundaciovilacasas.com

Opening hours vary depending on exhibition and season. Please check the website for most current information.

172   Centro de Artes Visuales—
Fundación Helga de Alvear

One of the world's most important collections
of contemporary art

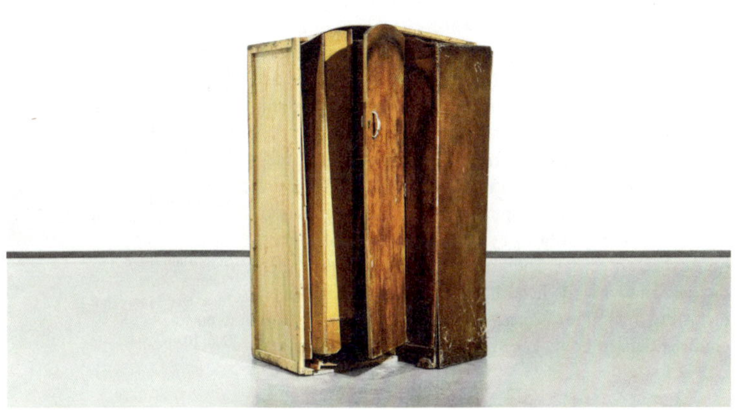

Collector:
Helga de Alvear

Address:
Calle Pizarro 8
10003 Cáceres
Spain
Tel +34 927 626414
general@fundacionhelgadealvear.es
www.fundacionhelgadealvear.es

Opening Hours:
June–September
Tues–Sat: 10am–2pm, 6–9pm
Sun: 10am–2:30pm
October–May
Tues–Sat: 10am–2pm,
5–8pm
Sun: 10am–2:30pm

The German Helga de Alvear has lived in Madrid for over fifty years. There she runs a successful gallery with an international art program. But de Alvear does not just sell art to collectors; she's often been her own best client. This is how her roughly 2 800 works of art have been assembled: Joseph Beuys, Jeff Wall, Juan Muñoz, or Louise Bourgeois—the remarkable list could go on. Since 2010 Alvear has been incrementally revealing parts of her collection in the city of Cáceres, in southwestern Spain. Her collection is housed in a 3 000-square-meter patrician villa, redesigned by the highly sought Madrid architects Mansilla and Tuñón. A 7 000-square-meter addition has just gotten underway.

S

173 Centro de Arte y Naturaleza— Fundación Beulas (CDAN)

Spanish postwar painting and rotating exhibits relating to landscape

Art and nature are the focus of activities of the Centro de Arte y Naturaleza—Fundación Beulas (CDAN), opened in 2006 near the northeastern Spanish city of Huesca. The core of CDAN is formed by a private collection owned by painter José Beulas, born in 1921. In the 1950s he began collecting the work of friends and companions: primarily regional landscape painters and sculptors, but also representatives of New Figuration and Informel, like stars Antonio Saura and Antoni Tàpies. In 2000, Beulas converted all of his assets and property into a public foundation. An organic, wavy building by star architect Rafael Moneo houses the art center. The surrounding landscape is spectacular, and with the help of the foundation, it has been blessed with land-art projects—eight so far—by artists including Richard Long, Per Kirkeby, and Ulrich Rückriem.

Collectors:
José Beulas & Maria Sarrate

Address:
Avenida Doctor Artero s/n
22004 Huesca
Spain
Tel +34 974 239893
info@cdan.es
www.cdan.es

Opening Hours:
May–September
Tues–Sat: 11am–2pm,
5–9pm
Sun: 10am–9pm
October–April
Tues–Sat: 11am–2pm,
5–8pm
Sun: 10am–2pm

174 OTR Espacio de Arte

Perpetual surprises in a manageable and modern project space

The aim of this downtown Madrid art space, opened in 2008, is not just to present a collection. Located near the Prado, the 300-square-meter OTR Espacio de Arte is dedicated to promoting young, not-yet-established art. Two to three thematic exhibits annually investigate artistic questions that cross into architecture. José Antonio Trujillo and Elsa López show the work from their own collection, as well as that of guest artists. Spanish and Latin American positions dominate, among them Montserrat Soto and Ernesto Neto. Artists like John Baldessari, Katharina Grosse, and Rémy Zaugg are also represented in the collection, displayed in exhibitions that nicely fuse concepts with sensual color.

Collectors:
José Antonio Trujillo & Elsa López

Address:
Calle de San Eugenio 10
28012 Madrid
Spain
info@espaciodearteotr.com
www.espaciodearteotr.com

By appointment only.

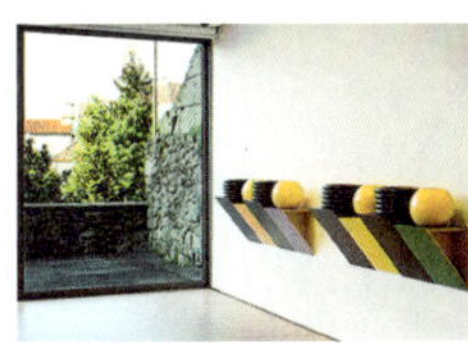

Collector:
Carlos Rosón Gasalla

Address:
Padre Sarmiento 41
36002 Pontevedra
Spain
Tel +34 637 717172
info@fundacionrac.org
www.fundacionrac.org

By appointment only.

175 Fundación Rosón Arte Contemporáneo (RAC)

An award-winning concept-art collection far from the Spanish art-metropolises

The Galician city of Pontevedra lies in the outermost region of northwest Spain. Here, you have to be brave to open an ambitious exhibition hall. Luckily, the Madrid-educated architect Carlos Rosón Gasalla is a risk-taker. His collection of 280 artworks from 160 Spanish and international artists opened on the ground floor of his house in 2007. It's not the simple artistic positions that triggered his passion to collect; rather, Gasalla favors art with conceptual and ironic leanings: work by Cildo Meireles, Karin Sander, and Liam Gillick, for example. Accolades have come quickly for the carefully curated exhibitions, which occur twice a year: in 2009 he received the collector award of the Madrid art fair Arco. Rosón Gasalla's foundation also sponsors an artist-in-residence program, which has hosted artists such as Tania Bruguera and Caio Reisewitz.

Collectors:
Manuel Chirivella Bonet &
Alicia Soriano Lleó

Address:
Calle deValeriola 13
46001 Valencia
Spain
Tel +34 196 3381215
info@chirivellasoriano.org
www.chirivellasoriano.org

Opening Hours:
Tues–Sat: 10am–2pm,
5–8pm
Sun: 10am–2pm

176 Fundación Chirivella Soriano

Spanish painting since 1957 in a beautifully restored gothic palace

Notary Manuel Chirivella Bonet and his wife, Alicia Soriano Lleó, had been collecting art for over twenty years before they purchased a piece of property containing a dilapidated gothic palace in the oldest section of Valencia, in 2001. The permission to destroy the palace came a few days later. Apparently, a misunderstanding: the couple did not want to tear down the building; they wanted to restore it. They opened their collection—spread across 1 000 square meters—in 2005. The focus is on Spanish painting since 1957. That is the year both collectors were born, but the selection also serves an art historical purpose: in 1957 the followers of the Informel movement founded a breakaway artist group dedicated to new geometric abstraction and new kinds of figuration. Artists like Antonio Saura are well represented in the collection, which also shows more recent Spanish art.

S

Sweden, Knislinge

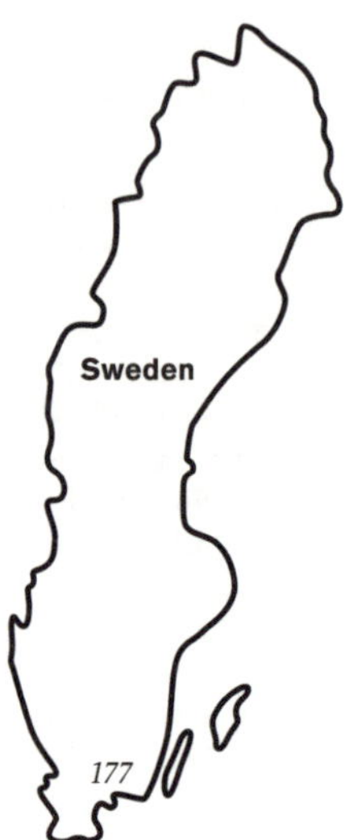

177 Wanås Foundation

Site-specific contemporary art on a castle estate in southern Sweden

Wanås castle in southern Sweden is a fortress from the fifteenth century. Charles and Marika Wachtmeister are the seventh generation to inhabit the residence. In 1987 Marika Wachtmeister began to exhibit sculptures on the sprawling grounds. Site-specific works by Jenny Holzer, Louise Bourgeois, Sissel Tolaas, or Dan Graham are scattered across the estate. The Wanås family is also fond of dense atmospheric sound works, such as an audio-walk by Janet Cardiff or an installation by Robert Wilson. Today, more than fifty permanently installed works comprise the continuously expanding outdoor collection. Since 2005, the spacious stable, built in 1759, has been used to house exhibitions. And since the Wanås castle is also the site of an eco-friendly agricultural business, guests who stroll around with map in hand looking at sculptures may just run into a few happy wandering cows.

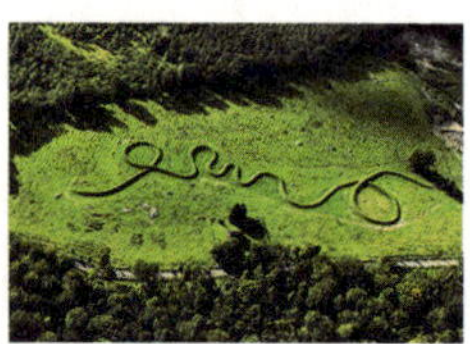

Collectors:
Marika & Charles Wachtmeister

Address:
Box 67
289 21 Knislinge
Sweden
Tel +46 44 66158
info@wanaskonst.se
www.wanas.se

Opening hours vary depending on exhibition and season. Please check the website for most current information.

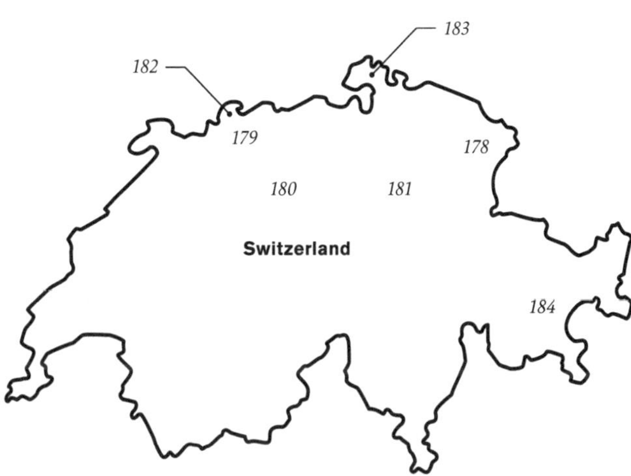

178   Museum Liner/Kunsthalle Ziegelhütte
*A perfect synthesis of modern and contemporary art
with avant-garde architecture*

Collectors:
Myriam & Heinrich Gebert

Address:
Ziegeleistrasse 14
9050 Appenzell
Switzerland
Tel +41 71 7881860
info@kunsthalleziegelhuette.ch
www.kunsthalleziegelhuette.ch

Opening Hours:
April–October
Tues–Fri: 10am–12pm, 2–5pm
Sat–Sun: 11am–5pm
November–May
Tues–Sat: 2–5pm
Sun: 11am–5pm

A must-see for architecture fans: inspired by the vision of functional museum architecture—as the Swiss artist Rémy Zaugg dreamed of—architect Robert Bamert of St. Gallen carved an exhibition complex out of a historic sixteenth-century brick-manufacturing building. Coarse wood, iron, brick, and exposed concrete are unified in a successful synthesis of modernity and local materials. Up to six special exhibitions a year showcase the broad range of the collection, which includes 1 200 works of classic modernism and contemporary art—from Hans Arp to Frank Stella, from Kerim Seiler to Beat Zoderer. A second example of successful museum architecture is located nearby: the Museum Liner, built by the Zurich architect-duo Annette Gigon and Mike Guyer, is devoted to the Appenzeller painters Carl August and Carl Walter Liner.

179   Kloster Schoenthal
Nature-inspired sculptures in a pristine landscape

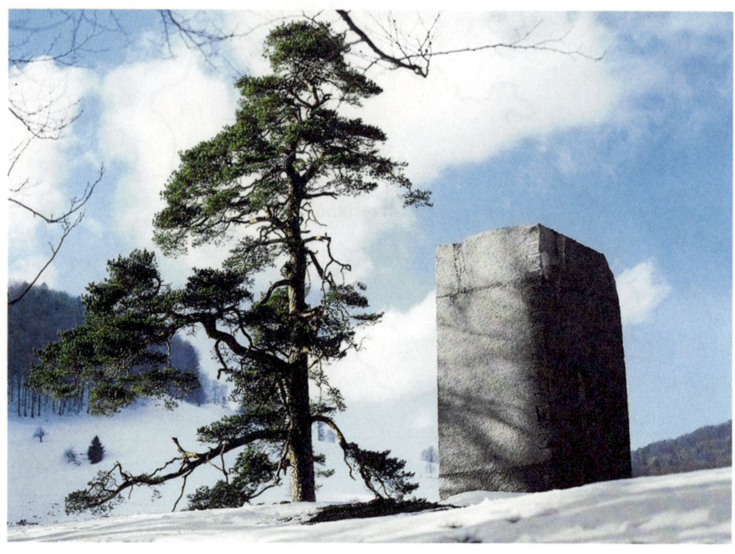

There is a special place about fifty kilometers southeast of Basel in the gentle foothills of Swiss Jura. Basel-based entrepreneur and collector John Schmid has created a sculptural landscape with 29 works by Swiss and international artists around the former Schoenthal monastery. But urban art lovers had better exchange their fine shoes for rubber boots to walk the sculpture trail, which meanders through twenty acres of fields, meadows, and forest. Twenty-one artists, from Richard Long to Roman Signer and Miriam Cahn, have engaged the natural environs with great sensitivity and realized works that meld perfectly into the landscape. Schmid, who maintains friendly relations with all the artists, acquired the estate and its landmark building in 1985.

Collector:
John Schmid

Address:
Schönthalstrasse 158
4438 Langenbruck
Switzerland
Tel +41 61 7067676
mail@schoenthal.ch
www.schoenthal.ch

Opening Hours:
Fri: 2–5pm
Sat, Sun, and holidays: 11am–6pm

180   Museum Sammlung Rosengart
The crème de la crème of classic modernism:
Picasso, Klee, and friends

Collectors:
Siegfried & Angela Rosengart

Address:
Pilatusstrasse 10
6003 Lucerne
Switzerland
Tel +41 41 2201660
info@rosengart.ch
www.rosengart.ch

Opening Hours:
April–October
Mon–Sun: 10am–6pm
November–March
Mon–Sun: 11am–5pm

The Lucerne-based Rosengart collection inhabits a neo-classical building formerly owned by the Swiss National Bank. Carefully remodeled by the Basel architecture firm Diener & Diener, the building, finished in 2002, offers perfect conditions for this impressive collection of classic modernism. Art dealer Siegfried Rosengart (1894–1985) didn't just *collect* Pablo Picasso, Georges Braque, and Henri Matisse; he and his daughter Angela, who entered the family business at age sixteen, were actually close friends with all of them. And thus, "all the paintings were chosen with the heart," Angela Rosengart says. The ground floor is devoted to Picasso, and the first floor contains paintings by his contemporaries Fernand Léger and Wassily Kandinsky. In the secure basement, where bolted safes used to hold gold reserves of the Swiss national bank, a fine collection of Paul Klee works hangs gently illuminated.

181   Kunst(Zeug)Haus
An extensive private collection of Swiss contemporary art
of the last thirty years

Collectors:
Peter & Elisabeth Bosshard

Address:
Schönbodenstrasse 1
8640 Rapperswil
Switzerland
Tel +41 55 2202080
info@kunstzeughaus.ch
www.kunstzeughaus.ch

Opening Hours:
Wed–Fri: 2–6pm
Sat–Sun: 11am–6pm

Zurich-based lawyer Peter Bosshard and his wife, Elisabeth, started collecting art in the 1970s. They had just completed a two-year stay in New York City and returned to Switzerland, where they began a decades-long engagement with the contemporary art scene. Today, the Bosshards support artists and art projects, in addition to having accumulated roughly 5 000 works of their own. In May 2008 they opened an art center in a former arsenal in the city of Rapperswil. Zurich architects Isa Stürm and Urs Wolf meticulously transformed the long and bulky building into a spacious 2 600 square meters, providing enough room for three to four exhibits each year. Aside from established Swiss art stars like Silvia Bächli, Fischli/Weiss, or Roman Signer, younger positions such as Mario Sala or Yves Netzhammer have also found a comfortable home.

S

182   Fondation Beyeler
*World-famous art in a building by Renzo Piano
outside of Basel*

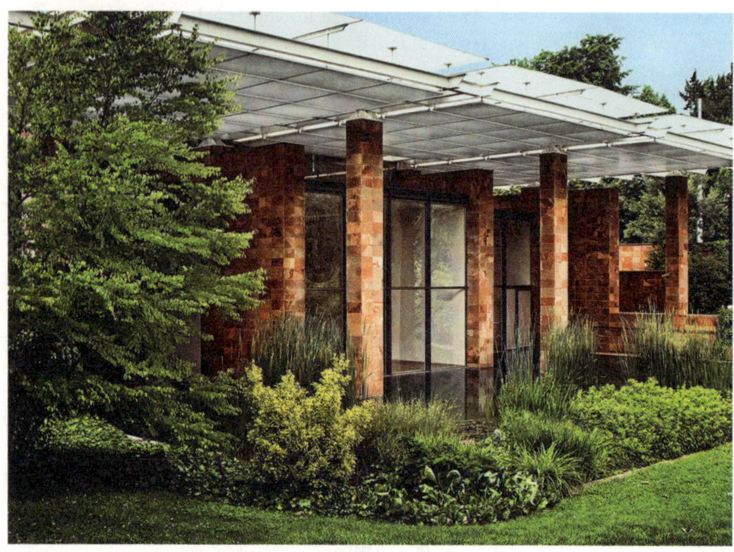

His standards were always high. Ernst Beyeler, who died in 2010, turned his gallery in Basel into one of the most important addresses of the international art market. Together with his wife, Hildy, he built an impressive collection of Modernist, Abstract Expressionist, and Pop Art works. Paintings by Pablo Picasso, Mark Rothko, and Andy Warhol have all found a home here. In 1997, the collectors opened the Fondation Beyeler in their hometown of Riehen, on the outskirts of Basel. The elongated Renzo Piano building blends perfectly into the landscape. Every year the foundation stages three large exhibitions of modern or contemporary art. In 2008, Sam Keller, a former director of Art Basel and a hyper-connected art-world figure, became the foundation's director, lending a sense of continuity and inventiveness to the collection. If you think the Museum of Modern Art in New York City is too far to travel, a visit here might be just as good.

Collectors:
Ernst & Hildy Beyeler

Address:
Baselstrasse 101
4125 Riehen, Basel
Switzerland
Tel +41 61 6459700
info@fondationbeyeler.ch
www.fondationbeyeler.ch

Opening Hours:
Wed: 10am–8pm
Thurs–Tues: 10am–6pm

183   Hallen für Neue Kunst Schaffhausen
*A pilgrimage destination for fans of large-scale
installations by top artists*

Collector:
Urs Raussmüller

Address:
Baumgartenstrasse 23
8200 Schaffhausen
Switzerland
Tel +41 52 6252515
contact@raussmueller.org
www.raussmueller.org

Opening Hours:
Sat: 3–5pm
Sun: 11am–5pm

Before Tate boss Nicholas Serota began planning the Tate
Modern, in London, he came here for a week of inspira-
tion: the Hallen für Neue Kunst Schaffhausen, opened
in 1984, which has become a template for art institutions
of cavernous factory space yearning to be filled with art.
Nearly thirty years ago, the Zurich-based Urs Raussmüller
was looking for a location where artists could present their
works with plenty of room to breathe. He found what he
was looking for in the contemplative town of Schaffhausen,
nestled along the Rhine. A former worsted-wool factory
of 5 500 square meters, the space offers the perfect conditions for showing groups of work by the superstars of
twentieth-century art: Joseph Beuys and Sol LeWitt, Mario
Merz and Robert Ryman. And yet Urs Raussmüller and
his wife, Christel Sauer, reject the label "collectors." They
think of themselves as facilitators of site-specific art that is
unlimited by space or time.

184   Sammlung Ruedi Bechtler—
Kunst im Castell
*Contemporary art of the highest quality
in a truly cool hotel*

Collector:
Ruedi Bechtler

Address:
Via Castell 300
7524 Zuoz
Switzerland
Tel +41 81 8515253
info@hotelcastell.ch
www.hotelcastell.ch/art07

Open visitation during hotel
hours. Guided tours every
Thursday at 5pm.

There are simply too many so-called art hotels showcasing
works by unknown regional artists usually purchased in a
blitz right before the hotel's grand opening. Hotel Castell,
in Zuoz, in the Engadin region, however, goes about things
differently. In the house and its surroundings, the visitor
bumps into works by Pipilotti Rist, Tadashi Kawamata,
Roman Signer, or Lawrence Weiner—most of them built
specifically for the place. Hotel owner Ruedi Bechtler is an
artist in his own right, and sensible enough not to feed his
guests standard artistic fare. In 1955, his father, Walter A.
Bechtler, started one of the largest Swiss art foundations,
whose mission is to make contemporary art accessible. Its
current president, Ruedi Bechtler, is deeply devoted to this
goal. One of the hotel's highlights, James Turrell's *Skyspace*,
offers the opportunity for a contemplative experience both
night and day.

S

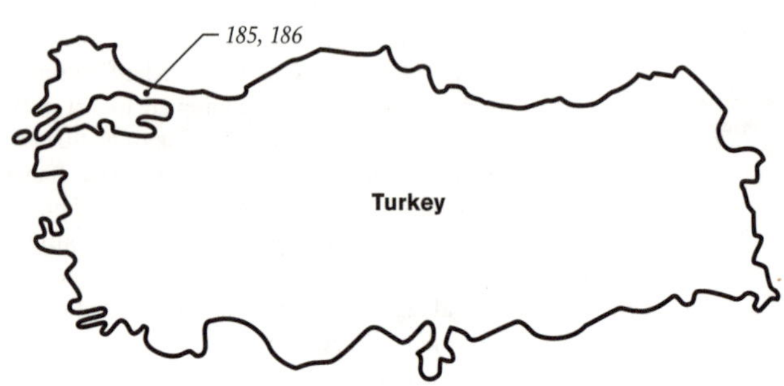

185 Proje4L—Elgiz Museum of Contemporary Art

Influential Turkish and international contemporary art

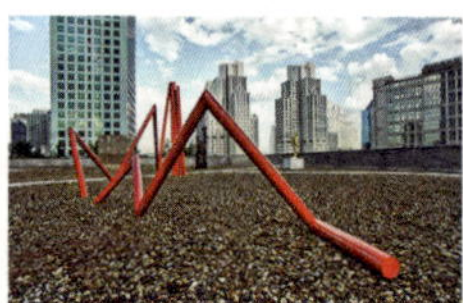

Long before contemporary Turkish art came into the spotlight, Sevda and Can Elgiz knew its inherent worth. The couple has been eagerly collecting since the early 1980s, even knocking down walls of their own home to fit the artworks inside, as they told the American magazine *Art+Auction*. Initially they focused on Turkish artists; at the end of the 1990s they began to acquire works by international artists. The private Elgiz museum—opened in 2001 as one of the first institutions for contemporary art in Turkey—now holds works by influential Turkish artists like Ömer Uluç and Güngör Taner, as well as that by international names like Tracey Emin and Barbara Kruger. In 2012, the museum was supplemented by 1 500 square meters of open-air, rooftop exhibition space.

Collectors:
Sevda & Can Elgiz

Address:
Meydan Sokak
Beybi Giz Plaza B Blok
Maslak
34398 Istanbul
Turkey
Tel +90 212 2902525
info@proje4l.org
www.proje4l.org

Opening Hours:
Wed–Fri: 10am–5pm
Sat: 10am–4pm
Tues: by appointment only

The development of the art scene in Istanbul can be
described in one word: speedy. Within the span of just a few years,
Turkish contemporary art has moved into the international spotlight,
and despite low support from the state, an active arts scene has
managed to emerge. This is due to the private sector, with both
corporations and banks generously subsidizing the city's art
institutions. Akbank Sanat, which has been around since 1993, is
sponsored by a financial institution. So is Istanbul Modern, a private
museum of modern and contemporary art established in 2004 by an
industry group in a former warehouse on the Bosporus. Both
institutions are located in the Beyoğlu district, considered one of the
most important addresses of the local scene. Here you'll find a
smattering of young galleries, such as Pi Artworks, Galeri Non,
Gallerist, Galeri Nev, and Pirosmani.
Additional art institutions in Istanbul reflecting the contemporary art
scene are Santralistanbul, located in a former power plant, or Borusan
Sanat, which houses artists' studios. There's also Salt, which has a
walk-in movie theater and a roof terrace, or Garaj, a non-profit center
that publishes the magazine *Gist*.
The Art Biennale, launched in 1987, made a decisive contribution to
the development of the Istanbul art scene. Today it's one of the most
important art biennials, alongside Venice, São Paulo, and Sydney. The
Istanbul Biennale, held from mid-September to mid-November, starts
at the same time as the annual art fair Contemporary Istanbul. Since
September 2013, the city has also been home to the Artinternational
Istanbul, a new art fair which sees itself as a bridge between East and
West.

Silvia Anna Barrilà

More Information: www.bmw-art-guide.com

186   Özil Collection
East and West, past and present in the heart of Istanbul

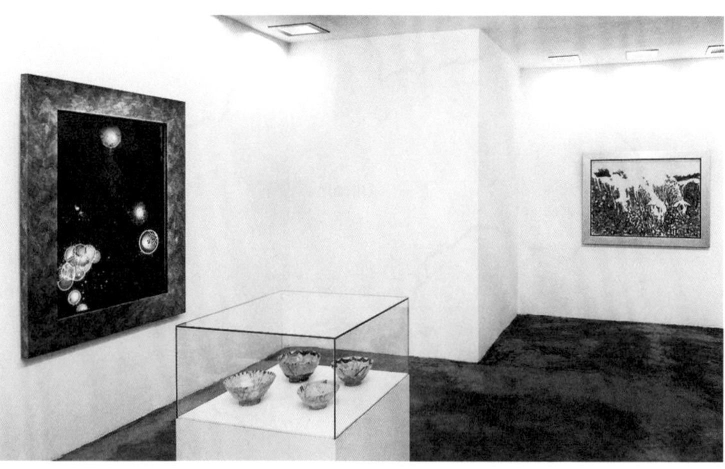

Collector:
Dağhan Özil

Address:
Ayazmadere Cad. 4
Fulya/Besiktas
34349 Istanbul
Turkey
Tel +90 212 2276852
eymur@ozilcollection.com
www.ozilcollection.com

By appointment only.

Istanbul is the place where East meets West. Art dealer and collector Dağhan Özil has been leveraging this knowledge since 1986, when he began exploring the interaction between Western and Turkish artists in his gallery, now headquartered in both Istanbul and Berlin. Özil's private collecting reflects his bifurcated interest: Islamic art, on the one hand; contemporary Western art stars, on the other. In 2007 Özil opened his private collection to the public, atop his Istanbul gallery, showing around 250 works of contemporary art and 500 pieces of Islamic ceramics and bronzes, displayed in thematic rooms that highlight the legacy of the Islamic–Western past and today's understanding of international art, including works by Wim Delvoye, Sarah Morris, Gerhard Richter, Markus Lüpertz, and Jan Fabre.

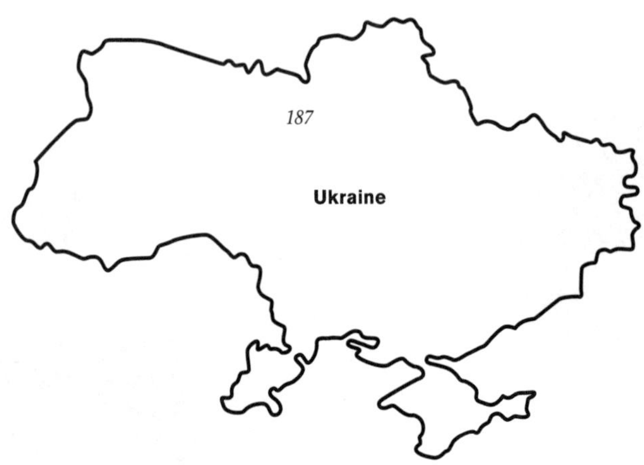

187   Pinchuk Art Centre
*Blue-chip contemporary in the first private museum
in the former USSR*

Within the span of a few years, Ukrainian billionaire Victor
Pinchuk has asserted himself as one of the most powerful
collectors on the international scene. He bought *Hanging
Heart (Magenta/Gold)*, by Jeff Koons, for a reported 23.6 million dollars, and *99 Cent II Diptychon*, by Andreas Gursky,
for a reported 3.3 million dollars, setting a record price for
both artists. Pinchuk has purchased other million-dollar
artworks by the likes of blue-chip stars Peter Doig and
Takashi Murakami. He reveals it all at his very popular
Pinchuk Art Centre, founded in 2006, a colossal six-storey
building that was the first private museum opened in the
former USSR, which has had nearly a million visitors come
through its doors. "There is only one queue in the country,"
Pinchuk told *The New Yorker* in 2009: "ours."

Collector:
Victor Pinchuk

Address:
1/3-2, "A" Block
Velyka Vasylkivska / Baseyna vul.
01004 Kiev
Ukraine
Tel +38 44 5900858
info@pinchukartcentre.org
www.pinchukartcentre.org

Opening Hours:
Tues–Sun: 12–9pm

188   The Farjam Collection

*A voyage from ancient Islamic art to contemporary
Middle Eastern and Western art*

Collector:
Farhad Farjam

Address:
DIFC Gate Village 4
Dubai
United Arab Emirates
Tel +971 4 3230303
info@farjamcollection.org
www.farjamcollection.org

Opening Hours:
Sat: 12–8pm
Sun–Thurs: 10am–8pm

Farhad Farjam, a Dubai-based Iranian industrialist, started his collection when he was still a student in New York in the 1970s. He had bought the first piece of his collection of Persian miniatures for 2 000 dollars, the cost of a semester's tuition. This resulted in, well, a lost semester. "It was a dramatic story for me that I never forget," he recalled during a panel at Art Dubai in 2010. Today Farjam owns one of the most important collections of privately held Islamic art in the world, an undertaking he considers a social responsibility. Over the years Farjam has turned to modern and contemporary art from the Middle East and the West. The Farjam Collection today includes artists like Mohamed Ehsai and Nja Mahdaoui, as well as Western icons Andy Warhol and Jean-Michel Basquiat. Moreover, Farjam was one of the earliest collectors of Farhad Moshiri, the wry Iranian artist who toys with pop culture.

U

189   Salsali Private Museum
A platform for collectors in Dubai's hub of creativity

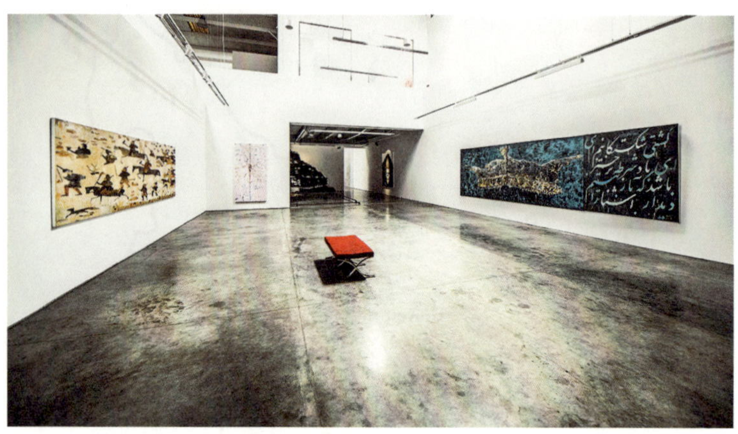

Located in the industrial area AL Quoz 1—Dubai's designated hub of arts and creativity—the Salsali Private Museum, which opened in November 2011, is not just an exhibition space for Ramin Salsali's collection of contemporary art. It is also a platform for collectors who want to meet and exchange ideas, or to exhibit their own collections. "An art collection is an art in itself," Salsali says. "It should reveal to its audience a story more significant than any individual viewpoint." An Iranian consultant for the petrochemical industry, Salsali started collecting when he was a twenty-one-year-old student in Germany. Today he owns over 300 works by Middle Eastern artists such as Reza Derakshani, Mona Hatoum, and Shirin Neshat, which sit alongside international stars like Arman, Niki de Saint Phalle, Jonathan Meese, André Butzer, Fischli/Weiss, Meret Oppenheim, and Daniel Richter.

Collector:
Ramin Salsali

Address:
Al Quoz 1, Road 8
Alserkal Avenue Complex/Unit 14
Dubai
United Arab Emirates
Tel +971 4 3809600
spm@salsalipm.com
www.salsalipm.com

Opening Hours:
Sat: 1–5pm
Sun–Thurs: 11am–6pm

U

190   Traffic
A multifunctional space for contemporary art and design

Collector:
Rami Farook

Address:
Umm Suqeim Road 179
Dubai
United Arab Emirates
Tel +971 4 3470209
info@viatraffic.org
www.viatraffic.org

Opening Hours:
Sat: 12–6pm
Sun–Thurs: 10am–7pm

Traffic is not only an exhibition space for over 300 artworks owned by its founder, Rami Farook; it is also a design store, art gallery, library, studio, and meeting place for lectures and screenings. "I have always loved the dialogue between art and design," Farook told the Dubai *Gulf News*. For this multipurpose venture Farook received the prestigious 2009 British Council's International Young Design Entrepreneur Award, which is fitting: it was after he visited a show curated by Damien Hirst at London's Serpentine Gallery in 2007 that Farook's genuine passion for collecting was ignited. "It is not the monetary worth but the intrinsic value of art that speaks to the heart," he said. "When it comes to art for art's sake, there are no rules." True, that: the Traffic collection ranges from Allora & Calzadilla to Roman Signer, and from Banksy and Tracey Emin to Louise Bourgeois.

191   Barjeel Art Foundation
Modern and contemporary art from four corners of the Arab world

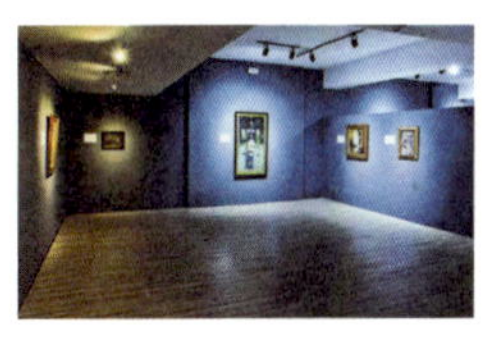

Collector:
Sultan Sooud Al-Qassemi

Address:
Maraya Art Centre
Al Qasba
Sharjah
United Arab Emirates
info@barjeelartfoundation.com
www.barjeelartfoundation.com

Opening hours vary depending on exhibition. Please check the website for most current information.

The term "Arab world" comprises a vast territory spanning from the Middle East to North Africa, subsuming the Levant, Maghreb, Egypt, the Gulf Arab, and Iraq—places strongly characterized by their own history and culture. This internal diversity of the Arab world's countries lies at the basis of Sultan Sooud Al-Qassemi's art collection, which includes over 500 works by both modern and contemporary Arab artists, such as Shakir Hassan Al-Said, Khaled Hafez, and Lara Baladi. Sultan Al-Qassemi spent over a decade amassing his collection, which was opened to the public in 2010, on the second floor of the Maraya Art Centre, in Al Qasba, the entertainment hub of Sharjah. "What's the point in art," he asked the Abu Dhabi *National*, "if it is not shared?"

U

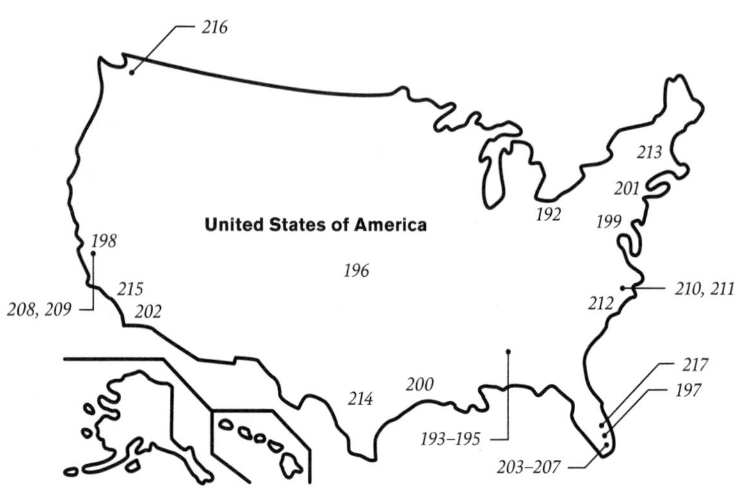

192   Transformer Station
*International photographic art and
a unique collaboration*

Fred and Laura Ruth Bidwell exhibit their collection in a former transformer station six months out of the year. Then they leave the exhibition rooms to the watchful eyes of the Cleveland Museum of Art, which uses the atmosphere of the old industrial building for exhibitions that fit the cool ambiance. This unique collaboration was decided before the Transformer Station's February 2013 opening, because both the Bidwells and the museum have the same goal of bringing smartly curated contemporary art exhibits to Cleveland. The collector couple's emphasis is on photography, having purchased works by Jessica Backhaus, Hiroshi Sugimoto, Philip-Lorca diCorcia, and Martin Parr. They also offer a perfect link to the curatorial mission of the museum by presenting historical positions like Walker Evans and Lee Friedlander.

Collectors:
Laura Ruth & Fred Bidwell

Address:
1460 West 29th Street
Cleveland, OH 44113
United States of America
Tel +1 216 9385429
info@transformerstation.org
www.transformerstation.org

Opening Hours:
Wed, Fri, Sat: 12–5pm
Thurs: 12–9pm

193 The Goss-Michael Foundation
*A must-see for everyone who loves
the Young British Artists*

Collectors:
Kenny Goss & George Michael

Address:
1405 Turtle Creek Boulevard
Dallas, TX 75207
United States of America
Tel +1 214 6960555
www.gossmichaelfoundation.org

Opening Hours:
Thurs–Fri: 10am–4pm
Sat: 11am–4pm
Mon–Wed: by appointment only

The strong contingent of Young British Artists in Dallas, Texas, is due to the longstanding alliance between art dealer Kenny Goss and the pop singer George Michael. Both have great sympathy for Damien Hirst's marinated cadavers that deal with death and ephemerality, and for Tracy Emin's eroticized installations. Sarah Lucas's feminist statements also make an appearance in the collection. Since 2007 you can catch a glimpse of the overall criteria of the Goss-Michael Foundation, where the two enthusiasts have assembled roughly 500 works, including those by Gilbert & George, Op Art queen Bridget Riley, or provocateurs Jake & Dinos Chapman. Many works are from the 1990s, which were formative years, says the collector duo, for an entire artistic generation.

194 Nasher Sculpture Center
*A private collection of masterpieces every museum
dreams of owning*

Collectors:
Patsy & Raymond Nasher

Address:
2001 Flora Street
Dallas, TX 75201
United States of America
Tel +1 214 2425100
www.nashersculpturecenter.org

Opening Hours:
Tues–Sun: 11am–5pm

Patsy and Raymond Nasher began obeying one command in the 1950s, and they have stayed true to it ever since: Only collect sculpture. More specifically, by modernist artists like Henry Moore, August Rodin, Pablo Picasso, and Raymond Duchamp-Villon. These works are accompanied by masterpieces by Alexander Calder, Richard Serra, and Claes Oldenburg. Every single object in this collection is museum-worthy; taken as a whole, they show the development of an entire epoch. Since 2003 the Nasher Sculpture Center has presented its holdings in exciting contrasts and supplemented by matching new acquisitions. Built by architect and Pritzker-Prize winner Renzo Piano, the pavilion-like structure, situated at the end of a park in Dallas's arts district, allows for a perspective that sets the robust outdoor sculptures in a relationship with the fragile objects inside.

U

195   The Warehouse
Two major United States collections in dialogue

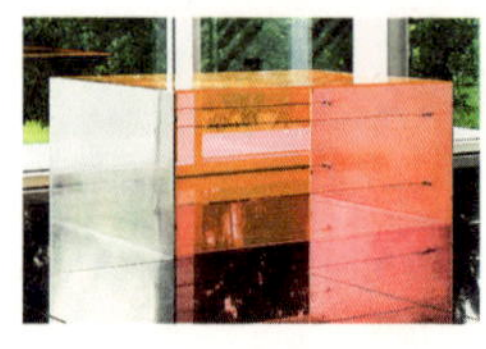

Cindy and Howard Rachofsky open their Rachofsky House, designed by Richard Meier, for events devoted to their charitable interests. But art lovers can find parts of the collection with works by Gerhard Richter, Lucio Fontana, Sigmar Polke, Piero Manzoni, Mario Merz, Kazuo Shiraga, and Atsuko Tanaka at a second address: since 2013 Cindy and Howard Rachofsky have shared a large hall called The Warehouse—divided into sixteen galleries—with fellow collectors Amy and Vernon Faulconer. Here the latter are interested in the art of Anish Kapoor, Bridget Riley, and James Turrell, among others. The result is an exciting dialogue of exhibits and, because collaborating collectors are rare elsewhere, a truly innovative experiment.

Collectors:
Cindy & Howard Rachofsky
Amy & Vernon Faulconer

Address:
14105 Inwood Road
Dallas, TX 75244
United States of America
Tel +1 214 4422875
www.thewarehousedallas.org

By appointment only.

196   The Dikeou Collection
Two artists collect artists they find to be important

One quickly recognizes that the Dikeou Collection has been selected by two artists acting as collectors. Devon and Pany Dikeou are less interested in establishing themselves than in making known the thirty photographers and concept artists they deem important: established names like Momoyo Torimitsu and Vik Muniz, but also more unconventional positions like Simon Periton, Dan Asher, or Jonathan Horowitz, whose works are often absurd or come in many parts—not exactly what collectors of big, representative works are looking for. The Dikeou's exhibition hall, in Denver, matches their taste in art: an unrenovated high-rise building from the 1950s that has retained its retro charm. Devon Dikeou initiated a project with each of the artists in their collection for *Zingmagazine,* which she publishes.

Collectors:
Devon & Pany Dikeou

Address:
1615 California Street, Suite 515
Denver, CO 80202
United States of America
Tel +1 303 6233001
info@dikeoucollection.org
www.dikeoucollection.org

Opening Hours:
Wed–Fri: 11am–5pm
By appointment only.

U

197   Girls' Club
*The name is the mission: to promote
and rediscover female artists*

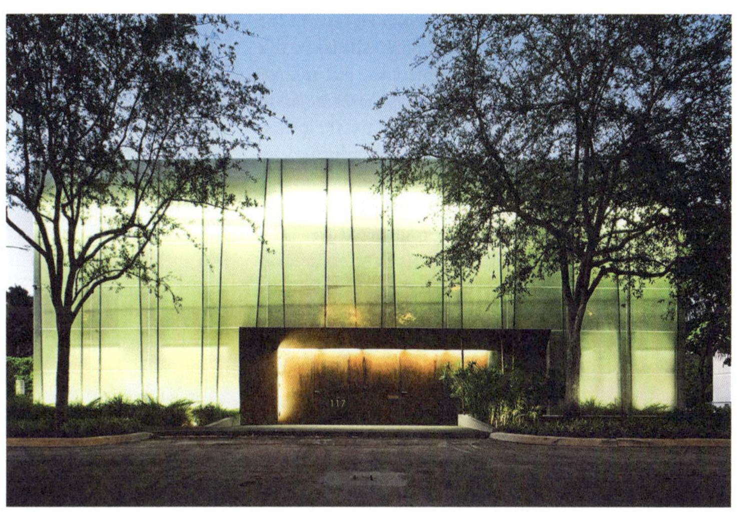

Collectors:
Francie Bishop Good &
David Horvitz

Address:
117 Northeast 2nd Street
Fort Lauderdale, FL 33301
United States of America
Tel +1 954 8289151
www.girlsclubcollection.org

Opening Hours:
Wed–Fri: 1–5pm
And by appointment.

With glamorous names like Beatriz Milhazes, Elizabeth Peyton, or the American concept-icon Barbara Kruger, you'll get noticed fast in the art business. But Francie Bishop Good and David Horvitz could name dozens of female artists who have been unjustly overlooked, which is why the American collector pair founded the Girls' Club in 2006. Here in this private foundation—comprised of spacious exhibition halls tucked behind a shimmering façade, designed by the fabulous architect Margi Nothard—the collectors show their holdings of women's art: the elaborate, cartoony paintings of Sandy Winters, or the stunning photography of Tracey Baran, who documented the inhabitants of a small New York town before her untimely death at age thirty-three, in 2008.

U

198   Oliver Ranch Foundation
A sculpture park where art responds to nature

Driving through the countryside of San Francisco to visit the region's vineyards is no longer a hidden secret. But Nancy and Steve Oliver's sculpture park still is. In the mid-1980s the two decided to complement the picturesque landscape with art. The first sculpture was *Shepherd's Muse*, by Judith Shea, an allusion to sheep farming, the collectors' shared hobby. This was followed by sculptures by Miroslaw Balka, Fred Sandback, Richard Serra, and Bill Fontana. The fixed principle of the Oliver Ranch Foundation is that art must directly respond to nature. Each work is created in dialogue with the artist. The realization of a work often takes several years, as was the case with Ann Hamilton's accessible *Tower*, the centerpiece of the Olivers' collection. Visitors can take a seat on one of two curiously constructed staircases, while performances and plays are presented on the other.

Collectors:
Nancy & Steve Oliver

Address:
22205 River Road
Geyserville, CA 95441
United States of America
Tel +1 707 8573975
www.oliverranchfoundation.org

Opening Hours:
Fri–Sun: Only guided tours with prior registration. Group tours upon request.

199   The Brant Foundation Art Study Center
Important American art from the 1960s to the present

He sits at the source and is one of the first to know who the artists of tomorrow will be: Peter Brant, owner of Brant Publications. His publishing house is responsible for art magazines such as *Art in America* and *Interview*. As a film producer, of the documentary *Andy Warhol*, for example, and a paper manufacturer, he can afford to purchase what is desired and in demand. This is how Brant, over the decades, has amassed over 1 000 works of American contemporary artists, one of the largest collections in the world, including works by Andy Warhol, Julian Schnabel, or Keith Haring. His focus on American art stems from his concern with an American sense of life, which he finds in every work anew. The spectrum runs from the positive attitude of Jeff Koons to the provocative criticism of performer–sculptor Paul McCarthy. Since 2009 a part of the collection has been exhibited in a former barn.

Collector:
Peter M. Brant

Address:
941 North Street
Greenwich, CT 06831
United States of America
Tel +1 203 8690611
info@brantfoundation.org
www.brantfoundation.org

Opening Hours:
Mon–Fri: 10am–4pm
By appointment only.

U

200   The Menil Collection
*An amazing collection with the format
of a metropolitan museum*

Collectors:
Dominique & John de Menil

Address:
1533 Sul Ross Street
Houston, TX 77006
United States of America
Tel +1 713 5259400
info@menil.org
www.menil.org

Opening Hours:
Wed–Sun: 11am–7pm

The legacy of the French-born pair is not only the imposing private museum with numerous individual galleries for works by Mark Rothko, Cy Twombly, or Byzantine art. Dominique and John de Menil began their collection in the 1940s and have amassed invaluable works of art over the decades: Fernand Léger, Henri Matisse, or Pablo Picasso mark the entry point of this incredible collection, and Jean-Michel Basquiat, Eric Fischl, Cindy Sherman, and Robert Gober belong to the list of later additions. Between the two groups hang the heroes of American postwar painting: Barnett Newman, Willem de Kooning, or Jasper Johns, among them. Outdoor sculptures by Mark di Suvero or Michael Heizer complete the history of art in the twentieth century. Dominique de Menil, who passed away in 1997, had survived her husband for more than twenty years. She founded their museum in 1987.

201   Fisher Landau Center for Art
*International stars from the 1960s on, in one of
New York's most important collections*

Collector:
Emily Fisher Landau

Address:
38-27 30th Street
Long Island City, NY 11101
United States of America
Tel +1 718 9370727
info@flcart.org
www.flcart.org

Opening Hours:
Thurs–Mon: 12–5pm

It all started with a robbery: over half a century ago, a few thieves relieved Emily Fisher Landau of her jewelry. The insurance company reimbursed the victim, who then wondered just what exactly she should do with her fresh funds. She decided on art, becoming one of the most important collectors and patrons in all of New York City. Pablo Picasso, Fernand Léger, Piet Mondrian, and Jasper Johns all hang in Fisher Landau's spacious Manhattan townhouse—big, but not big enough for the entire 1 300-work collection. So in 1991 the Fisher Landau Center of Art was opened in a remodeled factory. Its focus is on works after 1960, works Fisher Landau bought directly from the artists at the start of their careers, the timely result of good instinct, good advisers, or both: Donald Judd, Jenny Holzer, Ed Ruscha, Kiki Smith, Cy Twombly, and Sherrie Levine are all here.

U

202   Frederick R. Weisman Art Foundation
The Who's Who of Modernism, from Surrealism to Pop

It's as if Billie Milam and Frederick R. Weisman were still moving about their mansion. Paintings by Abstract Expressionists like Willem de Kooning or Mark Rothko hang together with Pop Art works over the fireplace and sectional sofas. Yet the collector couple had purchased the 1920s house only as an exhibition space. Weisman, the son of Russian immigrants, and a passionate art buyer, established a foundation in 1982 to preserve his esteemed collection after his death. Now, guided tours through the villa and adjacent gallery showcase the work that was most important to him: European Modernism from Paul Cézanne and Pablo Picasso, Surrealists like Max Ernst, and postwar art by Alberto Giacometti, Alexander Calder, or Robert Rauschenberg. Way too much art for a mansion, and all of it museum worthy, which why the forward-looking collector founded several American museums before his death, in 1994.

Collectors:
Frederick R. &
Billie Milam Weisman

Address:
265 North Carolwood Drive
Los Angeles, CA 90077
United States of America
Tel +1 310 2775321
tours@weismanfoundation.org
www.weismanfoundation.org

Opening Hours:
Mon–Fri: 10:30am and 2pm
Only guided tours with prior registration.

203   CIFO—Cisneros Fontanals Art Foundation
*Latin American art is not what you think
it is in this expansive collection*

Anyone who equates Latin American art with colorful, mythical painting will be taken to school by Ella Fontanals-Cisnero's collection. Forty years of continuous collecting offers stellar insight into the abstract, geometric language of Jesús Rafael Soto or Lygia Clark. The centerpiece is a work by Julio Le Parc, whose hulking sculpture at Documenta, the *Continuel-Mobile*, was comprised of flexible metal discs that pinged scattered light about the room. It was stored in boxes for decades. But now it fits perfectly in a former department store that was transformed into an exhibition hall by the prize-winning architect Rene Gonzalez in 2005. Photography, video, and installation art form the 1400-work collection, each given equal treatment. There's also an increasing amount of contemporary art—by Francis Alÿs or Ernesto Neto, for example—unrestrained by either geography or theme.

Collector:
Ella Fontanals-Cisneros

Address:
1018 North Miami Avenue
Miami, FL 33136
United States of America
Tel +1 305 4553380
info@cifo.org
www.cifo.org

Opening Hours:
Thurs–Fri: 12–6pm
Sat–Sun: 10am–4pm

Why does an art collector give away his or her art? Or hand it to a museum that in return names a room or sometimes even an entire section of a building after the donor? This is the reason the San Francisco Museum of Modern Art (SFMOMA) will be closed for three years beginning in 2013: the construction of new galleries for the Doris and Donald Fisher Collection, a private collection of over 1 000 works of modern and contemporary art. The Harvard Art Museums in Cambridge owe their outstanding artworks primarily to private collectors who have passed their treasures on to the university. And in the spring of 2013, Leonard A. Lauder announced that he will donate seventy-eight paintings and sculptures to the Metropolitan Museum of Art: masterpieces by Pablo Picasso, Georges Braque, and Juan Gris. The cosmetics tycoon explains the decision for the gift—worth an estimated one billion dollars—with a simple argument: it is a gift "to the people who live and work in New York."

That's a statement that the metropolis certainly likes to hear. Although many collectors live in New York, the number of private showrooms accessible to the public is slim, particularly when contrasted to Miami and its many public-private museums. Only during art fairs, such as the Armory Show, via its VIP program, is one able to catch a glimpse how many treasures are hidden in the lofts and apartments of New York City.

Discretion is appreciated, of course, and collectors maintain longstanding relations with museums—relationships, in many cases, now in the second generation. The willingness on the part of private collectors to share with public institutions has its roots in the history of American collecting: **nearly all the important museums in New York began as private collections.** But here, too, change is afoot: "It is much better to give twenty works to a small museum than to place 300 artworks in an extension of the MoMA or the Metropolitan Museum," says collector Aby Rosen.

Christiane Meixner

204 De la Cruz Collection—
Contemporary Art Space
Emerging artists meet solid positions like Neo Rauch or Jeff Koons

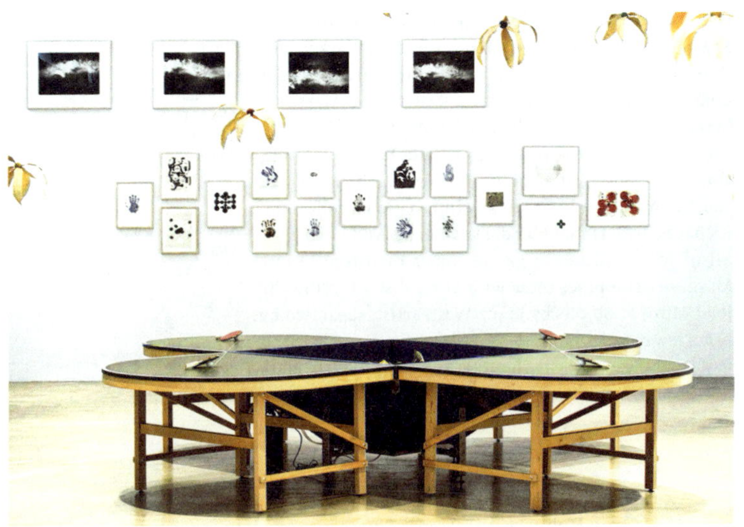

Collectors:
Rosa & Carlos de la Cruz

Address:
23 Northeast 41st Street
Miami, FL 33137
United States of America
Tel +1 305 5766112
info@delacruzcollection.org
www.delacruzcollection.org

Opening Hours:
Tues–Sat: 10am–4pm

Whenever Rosa and Carlos de la Cruz show up, art dealers get nervous. The American couple is part of the so-called group of "super collectors," people who might never think their holdings are quite large enough: there's always room for one more work, preferably a large one by Jeff Koons, Daniel Richter, or Neo Rauch. This quickly leads to the accusation of arbitrariness, or to the impression that private museums of this dimension lack a clear concept. But the fact is that the couple is quickly enthused over new trends and wastes no time in acquiring them. This is how the work of the up-and-coming artist Sterling Ruby or the Berliner Nikolas Gambaroff has made it into the collection. With purchases of Manfred Pernice, Thomas Eggerer, or Martin Creed, the de la Cruzes evidence their eagerness to acquire work that displays a theoretical complexity whose meaning only slowly dawns upon the viewer.

U

205   The Margulies Collection
at the Warehouse

Big-name photographers and sculptors
in curious combination

Old and new photography, from Helen Levitt to Cindy Sherman; videos and installations by Sara Barker, Bill Viola, or minimalistic light artist Iván Navarro count among the interests of the real-estate tycoon Martin Z. Margulies—a special niche not for everyone. His collection, which has been overseen by curator Katherine Hinds since the 1980s, is situated in a former warehouse. There you also find must-haves for any international collection: Richard Serra, Donald Judd, Dan Flavin, Andy Warhol—all of whose presence gauges one's own reputation. Margulies combines these with Surrealist sculptures by Joan Miró, or objects by Franz West, artists separated by just a few decades but also by entire artistic epochs. Such fissures, however, excite the collector and uniquely mark his rotating exhibits.

Collector:
Martin Z. Margulies

Address:
591 Northwest 27th Street
Miami, FL 33127
United States of America
Tel +1 305 5761051
mcollection@bellsouth.net
www.margulieswarehouse.com

Opening Hours:
October–April
Wed–Sat: 11am–4pm

206   Craig Robins Collection

A collection where art and design meet without angst

If anyone knows how art and design should be displayed together, it's Craig Robins. The real-estate agent founded Design Miami in 2005 as a companion to Art Basel Miami Beach and thereby managed to make a discredited Art Déco district chic and expensive once again. His collection, housed in his office building, brings together both fine art and fine design with consistency: paintings by Thomas Scheibitz, Kai Althoff, or Marlene Dumas meet classical furniture by Jean Prouvé, Charlotte Perriand, or Ron Arad, a contemporary design icon. Robins arranges the works with an eye toward form and content, both. It's not surprising that Cosima von Bonin or Mike Kelley are on the list of his favorite artists: both have extended their range to create sculptures that integrate furniture, plush, and even ambient music.

Collector:
Craig Robins

Address:
3841 Northeast 2nd Avenue
Suite 400
Miami, FL 33137
United States of America
Tel +1 305 5318700
tiffany@dacra.com
www.dacra.com

Opening Hours:
Mon–Fri: 9am–5pm
By appointment only.

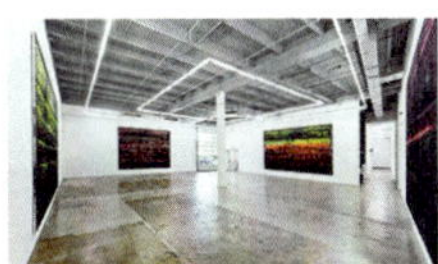

Collectors:
Mera & Donald Rubell

Address:
95 Northwest 29th Street
Miami, FL 33127
United States of America
Tel +1 305 5736090
info@rfc.museum
www.rfc.museu

Opening hours vary depending
on exhibition. Please check
the website for most current
information.

207 Rubell Family Collection/ Contemporary Arts Foundation

The most resonant names in Western art are present in this collection

They are America's super collectors, with museum-sized spaces, sponsors for exhibition projects, and a consistent and clear philosophy: for four decades Mera and Donald Rubell have only been purchasing art that speaks to both of them. They have agreed so far on over 1 500 works, including those by Bruce Nauman, Jeff Koons, Lawrence Weiner, Gerhard Richter, Richard Prince, and Keith Haring. Since 1993 a part of their collection has been shown in a remodeled warehouse and adjacent sculpture garden. Another highlight is German photography, from August Sander to the Düsseldorf Becher School, including Thomas Ruff and Andreas Gursky. The Rubells know that their market power can influence the artists' careers—even if they collect solely out of passion.

Collector:
Donald M. Hess

Address:
4411 Redwood Road
Napa, CA 94558
United States of America
Tel +1 707 2551144
info@hesscollection.com
www.hesscollection.com/art

Opening Hours:
Mon–Sun: 10am–5pm

Additional exhibition locations:
Salta, Argentina, p. 14
Klapmuts, South Africa, p. 147

208 The Hess Art Collection, Napa

Museum highlights from Europe and America in the gentle hills of Napa Valley

He sold the family brewery. He successfully began a Swiss mineral water brand and sold it to Coca-Cola. From that day on, Donald M. Hess, the son of Swiss-American parents, was able to devote his time to his two true passions: wine and art. Hess owns vineyards and art collections in the Argentine Andes and the South African cape region. Prior, in 1978, he invested in California's Napa Valley. At Mount Veeder, it's not just about sampling the wine; the two-hour drive from San Francisco is worth making for other reasons: integrated into the rustic 1903 building is one-quarter of Hess's 1 000-work art collection, spread over two spacious storeys. Works by Francis Bacon, Franz Gertsch, Anselm Kiefer, and Per Kirkeby are true jewels: nowhere else in California can you see them in such quality and density.

U

209 Di Rosa
Nature and art in almost equal standing

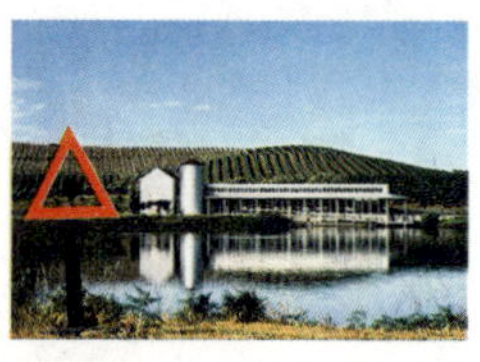

Since 1997 the collection of Veronica and Rene di Rosa
has invited visitors to descend upon their vineyards and
sprawling natural preserve. Everything here seems to be
focused on the local: the large outside sculptures as well
as the works housed in four elongated buildings were all
made by regional artists. The painterly landscape is just
as important to the collectors as the creatures that reside
there. Sculptors like Mark di Suvero, Bruce Nauman, and
Larry Sultan, or the painter Raymond Saunders have all
spent time in California, which is why they fit seamlessly
into the di Rosa portfolio, as do artists less internationally known, including Mildred Howard or Joan Brown.
Today the collection boasts over 2 000 works that can be
visited year-round, in guided tours of fewer than twenty-
five people.

Collectors:
Rene & Veronica di Rosa

Address:
5200 Sonoma Highway
Napa, CA 94559
United States of America
Tel +1 707 2265991
tours@dirosaart.org
www.dirosaart.org

Opening Hours:
November–March
Wed–Sun: 10am–4pm
April–October:
Wed–Sun: 10am–6pm

210 The Walther Collection—
Project Space New York
African and Asian photo art in dialogue
with Western classics

Having a second space in New York City makes sense,
particularly for globally connected collectors like Artur
Walther, founder of the Neu-Ulm-based Walther Collection,
a high-quality German space opened in 2010 that specializes in contemporary and classic photography. For Walther,
who has long lived on the Hudson, nabbing a space in New
York City was entirely logical. Here he sits on the committee
of the Whitney Museum and on that of the International
Center of Photography; here he grooms his international
contacts, from which his German location also profits.
Since 2011, the Walther Collection has been located in 160
square meters in a historical landmark, the West Chelsea
Art Building—ten floors of galleries and artist studios. The
collection's cosmopolitan perspective includes African and
Asian works, and its rotating three-month schedule offers
both new discoveries and modern masters.

Collector:
Artur Walther

Address:
526 West 26th Street, Suite 718
New York, NY 10001
United States of America
Tel +1 212 3520683
contact@walthercollection.com
www.walthercollection.com

Opening Hours:
Thurs–Sat: 12–6pm

Additional exhibition locations:
Neu-Ulm, Germany, p. 71

U

The **New York** art scene continues to grow. Two major art fairs per year even fit into the calendar: The coexistence of the storied Armory Show and Frieze New York—on Randall's Island, in the East River—illustrates how receptive the city remains to art. Over 1 000 private galleries have arrived at the same opinion, and now some have jumped the river to Bushwick—a multicultural district in Brooklyn where established Manhattan galleries like Luhring Augustine or Kesting Ray now entertain their branches. If you have time for just a short visit to Manhattan, you'd better be selective. A nice art walk could lead you to Paula Cooper, David Zwirner, or Larry Gagosian in the important gallery district of Chelsea. You could then head up to the vicinity of Central Park, where the galleries of Michael Werner and Hauser & Wirth reside on the Upper East Side. From there it's only a short hop to the grand institutions of the American metropolis: The Museum of Modern Art (MoMA) remains as attractive as ever, as does the Guggenheim Museum, and, of course, the Metropolitan Museum of Art, where the antique world meets American art from the twenty-first century. At the Whitney Museum of American Art you'll find contemporary American works of the twentieth century, and at the Sculpture Center you'll discover very fine exhibitions of current sculptors.

But you can also feel like a pioneer and discover art the way curious New Yorkers do. They look over Brooklyn to Queens, at MoMA's PS1, which, along with the New Museum of Contemporary Art, in Manhattan, is one of the most established museums for contemporary art. On the border of Bushwick and Queens you'll find young galleries like Regina Rex, who may already be presenting the stars of tomorrow, today. And, to return to Bushwick: here is where you will find space for project rooms like Chez Bushwick or Norte Maar, whose exhibitions are not subject to the selling pressure of the city. And on the other side of the Manhattan Bridge, just at the edge of Chinatown, you'll find the gallery Canada, known for its sensational program.

Christiane Meixner

More Information: www.bmw-art-guide.com

211 Zabludowicz Collection, New York
The corner of Broadway and Times Square: the office as an arena for international art

Collectors:
Anita & Poju Zabludowicz

Address:
1500 Broadway
New York, NY 10036
United States of America
ny@zabludowiczcollection.com
www.zabludowiczcollection.com/
new-york

Office building visits by
appointment only.

Additional exhibition locations:
London, Great Britain, p. 84

At 176 Prince of Wales Road, in London, in a Methodist church, a part of the 2 000-work collection belonging to Anita and Poju Zabludowicz has been on display via rotating exhibitions since 2007. One of the collector couple's recent exhibition addresses is located in the middle of Times Square, in New York City: 1500 Broadway. In the office of Tamares Real Estate, where Poju Zabludowicz oversees his investments, exhibitions offer visitors what he and his wife, Anita Zabludowicz, have gathered over the years. Aside from temporary projects, there are group shows spanning several floors that must assert themselves amidst the cool light of business offices. The rooms are open to the public, but anyone who wants a more penetrating view of the collection, featuring works by artists like Jeppe Hein or Josephine Meckseper, is required to hop on a jet and fly to Great Britain.

212 West Collection
Key names in international art meet new voices

Collectors:
Paige & Al West

Address:
1 Freedom Valley Drive
Oaks, PA 19456
United States of America
Tel +1 610 8837368
lee@westcollection.org
www.westcollection.org

By appointment only.

Financial services professional Al West is a man of action. He doesn't wait for gallerists or curators to recommend emerging voices to him; he lures them in himself. In 2011, for example, he and his daughter, Paige West, asked artists to apply for the West Collection Art Prize. Everyone who downloaded the app, looked at the art, and then gave an evaluation was part of the extended jury. This kind of participation is continued in the public spaces of West's business, SEI Investments. Approximately 1 200 works are installed in SEI's main building and can be viewed by appointment. The collection has grown since 1996, now encompassing nearly 3 000 works, including those by Donald Judd, Richard Artschwager, Martin Boyce, and Candice Breitz. Many of the works are loaned to museums or curated travelling exhibitions.

U

213 Hall Art Foundation
*Impressive presentations of art in an
eighteenth-century building*

Christine and Andrew Hall are not only longstanding collectors of art by Georg Baselitz. In 2006 the American commodity trader and his wife also bought the artist's former castle, near Hildesheim, Germany, to house works from their collection. More recently they bought and renovated Lexington Farm, in Vermont, an eighteenth-century structure that is now part of the Hall Art Foundation, where they show parts of their extensive collection. But unlike many of their peers, whose collected names read like a Who's Who of the international art scene, the Halls have decided to concentrate upon a few positions and prefer to collect them in depth. Here one finds notable Neo-Expressionist solo shows by the likes of A. R. Penck and Georg Baselitz, among other monographic exhibitions, including Neil Jenney's figurative paintings and Edward Burtynsky's photographs.

Collectors:
Christine & Andrew Hall

Address:
551 Route 106
Reading, VT 05062
United States of America
Tel +1 802 9521056
info@hallartfoundation.org
www.hallartfoundation.org

Only guided tours with prior online registration; currently Sundays at 12pm and 2pm.

214 Linda Pace Foundation
The legacy of a patroness who promoted young art

Linda Pace was an artist. But she wasn't just that. From 1993 onwards she organized a scholarship and exhibition program for artists in the Texan city of San Antonio. The artists often went on to have fantastic careers. Artist Isaac Julien, whose films can be found in Pace's collection—alongside art by Susan Philipsz, Arturo Herrera, Mona Hatoum, and Gabriel Orozco—called Pace an "artist-collector." The passionate patroness had procured roughly 500 works of art before she died, in 2007. Pace placed a part of her sculpture collection in a park owned by the foundation but accessible to the public. Other works are on loan to museums or installed in the private part of the foundation, which may be visited upon request. The foundation continues to purchase works by emerging artists in order to continue Linda Pace's legacy.

Collector:
Linda Pace

Address:
112 W. Combinatorial
San Antonio, TX 78204
United States of America
Tel +1 210 2266663
visit@pacefound.org
www.lindapacefoundation.org

By appointment only.

215   The Broad Art Foundation
Countdown to the private museum: a renowned collection of contemporary art stars

Collectors:
Eli & Edythe Broad

Address:
3355 Barnard Way
Santa Monica, CA 90405
United States of America
eschad@broadartfoundation.org
www.broadartfoundation.org

Visitation permitted only
occasionally. Please inquire
by e-mail or post.

One thing is certain: Eli and Edythe Broad are among the major collectors in the world. For about forty years, the couple has played an important role in Los Angeles, not only because they own almost 2 000 works by artists such as Christopher Wool, Cindy Sherman, and John Baldessari, but also because they serve as patrons in fields ranging from art to medicine. On the American West Coast, the Broads have been instrumental in the development of the region's museum landscape. They have donated or loaned works to the Museum of Contemporary Art and the Los Angeles County Museum of Art, among others. Now they are building a private museum for their collection, scheduled to open in 2014. Until this time comes, however, select art audiences may view parts of the collection at The Broad Art Foundation by setting up an appointment in advance.

216   Wright Exhibition Space
The collection of Seattle's "Patron Saint of the Arts"

Collectors:
Bagley & Virginia Wright

Address:
407 Dexter Avenue North
Seattle, WA 98109
United States of America
Tel +1 206 2648200

Opening hours vary depending on
exhibition. Please call on Fridays for
current information.

In Seattle, Bagley Wright was once known as a real-estate developer who vigorously promoted the 1962 construction of the Space Needle, the 184-meter-high tower that once stood as tallest building west of the Mississippi. When he died, in 2011, he was known for quite something else: namely, as Seattle's "Patron Saint of the Arts." Together with his wife, Virginia, Wright managed to assemble one of the largest collections of modern and contemporary art in the American northwest, boasting big American names like Willem de Kooning, Helen Frankenthaler, and Jackson **U** Pollock. The collection can be seen in temporary exhibitions at the Wright Exhibition Space and the Seattle Art Museum, to whom they bequeathed parts of their collection. Wright once wrote a personal essay about his life as a collector, detailing his run-ins with famous art protagonists of the twentieth century—Mark Rothko and Clement Greenberg among them.

217   Whitespace
*International art stars in a former warehouse
in Palm Beach*

The collector-couple Elayne & Marvin Mordes has assembled works by established artist-teams like Teresa Hubbard and Alexander Birchler, or Elmgreen & Dragset. Their collection also includes international names like Jonathan Meese, Thomas Houseago, Mat Collishaw, Christian Boltanski, and Anish Kapoor. The couple's treasures, comprised primarily of sculptures and installations, are housed in an unassuming warehouse in Palm Beach previously used for the manufacturing of one of the city's most in-demand products: dentures. Marvin Mordes was a long-time board member at the Hirshhorn Museum, in Washington. He brings this knowledge to bear not only upon his own collection; he and his wife also share their insights with guests on exclusive art tours during Art Basel Miami. Since 2009 they have opened their Whitespace rooms upon request for groups, private events, and, on Sundays, for all interested art lovers.

Collectors:
Elayne & Marvin Mordes

Address:
2805 N. Australian Avenue
West Palm Beach, FL 33407
United States of America
Tel +1 561 8424131
info@whitespacecollection.com
www.whitespace.com

Opening Hours:
Sun: 1–4pm

U

A project like this can never be **complete.** Almost every month, collectors worldwide open new showrooms or make their private collections available to the public in a variety of ways. If you know of any private collection of contemporary art that is publicly accessible and not listed here, we would be delighted to hear about it. We would be equally pleased to hear of any plans you might have for opening your own collection to interested art lovers. Doing so will help us keep the *BMW Art Guide by Independent Collectors* up to date. Please write to us at: bmwartguide@independent-collectors.com

Silvia Anna Barrilà is a freelance journalist who specializes in the art market. Since 2008 she has been writing for the Italian financial newspaper *Il Sole 24 Ore (ArtEconomy24),* in addition to several other magazines owned by the Mondadori publishing group. She also writes for international media covering art, including *Damn, Auction Central News, Artinvestor,* and *Monopol.* In this guide she covered the collections in southern and eastern Europe: Greece, Hungary, Italy, Poland, Russia, Turkey, and Ukraine. She also covered several countries in Asia—Bangladesh, China, India, Indonesia, and Japan—as well as a few collections in Germany, the Netherlands, Qatar, the United Arab Emirates, and the United States of America.

The journalist couple **Nicole Büsing** and **Heiko Klaas** have been writing freelance art journalism and art criticism since 1997 for a variety of national and international art magazines and newspapers, among which today include *Monopol, Artmapp, Artist Kunstmagazin, Dare, Zeitkunst, Artinvestor, Kunstmarkt Media, Photonews,* and *Next Level.* They also write catalogue essays for artists and institutions. In this guide they focused on collections from Europe and South America— Argentina, Austria, Belgium, Brazil, Denmark, Finland, France, Germany, Iceland, Israel, Luxembourg, Mexico, the Netherlands, Norway, Portugal, Puerto Rico, Spain, and Switzerland—and on a few institutions in Japan, South Africa, and the United States of America.

Christiane Meixner has been working as a freelance art critic since 1986 for a variety of magazines and newspapers, including *Der Tagesspiegel, Monopol, Weltkunst, Frankfurter Rundschau,* and *Zeit Online.* Since 2008 she has also served as a freelance editor of *Tagesspiegel's* "Art & Market" section. Her focus in this guide was on English-speaking countries: Australia, Canada, Great Britain, New Zealand, and the United States of America.

City

A
Alex 037
Alzano Lombardo 101
Appenzell 157
Aschaffenburg 044
Athens 085–090
Augsburg 045
Avignon 038

B
Baden-Baden 045
Barcelona 151–152
Bedburg-Hau 046
Beijing 030
Berlin 046–057
Bremen 058
Briosco 102
Brumadinho 026
Brussels 021–023
Buenos Aires 009–013
Busca 102

C
Cáceres 153
Camogli 103
Cascais 137
Catania 104
Città della Pieve 104
Cleveland 170
Copenhagen 034

D
Dallas 171–172
Denver 172
Deurle 024
Dhaka 020
Dörentrup 059
Doha 142
Donaueschingen 058–059
Dubai 167–169
Düsseldorf 061–062
Duisburg 060

E
Eberdingen-Nussdorf 062
Ecatepec 122
Edinburgh 080

City

F
Flassans sur Issole 038
Florence 105
Forlì 105
Fort Lauderdale 173
Freiburg 063

G
Gaiole in Chianti 106
Gars am Kamp 017
Geyserville 174
Greenwich 174
Gurgaon 094

H
Hafnarfjordur 092
Hamburg 064
Heerlen 125
Helsinki 035
Henningsvær 131
Hobart 015
Høvikodden 132
Houston 175
Hünfeld 067
Huesca 154

I
Ichikawa 119
Istanbul 162–165

J
Jakarta 096

K
Kagawa 120
Kemzeke 025
Kiev 166
Klapmuts 147
Klosterneuburg 018
Knislinge 156
Künzelsau-Gaisbach 067

L
Langenbruck 158
Lebring 018
Leinfelden-Echterdingen 068
Leipzig 069
Lisbon 138
London 083–084
Long Island City 175
Los Angeles 176
Lucca 106
Lucerne 159
Luxembourg City 121

City

M
Madrid 154
Magelang 097
Malo 107
Marines 039
Melbourne 016
Miami 176–181
Milan 107–108
Moscow 143–145
Munich 069–071

N
Napa 181–182
Naples 108
Neuhaus 019
Neumünster 072
Neuss 073
Neu-Ulm/Burlafingen 071
New Delhi 095
New York 182–185
North Auckland Peninsula 130

O
Oaks 185
Oslo 132
Ostend 025

P
Paiania 090
Paris 039–040
Pontevedra 155
Poznań 135

R
Rapperswil 159
Reading 186
Reggio Emilia 111
Reutlingen 074–075
Riegel am Kaiserstuhl 075
Riehen 160
Rio de Janeiro 027
Rome 111–112
Rotterdam 126

City

S
Saint-Paul-de-Vence 043
Salta 014
San Antonio 186
San Juan 141
Santa Monica 187
Santomato di Pistoia 113
São Paulo 027
Schaffhausen 161
Seattle 187
Senlis 043
Shanghai 033
Sharjah 169
Sindelfingen 076
Singapore 146
Soest 076
Stellenbosch 148
St. Georgen 077
St. Petersburg 145
Sydney 016

T
Tampere 036
Tel Aviv 098
The Hague/Scheveningen 127
Tokyo 120
Toronto 028
Traunreut 078
Turin 114–115

U
Ulm 078–079

V
Valencia 155
Vancouver 029
Varese 115
Venice 116
Venlo 128
Verzegnis 116
Veszprém 091
Vienna 019
Voorschoten 128

W
Waldenbuch 079
Warsaw 136
Wassenaar 129
West Palm Beach 188
Wijlre 129
Wolverhampton 084

Z
Zuoz 161

Collection

A

Fundación Alorda-Derksen 151
ALT Arte Contemporanea 101
Centro de Artes Visuales—
Fundación Helga de Alvear 153
Castello di Ama per l'Arte
Contemporanea* 106
Art4.ru 143
Art Stations Foundation 135
Astrup Fearnley Museum* 132

B

Barjeel Art Foundation 169
Ausstellungsraum
Céline & Heiner Bastian 046
Sammlung Ruedi Bechtler—
Kunst im Castell 161
Museum Beelden aan Zee 127
Benesse Art Site* 120
Museu Colecção Berardo 138
Berezdivin Collection—Espacio 1414 141
Centro de Arte y Naturaleza—
Fundación Beulas (CDAN) 154
Fondation Beyeler 160
Museum Biedermann 058
Museum Modern Art Hünfeld—
Sammlung Jürgen Blum 067
Museum van Bommel van Dam 128
Bonnefanten Hedge House Foundation* ... 129
Sammlung Boros 047
Michał Borowik Collection 136
Museum Brandhorst 069
The Brant Foundation Art Study Center 174
The Broad Art Foundation 187
Fondazione Brodbeck 104
Kunstraum Buchberg 017
Kunstraum Alexander Bürkle* 063
Museum Frieder Burda 045

C

Caldic Collectie* 129
La Casabianca 107
Fundación Chirivella Soriano 155
CIFO—Cisneros Fontanals
Art Foundation 176
Collectors House 125
Concordia Collection* 126
De la Cruz Collection—
Contemporary Art Space 179
The Cultural Foundation Ekaterina 144

D

Salon Dahlmann* 048
Casa Daros—
Daros Latinamerica Collection* 027
Das Maximum—KunstGegenwart 078
Deste Foundation for Contemporary Art 085
Devi Art Foundation 094
Museum Dhondt-Dhaenens 024
Didrichsen Art Museum 035
The Dikeou Collection 172
Djurhuus Collection 034
Museum DKM 060
Domus Collection 030
Dream House 119

E

The George Economou Collection* 086
Proje4L—Elgiz Museum
of Contemporary Art 162
Ellipse Foundation 137
Essl Museum—Kunst der Gegenwart 018
Schlosspark Eybesfeld 018

F

Sammlung Falckenberg 064
The Farjam Collection 167
Arbeitswohnung Federkiel* 069
Sammlung FER Collection 078
Sammlung Fiede* 044
Fisher Landau Center for Art 175
Deichtorhallen Hamburg—
Colección de Arte
Amalia Lacroze de Fortabat 009
Fondation Francès 043
Frissiras Museum 089
Sammlung Froehlich 068
Fürstenberg Zeitgenössisch* 059

G

Collezione Nunzia e Vittorio Gaddi* 106
Collezione La Gaia 102
Sammlung Arthur de Ganay 048
Herbert-Gerisch-Stiftung 072
Gibbs Farm* 130
Girls' Club 173
Fondazione Giuliani 111
Sammlung Goetz 070
Frédéric de Goldschmidt Collection* 021
Collezione Gori—Fattoria di Celle 113
The Goss-Michael Foundation 171
Sammlung Grässlin—
Kunstraum Grässlin & Räume für Kunst 077
Gratianusstiftung 074
Fondazione Morra Greco* 108

** new in the guide*

Collection

H
Hafnarborg—The Hafnarfjordur
Centre of Culture and Fine Art 092
Hall Art Foundation* 186
Hallen für Neue Kunst Schaffhausen 161
Sammlung Barbara und Axel Haubrok—
Haubrokprojects 049
Herakleidon—Experience in Visual Arts 089
Museo James Turrell—
The Hess Art Collection, Colomé 014
The Hess Art Collection, Glen Carlou 147
The Hess Art Collection, Napa 181
Sara Hildén Art Museum 036
Rolf A. Hoff Collection* 131
Sammlung Hoffmann 049
Karin und Uwe Hollweg Stiftung* 058

I
Independent Collectors 093
Inhotim—Instituto de Arte
Contemporânea & Jardim Botânico 026
Initial Access 084
Museum Insel Hombroich 073

J
JaLiMa Collection* 061
Jarla Partilager 050
La Colección Júmex 122
Jupiter Artland 080

K
Kienzle Art Foundation 050
Kunstwerk—Sammlung Alison &
Peter W. Klein 062
Fundación Federico Jorge Klemm 010
Stiftung für konkrete Kunst 074
KRC Collection* 128
Kunstsaele Berlin 051
Kunst(Zeug)Haus 159

L
Collection Lambert 038
Langen Foundation 073
Il Giardino dei Lauri 104
Museum Liaunig 019
Long Museum* 033
Lyon Housemuseum 016

Collection

M
MACBA—Museum Art Center
Buenos Aires 013
Fondation Maeght 043
Maison Particulière 022
La Maison Rouge 039
Sammlung Patrick Majerus 121
MALBA—Fundación Costantini (Museo de
Arte Latinoamericano de Buenos Aires) 013
Collezione Maramotti 111
The Margulies Collection at
the Warehouse 180
Prato d'Arte Collezione Marzona 116
Mathaf—Arab Museum of Modern Art 142
ME Collectors Room
Berlin/Olbricht Foundation 051
The Menil Collection 175
Messmer Foundation/Kunsthalle
Messmer 075
Morat-Institut für Kunst &
Kunstwissenschaft 063
Stiftung Museum Schloss Moyland 046
Casa Musumeci Greco 112

N
The Kiran Nadar Museum of Art 095
Nasher Sculpture Center 171
Nomas Foundation* 112
Novy Muzei 145

O
Özil Collection 165
OHD Museum of Modern &
Contemporary Indonesian Art 097
Museum of Old and New Art (MONA) 015
Oliver Ranch Foundation* 174
Henie Onstad Kunstsenter (HOK)* 132
Fondazione Opera* 107
OTR Espacio de Arte 154

P
Linda Pace Foundation* 186
Villa & Collezione Panza di Biumo 115
Coleção Particular 027
Collezione Peruzzi* 108
Peyrassol—Parc de Sculptures* 038
Philara—Sammlung zeitgenössischer
Kunst 061
François Pinault Foundation—
Palazzo Grassi & Punta della Dogana 116
Pinchuk Art Centre 166
Portalakis Collection 090
The Private Museum* 146

** new in the guide*

Collection

Q
Qiao Zhibing Collection 033

R
Alexander Ramselaar Collection* 126
Collection Regard 052
Fondazione Pier Luigi e
Natalina Remotti* 103
Rennie Collection at Wing Sang 029
Museum Ritter—
Sammlung Marli Hoppe-Ritter 079
Charles Riva Collection 023
The David Roberts Art Foundation 083
Craig Robins Collection 180
Rocca Stiftung* 053
Di Rosa 182
Rosenblum Collection 040
Museum Sammlung Rosengart 159
Fundación Rosón Arte Contemporáneo
(RAC) 155
Fondazione Pietro Rossini* 102
Rubell Family Collection/Contemporary
Arts Foundation 181
Rupert Museum 148
Sør Rusche Sammlung* 057

S
Saatchi Gallery 083
Fondation pour l'art contemporain—
Claudine & Jean-Marc Salomon 037
Salsali Private Museum 168
Samdani Art Foundation* 020
Fondazione Sandretto Re Rebaudengo 114
Schauwerk Sindelfingen 076
Kloster Schoenthal* 158
Sammlung Schroth 076
Sammlung Schürmann 053
Sammlung Christian Schwarm 054
Scrap Metal Gallery* 028
Sammlung Siegfried Seiz 075
Sensus — Luoghi per l'Arte
Contemporanea* 105
SIP Shpilman Institute of Photography* 098
Le Silo 039
Sammlung Springmeier* 054
Stella Art Foundation 145
Julia Stoschek Collection 062
Fundació Suñol 152

T
Takahashi Collection 120
Thyssen-Bornemisza Art Contemporary—
Atelier Augarten (T-B A21) 019
Traffic 169
Transformer Station* 170
Alexander Tutsek-Stiftung 071

V
Vanhaerents Art Collection 023
Collection Vanmoerkerke 025
Vass Collection 091
Verbeke Foundation 025
Centro Videoinsight* 115
Fundació Vila Casas 152
Vorres Museum 090

W
Kunstmuseum Walter 045
The Walther Collection 071
The Walther Collection—Project Space
New York 182
Wanås Foundation* 156
The Warehouse 172
Kunsthalle Weishaupt 079
Frederick R. Weisman Art Foundation 176
Schloss Wendlinghausen* 059
Sammlung Ivo Wessel 057
West Collection* 185
White Rabbit—Contemporary Chinese
Art Collection 016
Whitespace* 188
Wright Exhibition Space 187
Sammlung Würth* 067

Y
Yuz Museum 096

Z
Zabludowicz Collection, London 084
Zabludowicz Collection, New York 185
Museum Liner/Kunsthalle Ziegelhütte 157
Fondazione Dino Zoli 105

** new in the guide*

Collector

A

Sultan Soouд Al-Qassemi	169
Manuel Alorda	151
Sheikh Hassan bin Mohamed bin Ali Al Thani	142
Helga de Alvear	153
Jan-Holger Arndt	061
Mariam Arndt	061
Hans Rasmus Astrup	132
Philippe Austruy	038

B

Valérie Bach	038
Marc Barbey	052
Céline Bastian	046
Heiner Bastian	046
Ruedi Bechtler	161
José Berardo	138
Diana Berezdivin	141
Moisés Berezdivin	141
José Beulas	154
Ernst Beyeler	160
Hildy Beyeler	160
Fred Bidwell	170
Laura Ruth Bidwell	170
Margit Biedermann	058
Françoise Billarant	039
Jean-Philippe Billarant	039
Francie Bishop Good	173
Jürgen Blum	067
Dieter Bogner	017
Gertraud Bogner	017
Maarten van Bommel-van Dam	128
Reina van Bommel-van Dam	128
Christian Boros	047
Karen Boros	047
Michał Borowik	136
Elisabeth Bosshard	159
Peter Bosshard	159
Anette Brandhorst	069
Udo Brandhorst	069
Peter M. Brant	174
Edythe Broad	187
Eli Broad	187
Paolo Brodbeck	104
Gil Bronner	061
Frieder Burda	045

Collector

C

Joop N.A. van Caldenborgh	129
Rattan Chadha	128
Richard Chang	030
Aslan Chekhoyev	145
Manuel Chirivella Bonet	155
Cherryl Cohen	084
Frank Cohen	084
Bertrand Conrad-Eybesfeld	018
Christine Conrad-Eybesfeld	018
Claudio Cosma	105
Oswaldo Corrêa da Costa	027
Eduardo F. Costantini	013
Carlos de la Cruz	179
Rosa de la Cruz	179

D

Hanneke Derksen	151
Irma Dhondt-Dhaenens	024
Jules Dhondt-Dhaenens	024
Gunnar Didrichsen	035
Marie-Louise Didrichsen	035
Devon Dikeou	172
Pany Dikeou	172
Oei Hong Djien	097
Leif Djurhuus	034

E

George Economou	086
Paul Ege	063
Can Elgiz	162
Sevda Elgiz	162
Agnes Essl	018
Karlheinz Essl	018
Jo Eyck	129
Marlies Eyck	129

F

Eva-Maria Fahrner-Tutsek	071
Harald Falckenberg	064
Farhad Farjam	167
Rami Farook	169
Amy Faulconer	172
Vernon Faulconer	172
Anna-Belinda Firos	089
Paul Firos	089
Emily Fisher Landau	175
Ella Fontanals-Cisneros	176
Amalia Lacroze de Fortabat	009
Estelle Francès	043
Hervé Francès	043
Heiner Friedrich	078
Vlassis Frissiras	089
Anna Froehlich	068
Josef Froehlich	068
Christian zu Fürstenberg	059
Jeannette zu Fürstenberg	059
Soichiro Fukutake	120

Collector

G

Nunzia Gaddi 106
Vittorio Gaddi 106
Antoine de Galbert 039
Guido Galimberti 107
Arthur de Ganay 048
Heinrich Gebert 157
Myriam Gebert 157
Gerard De Geer 050
Brigitte Gerisch 072
Herbert Gerisch 072
Alan Gibbs 130
Giovanni Giuliani 111
Valeria Giuliani 111
Bruna Girodengo 102
Ingvild Goetz 070
Frédéric de Goldschmidt 021
Giuliano Gori 113
Kenny Goss 171
Friedrich Gräfling 044
Family Grässlin 077
Maurizio Morra Greco 108
Franz Joseph van der Grinten 046
Hans van der Grinten 046
Albert Groot 125

H

Francesca von Habsburg 019
Andrew Hall 186
Christine Hall 186
Axel Haubrok 049
Barbara Haubrok 049
Sonja Henie 132
Donald M. Hess 014, 147, 181
Sara Hildén 036
Rolf A. Hoff 131
Venke Hoff 131
Erika Hoffmann 049
Rolf Hoffmann 049
Karin Hollweg 058
Uwe Hollweg 058
Marli Hoppe-Ritter 079
David Horvitz 173

J

Dakis Joannou 085

Collector

K

Stella Kesaeva 145
Jochen Kienzle 050
Alison Klein 062
Peter W. Klein 062
Federico Jorge Klemm 010
Dirk Krämer 060
Grażyna Kulczyk 135

L

Yvon Lambert 038
Marianne Langen 073
Viktor Langen 073
Angela Lauro 104
Massimo Lauro 104
Tullio Leggeri 101
Herbert W. Liaunig 019
Elsa López 154
Eugenio López Alonso 122
Corbett Lyon 016
Yueji Lyon 016

M

Klaus Maas 060
Aimé Maeght 043
Marguerite Maeght 043
Sverrir Magnússon 092
Patrick Majerus 121
Achille Maramotti 111
Martin Z. Margulies 180
Igor Markin 143
Egidio Marzona 116
Giobatta Meneguzzo 107
Dominique de Menil 175
John de Menil 175
Jürgen A. Messmer 075
George Michael 171
Geraldine Michalke 051
Timo Miettinen 048
Daisuke Miyatsu 119
Franz Armin Morat 063
Elayne Mordes 188
Marvin Mordes 188
Karl-Heinrich Müller 073
Giuliano Musumeci Greco 112
Ines Musumeci Greco 112

N

Kiran Nadar 095
Patsy Nasher 171
Raymond Nasher 171
Kerr Neilson 016
Judith Neilson 016

Collector

O

Stefan Oehmen 051
Dağhan Özil 165
Julian Oggel 126
Thomas Olbricht 051
João Oliveira-Rendeiro 137
Nancy Oliver 174
Steve Oliver 174
Niels Onstad 132

P

Linda Pace 186
Lorenza Pallanti 106
Marco Pallanti 106
Giuseppe Panza di Biumo 115
Bernardo Paz 026
Vittorio Peruzzi 108
Donatella Picenelli 107
François Pinault 116
Victor Pinchuk 166
Anupam Poddar 094
Lekha Poddar 094
Zacharias Portalakis 090

R

Cindy Rachofsky 172
Howard Rachofsky 172
Fausto Radici 101
Alexander Ramselaar 126
Urs Raussmüller 161
Elisabeth von Reden 059
Joachim von Reden 059
Natalina Remotti 103
Pier Luigi Remotti 103
Bob Rennie 029
Friedrich E. Rentschler 078
Charles Riva 023
David Roberts 083
Craig Robins 180
Hanns-Gerhard Rösch 074
Eric Romba 053
Joëlle Romba 053
Rene di Rosa 182
Veronica di Rosa 182
Chiara Rosenblum 040
Steve Rosenblum 040
Angela Rosengart 159
Siegfried Rosengart 159
Carlos Rosón Gasalla 155
Alberto Rossini 102
Donald Rubell 181
Mera Rubell 181
Aldo Rubino 013
Anton Rupert 148
Huberte Rupert 148
Thomas Rusche 057
Rebecca Russo 115

Collector

S

Charles Saatchi 083
Claudine Salomon 037
Jean-Marc Salomon 037
Ramin Salsali 168
Nadia Samdani 020
Rajeeb Samdani 020
Patrizia Sandretto Re Rebaudengo 114
Maria Sarrate 154
Peter Schaufler 076
Christiane Schaufler-Münch 076
Maria Schlumberger 078
John Schmid 158
Ruth Schmidheiny 027
Karsten Schmitz 069
Lida Scholten 127
Theo Scholten 127
Carl-Jürgen Schroth 076
Gaby Schürmann 053
Wilhelm Schürmann 053
Christian Schwarm 054
Raffaella Sciarretta 112
Stefano Sciarretta 112
Siegfried Seiz 075
Ekaterina Seminikhin 144
Vladimir Seminikhin 144
Joe Shlesinger 028
Shalom Shpilman 098
Ingibjörg Sigurjónsdóttir 092
Amaury de Solages 022
Myriam de Solages 022
Alicia Soriano Lleó 155
Giovanni Springmeier 054
Julia Stoschek 062
Gabriele Straub 074
Josep Suñol 152

T

Ryutaro Takahashi 120
Budi Tek 096
Daniel Teo 146
José Antonio Trujillo 154
Alexander Tutsek 071

U

Iiris Ulin 048

V

Walter Vanhaerents 023
Mark Vanmoerkerke 025
László Vass 091
Carla Verbeke-Lens 025
Geert Verbeke-Lens 025
Matteo Viglietta 102
Antoni Vila Casas 152
Ian Vorres 090

Collector

W

Charles Wachtmeister 156
Marika Wachtmeister 156
Samara Walbohm 028
David Walsh 015
Ignaz Walter 045
Artur Walther 071, 182
Manfred Wandel 074
Wang Wei 033
Jutta Weishaupt 079
Siegfried Weishaupt 079
Billie Milam Weisman 176
Frederick R. Weisman 176
Ivo Wessel 057
Al West 185
Paige West 185
Nicky Wilson 080
Robert Wilson 080
Bagley Wright 187
Virginia Wright 187
Reinhold Würth 067

Y

Liu Yiqian 033

Z

Anita Zabludowicz 084, 185
Poju Zabludowicz 084, 185
Qiao Zhibing 033
Dino Zoli 105

p. 010 (l–r) Francesco Clemente, *Reconciliation*, 1991, © Francesco Clemente, Courtesy: Mary Boone Gallery, New York; Raquel Forner, *Mutante enajenado*, 1973; Antonio Berni, *La familia del peon*, 1975; photo: Gustavo Lowry **p. 013** photo: Candela Rubino, Courtesy: MACBA – Museo de Arte Contemporáneo de Buenos Aires **p. 014** photo: Florian Holzherr **p. 019** (l–r) Robert Schad, *SKINNE*, 2011; Robert Motherwell, *Open White and Black*, 1969; Tony Cragg, *Eroded Landscape*, 1998–2008; Dóra Maurer, *Double Double Nr. 33*, 2012 **p. 022** Daniel Arsham, *Pixel Cloud*, 2010; photo: Alexander van Battel **p. 023** Yinka Shonibare, *Leisure Lady (with Ocelots)*, 2001, life-size mannequin, 3 fiberglass ocelots, Dutch wax printed cotton, leather, glass, 160 × 80 × 80 cm (figure), 40 × 60 × 20 cm (each ocelot), overall dimensions variable, © Yinka Shonibare MBE, All Rights Reserved, DACS 2013; photo: Courtesy: Vanhaerents Art Collection, Brussels **p. 024** photo: Kristien Daem, Courtesy Museum Dhondt-Dhaens **p. 025** Jason van der Woude, *Open Space*, Open Function, 2010 **p. 030** Matthew Day Jackson, *Study Collection VII*, 2011; photo: Domus Collection **p. 033** Zhan Wang, *Garden in the Sky*, 2010 **p. 035** (l–r) Henry Moore, *Reclining Figure on Pedestal*, 1960, reproduced by permission of The Henry Moore Foundation; Eero Hiironen, *Island*, 1999 **p. 036** photo: Sara Hildén Art Museum **p. 040** Andrei Molodkin, *Cold War II*, 2007 **p. 044** Jorinde Voigt, *Symphonie Studie Var. XIII/1*, 2009, *Rhythmus (London) VIII*, 2010, *Subwoofer Studie 8*, 2010; Alicja Kwade, *Hemmungsloser Wiederstand*, 2010; Daniel Lergon, *Untitled*, 2009; Nathan James, *Safety in Numbers*, 2008; Alicja Kwade, *Option1-2*, 2011, Michael Sailstorfer, *Entwurf-sailstorfer (gelb)*, 2007; photo: indechs.org **p. 045** © Museum Frieder Burda **p. 047** (l–r) Danh Võ, *We the people (detail)*, 2011, *Trio*, 2010, *Numbers (1)*, 2011, *Number (6)*, 2011, all works Collection Boros, Berlin © NOSHE; photo: Andreas Gehrke **p. 048** (l–r) Candida Höfer, *Opéra Garnier, Paris VII*, 2005, *Opéra Garnier, Paris XXXI*, 2005 **p. 051** Friedrich Kunath, *Ohne Titel*, 2009, *Beim Erwachen in der Nacht*, 2009, *Fein raus*, 2010, *Vergegenwärtigung*, 2010, *Gestern ist ein fremdes Land*, 2010, *The Closest We Will Ever Be*, 2009; photo: Jan Brockhaus **p. 052** Hein Gorny / Collection Regard, ca. 1945; photo: Ludger Paffrath **p. 057** (l–r) Via Lewandowsky, *Last Call (Lomarov-Gedächtnisraum)*, 1997, *Beschleunigter Glücksfall*, 1996, *Geteilte Freude ist doppelter Spaß*, 2002; Florian Slotawa, *Tapes*, 2005; Via Lewandowsky, *Guter Geist geht aus*, 2003, *Schule des Houdini*, 2000, *An der Heimatfront gefallen*, 2000, *... und baute eine Stadt aus Pilzen*, 1993, *Fliege blickt in die Zukunft*, 1998; Julio Le Parc, *Forme en Contorsion sur Trames Noir*, 1968; Angelika Platen, *Julian Rosefeldt*, 2001; Mathieu Mercier, *Drum n'Bass Lafayette*, 2007; Timm Ulrichs, *Betreten der Ausstellung verboten!*, 1968/2007; photo: b p k Bildagentur für Kunst, Kultur und Geschichte **p. 058** Nunzio, *Senza titolo*, 2006, © Margit Biedermann Foundation / Museum Biedermann, Donaueschingen **p. 060** (l–r) Richard Long, *A walk of thirteen days in the Swiss Alps*, 2000, *Stones along the way*, 1998, (f.) *Cornish Slate Circle*, 1983; photo: Werner J. Hannappel **p. 061** Constantin Wallhäuser, *Boulevard of Broken Dreams*, 2008 **p. 064** (l–r) Wolfgang Tillmans, *Man Pissing on Chair*, 2000; Ed Ruscha, *Parking Lots*, 1967–1972, © Ed Ruscha; Martha Rosler, *Bringing the War Home*, 1967–1999; Richard Phillips, *Ingrid Green*, 2002, lithograph, 75,6 × 53,3 cm, © Richard Phillips; photo: Egbert Haneke, Hamburg **p. 068** Bruce Nauman, *Human Nature / Knows Doesn't Know*, 1983/1986; Zhan Wang, *Marmorfindling*, 2009, Frank Stella, *Lo Sciocco Senza Paura*, 1987; Foto: Maix Mayer, Leipzig **p. 070** exterior view Sammlung Goetz, architects: © Herzog & De Meuron, Basel; photo: Nic Tenwiggenhorn **p. 071** Jo Ractliffe, (f.) *Terreno Ocupado*, 2007, (b.) *As Terras do Fim do Mundo*, 2010 **p. 072** Menashe Kadishman, *Kissing Birds*, 1999/2000; photo: Marianne Obst **p. 073** photo: © Tomas Riehle / Arturimages **p. 074** (l–r / t–b) John Nixon, *Pink Monochrome*, 1994; Bernard Aubertin, *Carré, Or (Or Klassik)*, 2004–2006, *Carré, Or (Or Klassik)*, 2004–2006; Douglas Allsop, *Reflective Editor*, exhibition view, 931 round holes, square pitch, 2004; Bernard Aubertin, *Monochrome noir cachant un Monochrome rouge*, 1999, *Hiver N°28*, 2008; Aurélie Nemours, *Le mur*, 1978/88–1991; Ad Dekkers, *Verschoven diagonalen als zaagsneden*, 1967–1971; Bernard Aubertin, *Hiver N°28*, 2008, *Carré, Or (Or Klassik)*, 2004–2006; Josef Albers, *Hommage to the square*, 1965; Douglas Allsop, *Reflective Editor*, exhibition view, 3 vertical rectangular holes, parallel pattern 4/4, 2004; Bernard Aubertin, *Monochrome noir cachant un Monochrome rouge,* 1999; Tom Benson, *Cadmium Red Light,* 2003; Bernard Aubertin, *Carré, Or (Or Klassik),* 2004–2006, exhibition *Undsoweiter 4, 5, 6,* Stiftung für konkrete Kunst; photo: Steffen Schlichter **p. 077** © Sammlung Grässlin, St. Georgen; photo: Wolfgang Günzel **p. 079** (t) Robert Longo, *Untitled (Frank),* 1980; photo: Christoph Seeberger; (b) Museum Ritter, Ausstellungsraum mit Arbeiten von Rita Ernst, © Museum Ritter; photo: Tom Oettle **p. 083** (l–r) Keith Coventry, 1938, 1994–2006, Courtesy: David Roberts Collection, London; Ben Cain, *What Will We Do For Work Now,* 2012, Courtesy: the artist and Supplement, London; Keith Coventry, *Estates,* 1992–1998, installation view *A House of Leaves – Second Movement;* Courtesy: David Roberts Collection, London; photo: Courtesy: Mark Blower **p. 084** photo: Thierry Bal **p. 085** (l–r) Jeff Koons, *Chainlink,* 2003, *Kangaroo (Blue),* 1999, *Hair,* 1999; photo: Fanis Vlastaras, Rebecca Constantopoulou **p. 086** photo: Erieta Attali **p. 094** Hamra Abbas, *Please do not touch, stay out and enjoy the show,* 2004; photo: Devi Art Foundation **p. 095** Sheba Chhachhi, *The Water Diviner,* 2008; photo: Lucida, Photographers' Collective **p. 097** (l–r) Rudi Mantofani, *Looking at the Earth,* 2012, *Green Corners,* 2004–2012; Yunizar, *Tree,* 2012; Yusra Martunus, *04103,* 2004, *12104,* 2012 **p. 103** (l–r) Keith Haring, *Untitled,* 1983, Keith Haring artwork © Keith Haring Foundation; Barbara Kruger, *STAY/GO,* 2006, 2 c-prints, in artist's frame, 188 × 120 cm each panel, 188 × 254 cm overall dimension (framed), edition 10, Courtesy: Sprüth Magers Berlin London; Nam June Paik, *Buddah,* 1985; Tobias Rehberger, *Infection 1FR9,* 2008; photo: Paola Mattioli **p. 104** Adam Helms, *Zombies (American, 1861–75),* 2012; photo: Ornella Tiberi **p. 111** Colezzione Maramotti, North entrance, Courtesy: Collezione Maramotti, Reggio Emilia Ph. C. Claudia Marini **p. 113** photo: Carlo Fei, Florence, Italy **p. 116** photo: © Thomas Mayer **p. 119** Dominique Gonzalez-Foerster, *Moment Dream House;* Courtesy: © the artist, Gallery Koyanagi, Tokyo, and Tokyo Opera City Art Gallery; photo: Keizo Kioku **p. 120** Shinro Ohtake, *Art House Project Haisha, Dreaming Tongue / Bokkon-Nozoki;* photo: Osamu Watanabe **p. 121** (l–r) Ina Weber, *1 Orange, 1 Grauorange,* 2010; Sven Johne, *Demmin,* 2007; Renaud Regnery, *Le Plus,* 2008, © the artist and Klemm's, Berlin; Alexej Meschtschanow, *Blue Velvet,* 2010, © the artist and Klemm's, Berlin **p. 127** Jan Meefout, *Sluimerende Venus,* 1984 **p. 128** Ger Lataster, *Het haar van de vrouwen, de brillen van de dichters, de schoenen van de arbeiders en de as van ons allemaal,* 1987 **p. 129** Sol LeWitt, *2 × 7 × 7,* 1990, Caldic Collectie, Wassenaar **p. 131** Michael Sailstorfer, *KAVIFACORY,* 2013 **p. 132** Per Inge Bjørlo, *Larger Body,* 2003; photo: Øystein Thorvaldsen / HOK **p. 136** (l–r) Weronika Lawniczak, *Untitled (The one who struggles does not have to be a sad),* 2011; Mateusz Sadowski, *Looking to the end,* 2011 **p. 138** (l–r) Carl Andre, *The Way South,* 1975; Frank Stella, *Hagamatana II,* 1967; Joseph Kosuth, *One and Three Plants,* 1965, Museu Coleção Berardo (1960–2010), Courtesy: Museum Coleção Berardo; photo: David Rato **p. 144** (l–r) Antoly Zverev, *Lion,* 1979; Vladimir Yakovlev, *Flower,* 1974; Antoly Zverev, *Elephant,* 1952, Courtesy: The Cultural Foundation Ekaterina **p. 145** (l–r) Gregori Maiofis, *Studio of an Artist,* 2006; Dmitri Plavinsky, *Church of the Annunciation in a Village near Zagorsk,* 1975; Leonid Sokov, *Bear Beating a Sickle with a Hammer,* 1996 **p. 146** Charles Lim & Takuji Kogo, *Beaches,* 2012 **p. 153** Ángela de la Cruz, *Clutter with Wardrobes,* 2004, Courtesy: Centro de Artes Visuales Fundación Helga de Alvear Cáceres; photo: Joaquín Cortés **p. 155** Haim Steinbach, *together naturally (doubled),* 1986, plastic laminated wood shelves, 20 wooden trays, 4 ceramic vases, 61 × 140,3 × 36,2 cm **p. 156** Maya Lin, *11 Minute Line,* 2004; photo: Anders Norrsell **p. 158** Ulrich Rückriem, *Temple,* 1987 **p. 160** Fondation Beyeler, architect: Renzo Piano; photo: Todd Eberle **p. 162** Nuray Sevindik, *Breaking Off,* 2005; photo: Kayhan Kaygusuz **p. 165** (l–r) Jiri Georg Dokoupil, *Soap Bubles,* 1991, *Sheep,* 1990/91, *Sun in Wood,* 1990/91 **p. 168** (v. l. n. r) Reza Derakshani, *Hunting the Dust,* 2012, Courtesy: HH Sheikh Zayed Bin Sultan Bin Khalifa Al Nahyan, *Prayers,* 2013, *The Tomb of Cyrous, Passargad,* 2013, *The Peacock Throne,* 2013, *Titanic,* 2013, all works mixed media, all on canvas, except *The Tomb of Cyrous:* black sand; (f) Mies van der Rohe, *Barcelona Bench;* photo: Ali Zanjani **p. 169** (l–r) Seif Wanly, *Nocturne,*

1953, *Russian Ballet,* 1976; Fateh Moudarres, *Icons of Moudarres,* 1962; Mohammed Khadda, *Abstraction vert,* 1969; Chafic Abboud, *Kurdish Family,* 1950s, Courtesy: Barjeel Art Foundation; photo: Capital D Studio and Barjeel Art Foundation **p. 172** Donald Judd, *Untitled,* 1965 **p. 173** Girls' Club, Design: Margi Nothard of Glavovic Studio; photo: Robin Hill **p. 179** (t–b) Félix González-Torres, *Untitled,* 1994; Gabriel Orozco, *Bamboo Balls,* 2001, *Untitled,* 1998, *Untitled (Finger Rule),* 1997, *Untitled (Bunch $19.99),* 1994, *Puddle #43,* 1997, *Fear Not,* 2001, *Sin Titulo (Mano Azul Recortada y Pellizcada),* 2001, *Eroded Suizekis 12,* 1998, *Fear Not,* 2001, *Sin Titulo (Mano Azul Recortada),* 2001, *Untitled,* 1992, *Fear Not,* 2001, *Sin Titulo (Mano Azul Recortada y Pellizcada),* 2001, *Untitled,* 1998, *Untitled (Sin Titulo Circulos y Tinta),* 2000, *Untitled,* 2001, *Untitled (Mano Azul),* 2001, *Ping Pond Table,* 1998 **p. 181** Ruby Sterling, *SP170,* 2011, *SP177,* 2011, *SP173,* 2011, *SP171,* 2011, installation view, American Exuberance, Rubell Family Collection, Miami, 2011/12 **p. 182** photo: Erhard Pfeiffer, Courtesy: Di Rosa, Napa, CA

© 2013 for the reproduced works by Josef Albers / The Josef and Anni Albers Foundation, Carl Andre, Bernard Aubertin, Per Inge Bjoerlo, Keith Coventry, Tony Cragg, Kristien Daem, Ad Dekkers, Jiri Georg Dokoupil, Carlo Fei, Dominique Gonzalez Foerster, Werner Hannappel, Sven Johne, Donald Judd / Art Judd Foundation. Licensed by VAGA, NY, Ger Lataster, Julio Le Parc, Via Lewandowsky, Sol LeWitt, Richard Long, Robert Longo, Jan Meefout, Mathieu Mercier, Robert Motherwell / Dedalus Foundation, Inc., Bruce Naumann, Aurelie Nemours, Joseph Kosuth, Thomas Ruff, Michael Sailstorfer, Robert Schad, Yinka Rahman Shonibare, Florian Slotawa, Frank Stella, Nic Tenwiggenhorn, Timm Ulrichs, Jorinde Voigt, and Ina Weber: VG Bild-Kunst, Bonn; the artist and their legal successors.

Unless otherwise noted, image rights belong to the accompanying collection or to the photographer.

BMW Art Guide by Independent Collectors

Editors
BMW Group (Munich)
Independent Collectors (Berlin)

Conception & Implementation
Independent Collectors (Berlin)
Dorten (Stuttgart/Berlin)

Project Directors
Christian Cartsburg & Katrin Mechler,
BMW Group
Jana Hyner, Independent Collectors
Annette Kulenkampff, Hatje Cantz Verlag
Yvonne Sussmann, Dorten

Executive Editor
Jana Hyner (Berlin)

Authors
Silvia Anna Barrilà (Berlin/Milan)
Nicole Büsing & Heiko Klaas
(Hamburg/Berlin)
Christiane Meixner (Berlin)

Additional Texts
Independent Collectors

Graphic Design & Typesetting
Guido Negenborn & Bianca Wegner, Dorten

Reproductions
Wagnerchic Digital Artwork (Stuttgart)

Translation from the German
Tanja Maka & R. Jay Magill (Berlin)

Proofreading
Tanja Maka & R. Jay Magill (Berlin)

Production
Nadine Schmidt, Hatje Cantz Verlag

Printed by
Offsetdruckerei Karl Grammlich (Pliezhausen)

Binding
IDUPA Schübelin (Owen/Teck)

Typefaces
Arial by Robin Nicholas & Patricia Saunders,
The Monotype Corporation (Woburn)
Akzidenz Grotesk BQ by Hermann Berthold,
H. Berthold AG (Berlin)
LeMondeLivre by Jean-Francois Porchez,
Porchez Typofonderie (Clamart)

Paper
Invercote G, 180 g/m²
Fly 06, extraweiß, 90 g/m²
RC Offset, 80 g/m²

© 2013 BMW Group (Munich),
Independent Collectors (Berlin),
Hatje Cantz Verlag (Ostfildern),
and authors

Published by
Hatje Cantz Verlag
Zeppelinstraße 32
73760 Ostfildern
Germany
Tel +49 711 4405-200
Fax +49 711 4405-220
www.hatjecantz.de

Hatje Cantz books are available internationally at selected bookstores. For more information about our distribution partners, please visit www.hatjecantz.com

ISBN 978-3-7757-3623-7 (English)
ISBN 978-3-7757-3622-0 (German)

Printed in Germany

Additional Contributors
Sara Confalonieri, Jacqueline Fritz,
Julie Gaspard, Thomas Girst,
Katharina Knaus, Sarah Nussbaum,
Stephanie Schild, Deike von Glahn

Art is a gift. When we look at a work, are pulled into and interact with it, we say a wordless "thank you" to all the artists that fascinate, inspire, and sometimes even change us. With this book, BMW and Independent Collectors wish to thank everyone who lives with art and who has opened their spaces to like-minded spirits from around the world. Our heartfelt thanks go to all the collectors who appear in this edition of the *BMW Art Guide by Independent Collectors*. Your support and confidence in our project are what have made this book possible. Our deepest thanks go also to our committed team of authors and editors, and to the many contributors in the Independent Collectors and BMW network. You never turned away from the challenge.

Thank you.